THE ACCOUNTANTS' GUIDE
TO COMPUTER SYSTEMS

MODERN ACCOUNTING PERSPECTIVES AND PRACTICE

Gary John Previts, Series Editor

PRACTICAL ACCOUNTING FOR LAWYERS. Robert O. Berger, Jr.

INDEPENDENT AUDITOR'S GUIDE TO OPERATIONAL AUDITING.
Dale L. Flesher and Stewart Siewert

THE ACCOUNTANTS' GUIDE TO COMPUTER SYSTEMS. William E. Perry

THE ACCOUNTANTS' GUIDE
TO COMPUTER SYSTEMS

William E. Perry

President
William E. Perry Enterprises, Inc.

1807 1982

175 YEARS OF PUBLISHING

A Ronald Press Publication

JOHN WILEY & SONS

New York · Chichester · Brisbane · Toronto · Singapore

Library of Congress Cataloging in Publication Data:

Perry, William E.
   The accountants' guide to computer systems.

   (Modern accounting perspectives and practice)
   "A Ronald Press publication."
   Includes index.
   1. Accounting–Data processing.   I. Title.
II. Series. ,

HF5679.P42   001.64′024657   81–19859
ISBN 0–471–08992–3   AACR2

Printed in the United States of America

10   9   8   7   6   5   4   3   2   1

The green eyeshade has given way to the green hue
of the accountants' cathode-ray-tube terminal.
Accounting will never be the same.

PREFACE

Today's accountant barely resembles yesterday's accountant. The green eyeshade and quill pen image has been replaced by a cathode-ray tube and a program coding sheet. Both the function and the image of the accountant are changing as rapidly as is technology.

Since the late 1960s, data processing personnel have prided themselves on being change makers. They introduced computer technology to their organizations, they proposed important revisions to systems functions, and they worked with user personnel to install new system concepts. Since 1960, most organizations have changed dramatically the conduct of their businesses.

Accountants have the joint responsibilities of recordkeeping and control. The methods of filling these responsibilities have changed along with the methods of conducting business. Unfortunately, too many accountants have not participated in this change process.

As computer systems become more integrated and complex, the effects of poorly controlled systems can be catastrophic. The loss of traditional forms of evidence, the greater reliance on internal controls to verify the integrity of data, and the interconnection of organizations through communication lines all point to the increased need for accountants to become involved in control.

This book is the accountants' survival guide to computer systems. It is designed to provide accountants with immediately implementable solutions for today's technological control concerns.

WILLIAM E. PERRY

Orlando, Florida
January 1982

CONTENTS

THE ACCOUNTANTS' GUIDE
TO COMPUTER SYSTEMS

part one

THE PROBLEMS OF AUTOMATION

one

THE CHALLENGE
OF AUTOMATION

In the beginning, cavemen recorded the accounting records of their tribe on stone. With great care and precision, they hand-chiseled the results of their activities into stone. Whenever it was necessary to examine or reconstruct processing, the evidence was visible for all to see. The tribe controller had achieved an ideal system of internal control.

The complacency of the controller was short-lived. Technology raised its ugly head and struck a severe blow to control when the tribe technocrats introduced papyrus. Recording records on a fragile movable medium threatened the very foundations of accounting control. It wasn't until centuries later that the controller was able to restore control with the introduction of the bound journal and ledger. After 2,237 years of concern about papyrus technology, the controller again could sleep peacefully.

Unfortunately, the serenity was short-lived as another technocrat, Herman Hollerith, introduced the punched card in 1890. The bound journal concept was destroyed and in its place the technocrats introduced a card with holes punched in it. Not only had the controller lost the security of the bound journals, but the new method of recording information wasn't legible to the average accountant.

From 1890 until today, control over processing appears to have gone steadily downhill. The semiquestionable security of touching and feeling cards has been replaced by an electronic technology in which you can't even examine holes in the medium. The brief security of holding a reel of magnetic tape which contained your data has eroded into a technology in which the technocrats dump the data into a common pot called a data base. If only the good old days of chiseling into stone would return!

The methods of control have lagged and will continue to lag behind technology. This control lag has frequently been called the Bonnie and Clyde Syndrome. As you will remember, Bonnie and Clyde were robbing banks using automobiles while police were still on horseback. Too many accountants have been caught using the quill pen while the technocrats processed their organization's financial information on a computer.

CONTROL VERSUS TECHNOLOGY

A natural law of accounting is that control lags behind practice. The issuance of guidelines, standards, and controls usually emerges out of current practices and does not lead practice. This natural law needs to be recognized and effort made to change it.

The computer has challenged the cornerstones of control because people-oriented controls are not directly applicable to a machine. Control in a manual environment is based on the concepts of segregation of duties and supervisory approval procedures. Authorization frequently occurred when a supervisor affixed his or her signature or initials to a document. While these manual control concepts are workable, they need to be redefined when duties are concentrated in a single "black box" and no hard-copy documents exist for a supervisor to approve.

When the computer was first introduced, many organizations left control in the hands of the technicians. This is understandable because there was no practice to identify the problems requiring control. Remember the accounting law which states that control follows practice. When the effect of computer processing was recognized, the need for control became apparent. Unfortunately, there was no common body of control technology for automated systems.

Accountants having the control responsibility, but lacking technological skills and commonly accepted control practices, implemented those controls which they knew would work. These initial computer controls were financial controls over project initiations and charging users for their use of computer resources and services. These controls proved effective during the 1960s in restraining what appeared to be an uncontrolled growth in the computer function.

The 1970s introduced control over the systems development methodology. Design approaches such as the systems development life cycle introduced a series of checkpoints which enabled management to regain control over the developmental process. However, this control was based more on the process rather than the computer risks.

During the 1980s, accountants must learn to control the risks associated with automated technologies rather than the process. It's not good enough in an on-line data base environment to control the budget and to control the developmental process. The risks associated with integrating automation of day-to-day operations of an organization are too great to be ignored.

Control can no longer look at the past and say, "What has gone wrong that needs to be controlled?" With today's technological capabilities, accountants must look forward and say, "What could go wrong in the future and how can I reduce the impact of those problems on my organization?"

The computer technologies of the 1980s will pose greater risks than the 1970 technologies. Expansion of computer communication capabilities is introducing electronic mail and electronic messaging; data base technology permits the concurrent sharing of the same data by multiple users in an organization; and the coupling of the office of the future with existing data processing capabilities will drastically alter office methods.

VULNERABILITY OF THE ACCOUNTANT

Senior management expects the accountant to use the computer in the performance of the accounting function, and to provide guidance and direction for controlling automation throughout the organization. The accountant needs to be involved when new technology is implemented in the organization. The implementation of any technology normally goes through the following six steps:

1. *Wild Enthusiasm.* Everybody believes the new technology will solve all existing problems.
2. *Disillusionment.* The great hope is dissipated when people learn not only have all the old problems not been solved, but technology has introduced new problems.
3. *Total Confusion.* Nobody is sure how to get things accomplished quickly.
4. *Search for the Guilty.* The technological culprits causing the problem need to be identified.
5. *Punishment of the Innocent.* The technology can't be turned back; thus, any extra burden or effort is placed on those preparing or using the automated application.
6. *Promotion of the Nonparticipants.* Those standing on the sidelines watching the parade go by and telling everyone how bad it is are promoted in the hope that somehow they can restore order to the troublesome situation.

This costly developmental cycle needs to be broken. Organizations can no longer afford the huge costs associated with learning to use a new technology. The implementation of a new technology must identify and address the risks associated with that new technology. When the risks are known and addressed, it will help overcome human resistance to change, fear of technology, fear of being replaced by a machine, and fear of the unknown.

The accountant is viewed as the citadel of control. The ability to live up to those control expectations may be dependent upon the control environment in your organization. The following self-assessment questionnaire is designed to help evaluate your control environment:

		Yes	No
1.	Does your organization have a procedure for the design, implementation, and modification of control in automated systems?		
2.	Are your systems analysts and programmers trained in how to design, implement, and maintain controls?		
3.	Does your organization have a procedure to determine the cost/benefit of controls in automated systems?		
4.	Does your organization have formal guidelines and standards specifying the use of controls in automated systems?		
5.	Are the individuals in your organization responsible for control (i.e., the accountants) sufficiently trained in computer technology?		
6.	Does your organization have formal procedures designed to identify, document, and present to management control problems occurring in automated systems?		
7.	Are your organization's auditors adequately trained in computer audit and control concepts?		
8.	Is the adequacy of the controls in your automated applications and operating environment reviewed before placing them into production?		

The accountants must recognize and accept the control responsibility for automated controls. Most financial data are prepared by computer processing. Thus, the accountant has a dual computer control responsibility: first, as a user of financial data; and second, in the fulfillment of the comptrollership control responsibility.

The accountant's vulnerability to the lack of control over automation increases with each no answer to the above self-assessment questionnaire. Three or more no answers to the above questions signal a gap between the need for control and the probable existence of the needed control.

PLUGGING THE CONTROL GAP

Providing the control solution in an automated environment requires both learning and unlearning. The accountant must learn the new risks and how to control those risks. In addition, the accountant must unlearn the traditional methods of control.

The common method of control design is the "lock the door after the horse gets out" concept. Those responsible for control consider the sacred trust of the responsibility to mean not making the same mistake twice. Some controllers point with pride to a sign on their office wall which states "If you must make a mistake, let it be a new one." This concept is costing individual corporations thousands and even millions of dollars each year.

We have ingrained into our people that it is all right to make a mistake if it is a new one. Unfortunately, as systems become more integrated and complex the cost of a mistake rises significantly. A new mistake in the manual system might cost the company a few hundred dollars, but that same new mistake in an automated payroll system may cost the company tens of thousands of dollars. For example, a slip of a finger on a typewriter may add $1 to somebody's payroll check—not a very serious error. However, the same mistake on the computer might be repeated for every employee and, thus, an organization with 10,000 employees would lose $10,000. The same mistake but a significantly different consequence.

Accountants must *unlearn* full reliance on the traditional forms of control such as the segregation of duties. The concepts and methods of segregating duties among machines is significantly different from segregating duties among people. The concepts that were effective with people may not be effective with machines.

The accountant needs to *unlearn* the implementation of control using hard-copy documentation. The trend in automated systems is toward the elimination of paper. Even in banking systems, funds can be withdrawn without the traditional negotiable instrument and signature. As these time-honored concepts of control fail, new methods must be introduced to replace them. Control concepts that were effective with hard-copy documents may not be effective when those documents disappear.

The outlook is not bleak. The level of control available in automated systems is far greater than that possible with manual systems. The problem in many organizations has been trying to automate control using the same control methods that were effective in manual systems. We must *unlearn* those old methods and learn new methods.

The accountant has a unique opportunity to plug the organization's control gap. This control crossroad can be bridged by redesigning control concepts to complement the characteristics of the computer. The accountant possesses most of the skills needed to accomplish this task. The objective of this book is to provide the accountant with the insight, methodology, tools, and techniques to provide the organization the automated technology control solutions.

ROADMAP THROUGH THIS BOOK

This book was written to provide immediately implementable solutions to the risks associated with advanced technology. The book is divided into four parts which cover the following topics: The Automation Problem, Automation's Effect on Accounting, The Control Solution to Automation, and The Future.

The Problem: How Did We Get Into This Mess?

Whatever problem exists, it is man-made and can be man-corrected. The problems of technology have been with us since the beginning of time. A 1904 *Journal of Accountancy* suggested that accountants may wish to bring their own ten-key adding machine to the client's office in order to preserve their independence. This age-old need was echoed in the 1960s when accountants introduced their own software to assure their independence.

We can't develop a solution until we know the problem. This part of the book explains what happens when a computer is introduced into an organization. The evolving changes are described, together with the risks they pose to the organization.

The Accountant: What Have You Done to My Job!

Accountants used to prepare journal entries, close, and consolidate the organization's books. Now these are done by the computer. Today's accountants place numbers into little boxes and somehow the data magically end up in a consolidated financial statement. It's not even necessary to enter both the debits and credits. By entering one side of an accounting transaction the computer automatically knows what the other side should be.

The accountants' working world has changed. This part explains the effect of automation on the accountant and the organization, and how automation has changed the traditional forms of evidence from paper to electronic evidence. The accounting function will never be the same.

The Solution: There Is Hope

Properly designed, control in an automated environment is far superior to that dreamed about in a manual environment. However, control doesn't just happen—it must be planned. Control should not be a backward look at what has happened to avoid repeating previous errors but, rather, a forward look anticipating problems and correcting them before they cause losses.

This part of the book explains the risk of using automated technologies. Based upon the identification of risk, cost-effective controls can be established. While the objectives of control automation do not change, the methods change significantly. Control solutions are presented for all segments of automated operations including the design process, automated applications, computer operations, and the security over operations.

The Future: You Ain't Seen Nothing Yet!

The rate of change is accelerating. The accountant must learn to manage and control that change in the organization. The accountant of the future will be a change maker. In order to protect organizations from catastrophic risks, the accountant should lead the pack of technocrats suggesting new methods of control to ensure that the use of automated technology is controlled, achieves the organization's requirements, and is implemented in a cost-effective manner.

two

THE CHANGING
BUSINESS ENVIRONMENT

The word ubiquitous means ever-present or occurring everywhere. This term could be used to describe the use of the computer in the business environment. There are few activities left in the business world that are not affected by the computer.

Most of us have witnessed the computer revolution. We have seen the automation of order entry and billing systems. We have learned how to put our numbers and letters into boxes, being careful not to have more characters than boxes. But this was only the beginning of automation.

The supermarket has automated the checkout counter. Magnetic codes identify the product to the automated checkout register. This permits a price recorded in the computer to be used rather than the price on the product. Students learn to operate computers in elementary school. High-school students interact with the computer to help them select a potential career, then review the educational opportunities available to study for that career. Machines disburse money on street corners; we can pay our bills using a push-button telephone in our home; even our cars have small computers to tell us the number of miles we can travel before we run out of gasoline.

Accounting is still our method for recordkeeping in this computerized society. Someone must ensure the integrity of those numbers whether they are manually or automatically generated. Regardless of technology, people still want to know that the amount on the bottom line is accurate. Some areas have experienced a supermarket revolution by shoppers who still want the dollar prices marked on the products. They don't "trust" the computer.

MANUAL VERSUS AUTOMATED SYSTEMS

To paraphrase Carl Sandburg, the computer has crept in on little cat's feet. At first it wasn't there, and then it was. At first it changed very little, and then it changed a lot.

The computer is like a growing and maturing child. As the child grows, so do the child's problems. In addition, it costs more money to clothe, house, and feed an older child than it does a younger one. Fortunately, parents don't know the problems of older children when they have babies. If they did, they may choose to go childless.

My wife wanted to redo our living room. However, she knew that the $5,000 price tag would be unacceptable and, therefore, never presented the full cost proposal. What she suggested was that we buy a new $99 lamp. Eager to please and reward, I quickly agreed that was a viable use of our money. Shortly thereafter came a second request — for a new $279 table which was needed to properly show off the lamp. I didn't realize that the table and lamp clashed with the sofa, but was assured that an expenditure of $569 would remedy that situation. Next we got new chairs to match the sofa, followed by a rug. Of course, this then clashed with the walls and drapes, and within a matter of months we had spent $5,000. It crept in on those little cat's feet, with me not aware of what was happening until after it was over. This phenomenon is called the creeping commitment concept, and many EDP managers use this concept to introduce significant new EDP concepts that are hard to comprehend until they are installed.

The computer, like a growing child, requires an ever-increasing commitment because of the change it introduces into an organizational structure. The more we understand about the changes caused by a computer, the better equipped we are to deal with those changes. Most of the computer problems organizations suffer from are due to a lack of knowledge about the characteristics of our maturing child — the computer.

The New Technology Cycle

The problems caused by the introduction of new technology into organizations are well known. Unfortunately, few organizations take the time and effort to think through the full impact of introducing new technology, just as the new parent does not think about teen-age problems. This is the principal cause of the disillusionment with technology.

The introduction of new technology into an organization is illustrated by the new technology cycle (Figure 2-1). Associated with the introduction of new technology are new technological capabilities. These, of

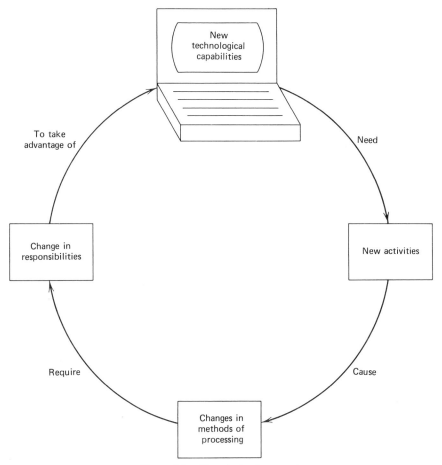

Figure 2-1. New technology cycle.

course, vary with the type of technology. Some equipment offers data recording capabilities, others unattended processing such as the cash dispensing terminals, while other technology provides the capability to store and retrieve huge amounts of data.

New technological capabilities can be obtained from the introduction of new equipment or the upgrading of existing equipment. For example, introducing word processing into an office environment currently using typewriters provides a brand-new capability. On the other hand, increasing the speed of computers does not provide a new concept, but does make applications economical that were previously uneconomical.

New technological capabilities need new activities to support those capabilities. These new activities can be as simple as training individuals in the use of technology, to as radical as transferring the control of data from the organizational users to a centralized data-administration group.

The new activities cause changes in the methods of processing. For example, the introduction of the programming activity required users to work with the programming activity in order to get changes to their system implemented. As the new activities mature, the methods of processing continue to change.

The changes in activities and the methods of processing usually require changes in the assignment of responsibilities. Unfortunately, this aspect of the new technology cycle is often overlooked. This sometimes poses dilemmas when no one is sure who is responsible for a specific area or task. Normally the changes in responsibilities are needed to take advantage of the new technological capabilities.

In most organizations, technology creeps slowly into all parts of the organization in a slowly revolving cycle that continues repetitively as the organization improves its technological skills. It is the time span between each part of the cycle that determines how smoothly new technology is installed. The greater the time span, the more chaotic the installation. For example, if changes in methods of processing are initiated without the corresponding change in responsibilities, some functions may have to fulfill a role for which they have no authority. In those instances, things may or may not happen properly. We will see this more clearly as we examine the specific differences between a manual and computer system.

Manual/Computer Differences

An automatic transmission in an automobile functions differently from a manual transmission. If you had driven a car with a manual transmission all your life and then stepped into a car with automatic transmission, you would feel lost. The same confused feeling exists when one attempts to function in an automated environment without understanding the differences between a manual and an automated environment.

A few moments of instruction on how to use an automatic transmission in an automobile demystifies the process. While computer technology is more complex than an automatic transmission, one must go through the process of understanding the differences before one can effectively use and control the automated processing environment.

The differences between manual and automated systems can be expressed in terms of the systems characteristics. We will examine each difference and discuss its effect on systems. (See Exhibit 2-1 for the differences between manual and computer systems.)

EXHIBIT 2-1   **Manual/Computer Differences**

Manual System Characteristics	Computer System Characteristics
Inconsistency	Consistency
Logical	Illogical
People	Machines
Paper	Electronics
Slow	Fast
Simple	Complex
Reactive	Predefined
Single	Multiple

Inconsistency Versus Consistency

Most of the procedures, guidelines, controls, standards, and audit procedures in use today were designed around the inconsistency of processing.
Organizations could not trust people to do the same thing correctly on a
consistent basis. Industrial psychologists tell us that people have up and
down periods during the day and during the week. Immediately preceding
lunch and Friday afternoon have been identified as two error-prone periods for people.

The computer, on the other hand, is consistently consistent. Given the
same set of circumstances, the computer will perform the identical act
every time. The major attribute of the computer has been its ability to
rapidly repeat the same tasks in the same manner.

Let's look at how we manage, control, and audit based upon the inconsistency principle. Recognizing that people will make mistakes, we initiate those procedures necessary to provide reasonable assurance of consistency. Some of these inconsistency control procedures are:

Redundancy.   In other words, the same task is performed twice with
the two results compared and differences investigated.

Supervisory Review.   A supervisor reviews either completely or ran-
domly the work performed by a subordinate in order to verify or test
the accuracy and completeness of processing results.

Statistical Sampling.   Ramdom samples are taken of work and verified to statistically determine the accuracy or inaccuracy of processing.

Division of Duties.   One individual performs part of the task and another individual performs the second part. Each checks on the work of

the other. For example, when a customer places an order, one individual may deliver the merchandise and another collects the money.

The consistency of computer processing makes many of these control concepts obsolete. The concern is no longer inconsistency but, rather, erroneous consistency. For example, if a wrong product price is in the computer, all sales of that product type will be priced erroneously. Under these circumstances, it may be more important to verify the accuracy of the process than to verify the accuracy of the results of processing.

One of the greatest misconceptions about the computer is the one that compares computer processing to an individual's ability to think and reason. This leads the uninitiated to believe that the computer has some sort of intelligence and, therefore, can provide some assistance in performing tasks correctly. Exactly the opposite is true. The computer has no ability to think or reason, but is truly a machine which performs those tasks and in that manner in which it has been instructed. If the machine is instructed correctly, it will perform the tasks correctly. On the other hand, if the computer has been improperly instructed, it will continue to repeat those errors until instructed otherwise.

We understand the consequences of inconsistent processing. These are a series of minor annoying problems which can ordinarily be addressed through increased supervisory attention or training. We may not know how to handle erroneous consistency problems. The kinds of problems caused by the consistency characteristics of computer systems include:

1. Large number of documents all containing the same error, such as invoices with the sales tax calculated using the wrong percentage.
2. Omission of part of processing, such as the omission of adding sales tax to invoices.
3. Rejection of certain types of transactions from the system erroneously, such as rejecting all orders for a newly introduced product.

Logical Versus Illogical Processing

People usually operate in a logical manner. You expect them to differentiate between right and wrong, company policy and violations to that policy, and so on. When things start to go wrong, we depend on people to identify those problems and take action.

The computer is not logical from the perspective of reasoning. The computer would just as soon perform an illogical act as a logical one. For example, we read about computer systems producing a weekly payroll check for an hourly worker for $1 million, computers eating a bank official's personal identification card, and computers ordering large amounts of unneeded product.

The employee relations department of a large corporation decided to permit employee families to tour the plant. To reduce the potential for damage, the work areas were to be roped off so family members could not get at the equipment and thus reduce the probability of injury or damage. The employee relations department withdrew 20,000 feet of cord to rope off the employee area. However, unknown to them, this triggered the automatic inventory requisition system to reorder a six-months' supply of cord based upon this one-time very large special requisition. The computer eagerly ordered 120,000 feet of cord without the blink of an eye or the slightest care, even though that was enough cord to satisfy the company's rope requirements for ten years.

Illogical processing has not been a major concern in manual environments. When the computer is introduced, this computer characteristic introduces a difference that requires management attention.

People Versus Machines

In manual systems, people initiate transactions, process the transactions, store information, and prepare system outputs. As machines begin to assume the systems functions, these tasks are removed from people and reassigned to machines. Initially, people still prepare transactions, but machines do the processing, storage of data, and preparation of output. People still oversee the processing, but even that manual system characteristic slowly diminishes as the systems become more complex and integrated.

Manual systems were people-oriented systems, while computer systems rely upon machines for processing. People can provide oversight, but are inconsistent, while machines consistently perform exactly what they are instructed to perform.

An important change that occurs as computers take over processing is the switch from people-initiated transactions to computer-initiated transactions. It has been estimated that in the larger computer systems, nine out of ten transactions are computer generated. For example, a customer may enter an order which is given to a clerk and put into the computer system. Based on that one entry, the computer may generate transactions to ship the product, post the amount to the customer's account, reorder inventory, change the amount of available credit for the customer, initiate a back order if necessary, and produce transactions to charge sales tax and shipping charges.

The computer-generated transactions eliminate a lot of people work, but in the process some of the control provided by people is lost. For example, a military depot initiated a program to scrap obsolete stock. Following regulations, the material classified as scrap was sold at bargain rates. What the military depot did not know was that the higher army level had an automatic inventory replenishment system. Therefore, as quickly as the depot could scrap stock it was replenished by the higher army level. All systems worked as designed, but the incident cost the taxpayers several hundred thousand dollars. While there is no assurance that people would not make many of the same mistakes, it is less likely that people would initiate a purchase order for a product being scrapped.

The control characteristics that are lost when people are removed from the system processing include:

Human oversight of processing

Analyze symptoms to identify the source of a problem

Correct unplanned-for erroneous conditions

Recommend the system changes in order to improve the effectiveness, economy, and efficiency of operation

On the other hand, machines have advantages over people, which include:

Consistency of processing

Speed of processing

Ability to handle fluctuations in volume with minimal extra effort or time

Paper Versus Electronic Media

Manual systems use paper as a basis of recording input, processing, and output. When a transaction occurs, the information is recorded on a form; frequently processing is recorded on the same form, or may be attached, such as adding machine tape; and the form may also be used as output. At least output will be another piece of paper. When you want to inquire, verify, or use information, it is available on paper. People can retrieve it and use it without interpretation.

Computers use electronic media for recording much of the information previously recorded on paper. For example, the information used to generate a transaction is recorded electronically by a computer terminal. Processing is performed within computers and the results stored electronically on tapes or disks. Output information can be retrieved electronically and displayed on a terminal display tube, making hard-copy documents less necessary. Transactions occurring between organizations can be performed electronically, such as electronic transfer of funds. Processing can occur without any supporting paperwork. People wanting the electronic information must know how to obtain and decode the information contained on electronic media.

Auditors have been particularly hard pressed with the new forms of evidence. In an effort to retrieve, analyze, and use information contained on electronic media, they have developed auditor software packages. These are special languages that use auditor terminology. Other users of computer information have experienced the same problems, except where systems capabilities make the desired information readily accessible.

Paper is being replaced by electronic media for the following reasons:

1. The cost of purchasing and storing paper is rising.
2. The difficulty of finding a single document among file cabinets of documents.
3. The cost of recording the same information many times on paper.
4. The difficulty and cost of destroying paper when it is no longer useful.

Properly structured, electronic evidence can provide extensive benefits over paper. The problems, as with other aspects of computer systems, are caused by the inadequate planning for the use and retrieval of electronically stored information.

Slow Versus Fast Processing

People process at people speeds, and machines process at machine speeds. Obviously, machines are faster than people and thus the processing time to perform a transaction can be substantially reduced. This offers both advantages and disadvantages to the accountant.

The slow processing by people allows for interaction and think time. If an employee is concerned over some aspect of processing or the validity of input, those concerns can be discussed and resolved with supervision. The individual can also interact with other people to be sure that the intents of processing have been properly understood.

Machines can complete transactions in fractions of a second. Let's look at a cash-dispensing terminal at a bank. Individuals enter their identification card, then indicate the secret password and the amount of funds desired to be withdrawn. The computer rules have been followed and the funds are instantaneously disbursed. There is no time to question, no time to challenge, and no time to think; action is immediate.

The positive side of the rapid processing of machines is that the transaction can be complete in a fraction of a second. There is no need to wait in line for people, there is no need to deal with a poorly trained employee, or any of the other limitations of dealing with people. On the other hand, whatever the rules are, that is what processing will be. If the rules are wrong or improperly enforced and secured, the potential losses can be large.

One large insurance company believes we are in an "IWIN" society. IWIN stands for I Want It Now. Their argument is that their employees, their customers, and management are demanding an instantaneous response. Writing letters is no longer acceptable. Calling one individual and being referred to another, and then another, is not acceptable. People want information when they want it, and only machines provide that kind of capability.

Simple Versus Complex Processing

Business systems over the past several hundred years have been attempting to simplify processing so it is easy for people to perform their job. The more complex the processing, the more people are prone to make errors. Organizations have tried to develop systems that can be used by their least skilled individual. This often involved limiting the systems' capabilities to the capabilities of people.

When the computer was introduced, the complexity of processing in most organizations was increased. The characteristics of the computer enabled it to perform very complex tasks repetitively with great accuracy. Complexity was no longer a systems concern as it had been in manual systems.

Let's look at what has happened to the pricing of products in most large corporations. Using manual systems, corporations attempted to establish one or two prices for each product. One might be a regular price, and the second a quantity discount price. In some instances, quantity discounts were available at different quantity levels. However, a simple look-up in a catalog would tell a billing clerk the appropriate price to charge. With the computer, this simplicity was no longer necessary. Special prices based on families of products could be offered. For example, if you ordered product X, product Y, and product Z at the same time, you would get a different price than if you ordered them alone. In addition, you might get discounts if during a year you ordered X amount of a certain product, or families of products. In some corporations today, the pricing structure is so complex that even the marketing force is uncertain what price to charge a customer.

The complex pricing provides competitive advantages to corporations, but at the same time raises some systems concerns. With the complex processing, there may be only a limited number of people in the organization that understand how the process logic works. In some organizations, many of these people are resident in the computer department. The users of the system, being responsible for only a part of the system, may not understand how the other parts work. Therefore, when changes are being considered, either a task force of multiple users must be assembled or the change responsibility falls to the data processing systems personnel.

Reactive Versus Predefined Processing

People react to situations when they occur. It's not necessary for people to make every decision ahead of time. This would not be a good use of people time because people can react and take action based upon unusual conditions. For example, if you are going from home to work over a certain route you don't predetermine what to do for each and every problem that could occur. If an accident occurs at intersection X you can decide when you arrive at the accident scene which alternate route to take. Unfortunately, the computer doesn't work this way.

Computers are machines following predetermined rules. If there is no rule, the computer flounders. In our going to work example, people would find an alternate route. However, if the computer had been instructed to go through intersection X, it would wait there until the accident was cleared, even if it took two or three days.

Many computer problems are associated with the fact that some abnormal processing conditions have not been predefined. For example, if space is allotted to indicate the sex of an individual, and those codes are indicated as M or F, the computer system must be instructed what to do should a code other than M or F appear. If those instructions are not provided, the computer might do anything. It might indicate that individual is male or female, or do some illogical kind of processing.

It has been estimated that as much as 50 percent of the development effort for automated systems is expended in predefining what to do for extraordinary processing conditions. These nonnormal processing conditions include:

1. *Invalid Data.* Defining invalid data and determining what to do for each type of invalid data.

2. *Mathematical Overflow.* Mathematical accumulations that exceed the predetermined number of positions, such as when space is allotted for $1–99 and a transaction occurs for $100.

3. *Undefined Codes.* Transactions include codes or identifiers which have not been predefined to the computer, such as when a new customer purchases a product on credit but that customer's credit information has not been entered into the computer.

4. *Undefined Processing.* Categories of processing that should not occur but do, such as customers ordering a product which they are not eligible to buy.

The luxury of manual systems in dealing with problems as they occur cannot exist in an automated system. From a systems development viewpoint, the predefinition of problem processing is the major difference betweeen a manual and a computerized system. Manual systems determine how to process ordinary transactions, while computer systems must do this and, in addition, process all unusual conditions. Because no one systems group can possibly identify all unusual conditions, the probability of problems in computer systems is ever present.

Single Versus Multiple Transaction Processing

People-oriented systems are designed to process a single transaction at a time. When the transaction has been processed, the paperwork may be forwarded to another individual who will process the next step as a single transaction. This process continues until the processing is completed. For example, when a customer buys a product on credit, the sales clerk processes the order and gives the customer the merchandise and a copy of the invoice. This completes the marketing transaction. A copy of the invoice is then transmitted to the accounting department who initiates the necessary processing to post that invoice to the customer's account. That transaction is processed in a different time frame, by a diferent individual, as if it were a single transaction.

Computer systems are connected, enabling information to flow from one system to another. This enables the entry of a single transaction into a computer system to cascade through the system, generating a series of additional transactions without human interaction. A single human transaction can initiate multiple computer transactions. This increases the impact of an error in any single transaction.

Data base technology introduces the same multiplier effect as exists with. multiple transactions. Data base technology reuses the same data element in multiple applications. If the data are correct they are correct more consistently, but if they are incorrect they are incorrect in each transaction that uses the information. As corporations consolidate their computer systems and data, this multiplier effect of data error increases.

IMPACT OF THE DIFFERENCES

The importance of the differences between manual and automated systems should be apparent to accountants from the discussion of those differences. The plans, procedures, and controls that were effective in a manual environment may not be effective in an automated environment. The differences in processing help explain the automation risks.

The impact of those differences on the organization may be insignificant or they may be catastrophic. The magnitude of the impact is dependent upon the amount of planning the organization has performed to deal with those differences. Experience has shown that those organizations that have a positive attitude about the control of and the use of technology minimized the impact of those differences. On the other hand, those organizations who use new technology with minimal planning experience the greatest difficulties.

Accountants have the responsibility to safeguard the assets of their corporation. One area in which that responsibility needs to be fulfilled is assuring that adequate planning occurs over the use of data processing technology. This planning provides organizations with the greatest opportunity for success in the use of automated technology.

Technological Rule of Thumb 1. Adequate planning is the most important step in assuring the successful use of computer technology. Accountants, as the guardians of purse strings, should require that adequate planning occurs before releasing the funds to acquire or upgrade computer technology.

ADDRESSING THE DIFFERENCES

The first step in addressing the differences between manual and automated systems is to identify those differences and the effect caused by those differences. The differences cause problems, and problems don't go away. They can be buried, as is frequently the case, but they will eventually reappear.

The use of automated technology has been compared to placing the operations of an organization under a microscope. All of the problems that are hidden quickly become visible. In manual systems, people are able to correct and conceal problems. In computer systems, it is significantly more difficult to conceal and correct problems. This is because data processing personnel are processing intermediaries and as such usually establish a formal correction process.

The frequency and severity of problems vary from organization to organization and from month to month within those organizations. These problems are often called risks which, if properly controlled, need not cause losses, but if improperly controlled can result in large losses.

Manual control design used what had happened in the past as a basis for designing controls to assure that those problems did not occur in the future. Automated control design suggests that you attempt to identify and control problems before they are problems. The differences discussed in this chapter are mini-time bombs which, if not adequately controlled can explode into serious problems at some future date. Control solutions are included in Part 3 of this book.

PEOPLE AND TECHNOLOGY

As of this date, there has been no recorded case of a computer defrauding its owner. The problem has been with people, and will be with people in the foreseeable future. The proper use of technology and the proper control of technology evolve from people.

People should not be bystanders when advanced technology is introduced into their area. Those organizations most successful in the use of automated technology involve the users in the design of those systems. Some organizations will not install computer systems in areas where the users will not become actively involved in the installation of those systems.

People resent things that are forced upon them. When the attitude about a system is, "It's not *my* system," the area is in trouble. Unless the people in the department feel it *is* "their system," they will do little to support and to make that system successful. They will devote their time and energies to those things they believe to be "theirs."

Technological Rule of Thumb 2. The effective use of computer technology requires user involvement. Without users heavily involved in the design, operation, modification, and control of automated technologies, the probability of success is substantially reduced.

Computer technicians tend to be machine oriented. Their training, their mission, and frequently their job satisfaction center around optimizing the use of machinery. Their interest in people is minimal.

Many computer technicians believe that their responsibility begins when transactions are received in the computer department, and stops when reports leave the computer department. They neither accept nor want responsibility for the origination of accurate, complete, and authorized transactions, or responsibility for the correctness and usefulness of information within the user area.

Computer people have coined a term which describes their philosophy of business processing. The term is "GIGO" which means Garbage In, Garbage Out. The underlying concept of GIGO is that you, the user, are responsible for providing me, the data processor, with good information. If you don't, I'm not responsible, you are. This attitude is not healthy in building good automated systems.

Many organizations have experienced problems in developing solid employer–employee relationships with data processing personnel. Many data processing personnel profess that their primary allegiance is to the data processing profession, and they have only a secondary allegiance to their employer. With this attitude, the usefulness of the systems within the organization may come second to the desire to master and use technology.

The people part of automated systems must be recognized and managed. There are many good practices that have proved effective in reducing the turnover rate of data processing personnel and increasing their organizational loyalty. These will be discussed in later sections of the book. Time spent in addressing and managing the people problem is usually significantly rewarded in productivity dividends.

Technological Rule of Thumb 3. Automated systems that concentrate on the automated segment to the exclusion of the people segment have a lower probability of success. Managing people is equally as important as managing machinery.

three

THE AUTOMATED ACCOUNTING RISKS

A large corporation in the northeast was blanketed by a severe February snowstorm. The factory machines ran continuously. A shutdown of the factory meant a great expenditure of funds to restart the process, as well as the loss of needed production during the downtime. In an effort to avoid this costly process, the corporation's management pleaded with the employees in the factory to stay at their work stations until relieved. It wasn't until four days later that the city streets were cleared and other employees could get in to work and take over the operations. The corporation promised to pay the employees for every hour they were at their work station during the week which, for most of the employees, came to well over 100 hours of work. Unfortunately, the computer system could only handle up to 99 hours and, therefore, dropped the hundredth digit. Thus, if employees worked 118 hours, they were paid for only 18 hours. You can imagine the complaining and morale problem among those employees who worked abnormal hours, yet received subnormal pay.

This kind of risk is unique to the automated processing environment. If the corporation had recognized this risk, they could have addressed it and produced the proper paychecks. However, not recognizing the risk, and the condition never having previously occurred, they had to live through a very painful and costly period of correcting the problem, apologizing to those affected, and restoring employee morale.

WHAT ARE RISKS?

A risk is an ever present condition which may result in a loss. Risks are not conditions which can be prevented but, rather, conditions whose impact can be minimized. For example, fire is a risk which is ever present.

No one knows when or where a fire may start, yet the impact of fire can be significantly reduced. For example, a fire risk can be reduced by constructing buildings of fireproof material, installing fire alarms and sprinkler systems, as well as fire breaks.

The ever present nature of a risk is a difficult concept for many people to grasp. However, once this concept is understood, then countermeasures can be installed to reduce potential losses from the occurrence of that risk. Risks are widespread and numerous. There are environmental risks, technological risks, business risks, and accounting risks. This chapter will discuss accounting risks.

Accountants should concentrate upon those risks which they can help minimize. These are the risks which directly affect financial applications. Obviously, technological risks affect financial applications but the solutions to many of those risks are outside the scope of the regular accounting function. For example, there is a technological risk that data will be garbled during transmission over communication lines. The solution to this risk is highly technical, and the full impact of the risk may not be recognized by the nontechnician. Thus, the accountant must rely upon the technical people to identify and address technological risks. On the other hand, the accountant has a responsibility to identify and assist in the minimization of accounting risks.

An accounting risk is defined as a risk that affects the integrity of financial information. Automated systems add to the financial information risk. Accountants can help design countermeasures to reduce losses associated with those risks.

The accounting risks in this book are described to emphasize the potential problems in maintaining the integrity of automated financial data.

THE THREE Rs OF RISK

The three Rs of the academic world are reading, writing, and arithmetic. The three Rs of automated system concerns are risk, result, and restraint. In addressing the new risks in the automated accounting environment, the accountant must remember to work with the three Rs.

R_1 = A risk is a situation through which a loss can occur.
R_2 = The result is the amount of projected or actual loss due to the risk.
R_3 = The restraints are the controls, procedures, and standards installed to reduce the potential loss due to a risk.

For the risk of a fire, let's examine the three Rs. The risk is the fire. The result of the risk is the plant and material loss and any injury to people.

The result can be measured in quantitative terms. The restraints are those countermeasures installed to minimize the result, such as fire drills, fire walls, and fire alarms.

All three Rs must be included in the accountant's solution to problems in the automated accounting environment. Many organizations attempt to install restraints without first identifying the risk or determining the potential result of that risk. In those instances, the restraints may or may not be effective, but experience has shown that they tend to be less effective against the new risks.

Risks are evaluated in terms of frequency of occurrence and expected loss. The multiplication of these two factors provides you with the expected results from the realization of a risk. For example, if data entry errors is the risk, then the accountant must know the expected frequency and the expected loss in order to calculate the probable result. For example, if ten data entry errors can be expected each week and the resources needed to correct each error cost $25, then the expected loss per week because of data validation errors is $250 (10 errors times $25 loss per error equals $250).

Risk can be divided into four categories involving frequency and expected loss. Risks can have either a high frequency or a low frequency of occurrence. Risks can have a high or low expected loss. This categorization of risk and the expected result is illustrated in Exhibit 3-1.

EXHIBIT 3-1   Categorization of Risks

Frequency of Occurrence

		High	Low
	High	Catastrophic	Dangerous
Expected Loss			
	Low	Routine	Unimportant

The categorization of risk illustration shows that high-frequency, high-loss risks are catastrophic. For example, if an airline were to lose a large number of airplanes the result would be catastrophic. If organizations do not learn how to deal with these high-frequency, high-loss risks quickly, they are out of business. On the other hand, low-frequency, low-loss risks are relatively unimportant. Examples include the potential loss of pencils, and employees pilfering scotch tape. These are annoying losses and ones which management must attempt to reduce, but the effect on the organization is minimal; thus, the losses are unimportant and don't require much management attention.

The high-frequency, low-loss risks are everyday occurrences and must be dealt with accordingly. For example, keystroke errors, addition errors, and improper recording of numbers are high-frequency, low-loss risks. These problems become routine and are quickly dealt with because they occur repetitively and invoke a large number of complaints. For example, keystroke errors can be reduced quickly through key verification. Addition errors can be dealt with through performing the additions twice and comparing the results, and the incorrect entry of numbers such as employee number or part number can be improved through the use of check digits which enables the automatic checking of the correctness of entered data. The check digit catches both transposition of digits errors as well as entering the wrong digits.

This leaves the low-frequency but expected-loss risk. This type of risk is potentially dangerous because it occurs infrequently and often the needed countermeasures are not in place. This occurs because these are the high risks that are neither obvious nor have occurred previously, so it is believed they will not occur. These are the kinds of risks that are associated with automated accounting applications and need to be controlled. Examples of these low-frequency, high-loss risks include computer fraud, issuing hourly paychecks for a million dollars, and the erroneous order of unwanted and unsalable inventory.

Accountants' Computer Guideline 1.   Learn and practice the three Rs of risk as a defense against unanticipated losses.

DIFFERENCES CAUSE RISKS

The origin of the new risks in automated applications can be traced to the differences between manual and automated processing. (See Risks/Differences Matrix, Exhibit 3-2.) The Risks/Differences Matrix shows the relationship between the identified differences and the automated accounting risks.

The Risks/Differences Matrix shows which differences cause the auto-

EXHIBIT 3-2 Accounting Risks Differences Matrix

Accounting Risks \ Differences Between Manual and Automated systems	Inconsistency/Consistency	Logical/Illogical	People/Machines	Paper/Electronic	Slow/Fast	Simple/Complex	Reactive/Predetermined	Single/Multiple
1. Data entry error				✓		✓		
2. Improper code				✓		✓		
3. Unidentified data		✓						
4. Unauthorized transaction							✓	
5. Control level violation			✓			✓		
6. Lost transactions			✓	✓			✓	
7. Erroneous output	✓	✓	✓	✓	✓	✓		✓
8. Processing mismatch						✓		
9. File out-of-balance			✓	✓	✓			
10. Inadequate audit trail			✓	✓				
11. Cascading of errors	✓	✓						✓
12. Incomplete accounting entry			✓			✓		
13. Repetition of errors	✓							✓
14. Improper cutoff		✓				✓		
15. Fraud			✓	✓	✓	✓	✓	✓
16. Noncompliance with regulations			✓			✓		
17. Noncompliance with policies/procedures			✓			✓		
18. Inadequate service level						✓		
19. Improper accounting			✓			✓		

mated accounting risks. For example, one of the new accounting risks is the risk of data entry error. Because data must be transcribed to computer media, there is a risk that in this process an error will occur.

The data entry error risk exists because of two of the differences between manual and automated systems. The first difference causing the risk is that information is stored on electronic media rather than paper.

This difference is the reason for the entry of data into the computer. The second difference causing the risk is the complex computer processing. The complex process affects the type, scope, and makeup of data going into computer systems, which adds to the data entry risk. For example, if to enter data it is necessary for an individual to perform some complex search or processing before entering the data, the risk of error increases.

ACCOUNTING RISKS IN AUTOMATED APPLICATIONS

Problems in an automated accounting environment stem from the risks within that environment. The accounting risks can be divided into general accounting risks and application risks.

Most accountants are familiar with the application risks. These have been widely publicized and the lists of these risks are available from most of the major accounting firms. For example, in a computerized merchandise billing system, the application risks that would be of concern to the accountant include:

Items are shipped but not billed
Items are billed but not shipped
Items are billed at the wrong price

The general accounting risks may not be familiar to many accountants. The accounting manual of most organizations addresses the application risks, but may not address the general accounting risks in automated applications. These risks are briefly described in Exhibit 3-3 and discussed below. (Exhibit 3-3 lists the risks, provides a brief explanation of each risk, and gives an example of the risk.)

INSTRUCTIONS FOR RISK SELF-ASSESSMENT QUESTIONS

Included with the discussion of each risk will be a series of self-assessment questions for the accountant to answer about the risk. The objective of these self-assessment questions is to help accountants assess the existence and severity of these risks in their organization. At the completion of the discussion of each new accounting risk, accountants should answer the self-assessment questions about their organization. A section at the end of the chapter explains how to interpret the answers to these questions.

Some of the questions may be difficult to answer yes or no. In those

EXHIBIT 3-3 Automation's Accounting Risks

Accounting Risk	Description	Example
1. Data entry error	Input being entered into the computer system contains an error.	An order quantity of 5 was entered when only 3 were desired.
2. Improper code.	The code used to represent a name, product, etc. is improper.	The address was in New York State, and a code 35 was entered when 36 means New York State.
3. Unidentified data	The information entered into the computer system cannot be identified with any existing entity within that system.	Cash was received from customer 123, but the accounts receivable system does not show a customer with that number.
4. Unauthorized transaction	A transaction was entered into the automated application which is not in accordance with the intent of management.	A payment for first-class airfare was entered for reimbursement, but the company has a policy to fly coach.
5. Control level violation	People circumvent control levels by entering multiple transactions.	A product in short supply is limited to 100 units per customer. A sales person enters two orders of 75 so a favorite customer can get 150 units.
6. Lost transactions	Information is lost before entry into a computer system, or lost after rejection from a computer system.	A transaction is rejected because an improper code is detected and then lost during the correction process.
7. Erroneous output	System outputs either contain erroneous information or the meaning is misunderstood, resulting in erroneous decisions.	A manager believes an output report shows product sold while it actually shows product sold plus commitments.
8. Processing mismatch	Information is processed against the wrong master information.	A payroll increase for employee 123 matched against employee 128 and the increase given to employee 128.

33

EXHIBIT 3-3   Automation's Accounting Risks (Continued)

Accounting Risk	Description	Example
9. File out-of-balance	The sum of detail records does not equal the computer control total, or the computer control total does not equal the manually maintained total.	The individual accounts receivable detail records do not equal the accounts receivable control total.
10. Inadequate audit trail	The audit trail is insufficient to permit reconstruction of transaction processing.	A customer asked for supporting information on amounts billed to that customer, but the computer system is unable to locate the supporting documentation.
11. Cascading of errors	The error in one system causes no problem in that system, but is transmitted to another system and causes a problem there.	An alphabetic character is included in the order quantity field in a billing system. The alphabetic character is ignored in that system and product is shipped. However, when the alphabetic quantity is transmitted to the inventory replenishment system, it causes an error.
12. Incomplete accounting entry	The information entered into the computer is not a complete accounting transaction.	The checks attached to a bank deposit slip do not equal the total of the deposit.
13. Repetition of errors	The error within the computer system is repeated for all conditions with the same characteristics.	A wrong product price is entered into the computer and all of that type product shipped are billed at the wrong amount.

EXHIBIT 3-3 Automation's Accounting Risks (Continued)

Accounting Risk	Description	Example
14. Improper cutoff	Information is placed into the wrong accounting period.	An order is entered into the computer system on the last day of the month, but not shipped until several days into the following month. However, the sale is recorded in the previous month.
15. Fraud	A scheme is initiated to remove money or resources from the organization.	An employee deletes unpaid open items in an accounts receivable system so that a colleague will not have to pay for items purchased.
16. Noncompliance with regulations	Procedures required by regulatory agencies are not complied with in the automated applications.	An organization is required to delete certain types of information about employees after one year, but fails to do so.
17. Noncompliance with policies/procedures	The policies and procedures of the organization are not complied with in the automated applications.	An accounting system fails to keep the type of information specified by the controller's accounting procedures.
18. Inadequate service level	Users of automated applications do not receive the desired results on time.	A credit manager does not receive the accounts receivable aging report on the desired date because of the unavailability of computer time.
19. Improper accounting	Accounting information is not processed in accordance with generally accepted accounting procedures.	Funds given to a customs official to get a boat unloaded are recorded as legal fees.

instances, the accountant should use judgment as to whether the conditions presented are generally applicable for the organization, in which case a "yes" answer should be given, or whether the condition posed has not been adequately addressed, in which case a "no" answer should be given.

The discussion of each risk and the self-assessment questions follow.

Data Entry Error Risk

People have needs to satisfy, and the computer system is the vehicle for satisfying those needs. The process of transcribing needs to the computerized application is the data entry process. This involves two steps: first, defining the need in a form acceptable to the computerized application data entry specifications; and second, transcribing that information into computer media.

For example let's assume an accountant wants to make a journal entry. The first data entry step involves finding the appropriate codes for the accounts, getting the proper input form, and then preparing the data according to the rules of the computerized application. During the second step, the information is entered into the computer using the available input device. For example, if a key-to-disk unit is available for input the journal entry information is keyed onto a disk. If a terminal is used the information is keyed directly into computer storage.

Errors can be made at the following points during this process:

Origination of data
Data recording in preparation for entry
Placing data onto the input form
Transcribing the data to computer media
Recording by the mechanical or electronic equipment

The self-assessment questions for the data entry error risk are listed in Exhibit 3-4.

Improper Code Risk

Names, descriptions, and locations are no-no's in computerized systems. Codes are in. Everything is a code because computer systems operate more efficiently and economically using computer codes. Some people feel this is a depersonalization process, but regardless of the outcome, that's the way systems are designed. Employees are numbers, insurance

EXHIBIT 3–4   Accounting Risks Self-Assessment Questionnaire

Risk Assessment Category   Data Entry Error

Item	Yes	No
1. Have formalized procedures been established for the entry of data into automated accounting systems?		✓
2. Have data validation programs been written that evaluate the incoming data for the most common errors?	✓	
3. Are the people preparing input adequately trained?		✓
4. Are the number of data entry errors recorded and evaluated so that the process can be continually improved?		✓
5. Does user management regularly review data entry errors in order to improve the process?	✓	

EXHIBIT 3–5   Accounting Risks Self-Assessment Questionnaire

Risk Assessment Category   Improper Code

Item	Yes	No
1. Do identical items, product, and description throughout the company use the same code?	✓	
2. Is the documentation provided to look up codes easy to use?	online ✓	
3. Are code structures readily expandable should additional codes be needed?	✓	
4. Are code structures used for different purposes significantly different so that the code for one item could not be mistakenly used for a different purpose?	✓	
5. Are coding errors continually analyzed to determine and correct the causes of coding errors?	✓	

policies are numbers, and if you forget your number processing can be extremely difficult.

If the wrong code is used, it is highly probable that the wrong processing will occur. If a customer wants product 123, but orders product 234, the computer system will initiate the procedures to ship that customer product 234. The proper structure and use of codes is important in assuring accurate processing.

The improper code risk self-assessment questions are listed in Exhibit 3-5. ·

Unidentified Data Risk

A methodology within data processing has evolved to deal with unidentifiable data. The method is to place 9 in the identification field to indicate that this source of the transaction is unknown. Many systems are constructed so that this unidentified data can live for years within the system.

Anyone analyzing control in an automated application immediately searches out the 9 identifiers. Those transactions are usually orphaned data.

The causes for data being unidentifiable are numerous and include:

Data sent to an organization but not identified, such as sending an organization a check but not telling what those funds are to be used for or whom they are from

Transactions with an erroneous identifier such as an invalid customer number

Data entered before the proper identifier is established, such as purchasing an item on credit before one's customer account is established

These unidentified transactions pose several risks. First, they can cause the loss of customer goodwill because to the individual entering the transaction it appears the organization cannot process data properly. Second, the cost and effort to identify the data can be expensive. Third, those accounts are susceptible to fraud and abuse.

The unidentified data risk self-assessment questions are listed in Exhibit 3-6.

Unauthorized Transaction Risk

The authorization rules should define for each data processing resource which transactions are authorized to have access to the resource and

EXHIBIT 3-6   Accounting Risks Self-Assessment Questionnaire

Risk Assessment Category   Unidentified Data

Item	Yes	No
1. Have special accounts or identifiers been established to hold unidentified data?	✓	
2. Does the unidentified data include the date of entry so its aging can be monitored?	✓	
3. Are control totals established for unidentified financial data?	✓	
4. Are regular reports prepared and presented to management that list the unidentified data?		✓
5. Have procedures been developed, implemented, and monitored that assure the timely disposition of unidentified data?		✓

Cash?

Cash?

which are not. These authorization rules should be enforced by the operating environment application because they apply to all application systems. The proper enforcement of the rules ensures that only authorized transactions are processed. However, if the rules are not enforced or there are weaknesses in the enforcement process, then unauthorized transactions may be processed by the application system.

Unauthorized transactions are defined as those transactions which are not processed in accordance with the intent of management. It is possible that transactions are within the scope of authority of an individual and within the rules of the system, but still not within the intent of management. For example, a supervisor may give an employee a raise greater than the maximum amount authorized by management. The supervisor may be authorized to give raises, the payroll system may accept the raise given, but the amount is in violation of the intent of management.

Unauthorized transactions may be intentional or accidental. Many times, people don't understand the rules of the system or the intent of management, and thus enter transactions that are unauthorized. The solution is a detailed definition of what is and is not an authorized transaction and then enforcing that definition.

The unauthorized transaction risk self-assessment questions are listed in Exhibit 3-7.

EXHIBIT 3-7   Accounting Risks Self-Assessment Questionnaire

Risk Assessment Category   Unauthorized Transaction

Item	Yes	No
1. Have limits been placed on the transaction values entered into the system?		✓
2. Have the limits of processing authority of individuals been defined?		✓
3. Has a profile been prepared showing which resources each individual or transaction can access?		✓
4. Has that user authorization profile been enforced in the operating environment?		✓
5. Are violations of transaction authorizations identified and reported to management for appropriate action?		✓

Control Level Violation Risk

Many organizations place limits on the scope of authority of an individual or transaction. For example, a sales manager may be authorized to issue a customer a goodwill credit of up to $100. Over $100, the credit must be approved by the corporate controller.

The control limits can be violated by creating several transactions within an individual's scope of authority. For example, if the sales manager wished to issue a specific customer a $240 goodwill credit, he could accomplish the objective within the system rules by issuing that customer three goodwill credits for $80 each. In this situation, the marketing manager technically is issuing credits within his scope of authority, yet he has circumvented the intent of the management policy.

Control level violations are easier to execute in an automated application because people may not see them. It would be difficult to submit to an individual those three $80 credits, yet the computer, unless programmed to look for those situations, treats each one individually and processes it according to the rules. The computer does not think that it just processed an $80 credit for the same customer. Thus, the three $80 credits could be processed sequentially without the slightest concern by the application system.

The control level violation risk self-assessment questions are listed in Exhibit 3-8.

EXHIBIT 3-8   Accounting Risks Self-Assessment Questionnaire

Risk Assessment Category   Control Level Violation

Item	Yes	No
1. Have the control level limits in financial applications been identified?		✓
2. Have employees been instructed on not violating control level limits through the issuance of multiple transactions?		✓
3. Are monitoring procedures established to identify control level violation situations?		✓
4. Are control level violations summarized and reported to management for appropriate action?		✓
5. Are control level violators punished?		✓

Lost Transactions Risk

Transactions can be lost for three reasons: first, transactions can be lost before entry into the computer system; second, transactions can be lost during processing; and third, transactions can be lost after they have been rejected from the system for correction. While this risk is not unique to automated applications, it is increased due to automation.

Control over transactions before entry into the automated application can be difficult and costly. Many organizations believe they should not attempt to control transactions before being prepared for entry into the automated application. For example, if customers send in orders which are never received or are lost in the mail room, these are difficult situations to control. However, controls can help prevent and detect transactions lost in the recording and entry procedures.

Transactions can be lost during processing because of both application system problems and hardware and software problems. Data base technology poses some unique concerns regarding loss of information. The data can be within the data base, but because of structural problems of the data base those data are not retrievable.

Transactions not meeting the rules of the system are rejected for correction. Some systems do not maintain control over rejected transactions but, rather, assign the control to the people who have the responsibility to correct and reenter those transactions. This may result in lost transac-

EXHIBIT 3-9   Accounting Risks Self-Assessment Questionnaire

Risk Assessment Category ___Lost Transactions___

Item	Yes	No
1. Is control over transactions established during the recording process?	✓	
2. Are controls maintained over data during processing so transactions cannot be lost during processing?	✓	
3. Is control maintained over transactions rejected from application systems?	✓	
4. If controlled transactions are lost, or not reentered promptly, does management investigate the cause?	✓	
5. Are statistics maintained over the frequency and type of lost transactions so system corrections can be made if appropriate?	✓	

tions or transactions delayed for extended periods of time before reentry.

The lost transaction risk self-assessment questions are listed in Exhibit 3-9.

Erroneous Output Risk

The objective of an automated accounting application is to produce some desired result. If this result is erroneous, the system has failed to fulfill its requirements.

The term *erroneous results* is used to mean the system did not fulfill its requirements. The reasons this can happen include:

The data on the report are erroneous

The information arrived too late to be meaningful

The user did not understand the data presented

The reports were issued to the wrong people

The erroneous output risk self-assessment questions are listed in Exhibit 3-10.

EXHIBIT 3–10   Accounting Risks Self-Assessment Questionnaire

Risk Assessment Category ___Erroneous Output___

Item	Yes	No
1. Are procedures taken to ensure the accuracy and completeness of systems output?	✓	
2. Do reports indicate the intended recipient of the report?	✓	
3. Have users of the report been instructed on how to interpret the information on the report?	✓	
4. Has the date the report is needed been determined?	✓	
5. Do report recipients have a formal method to report problems and recommend improvements in systems outputs?		✓

Processing Mismatch Risks

Much of computer processing involves matching one set of information with another set of information. For example, when payroll rate increases are entered, they must be matched against the employee's master record so that the old pay rate can be changed.

An inaccurate match, or inability to match information, can lead to erroneous processing. The reasons an inaccurate or no match may occur include:

Programming error

Wrong key used to match information

Out of sequence condition on one of the two sets of information

Information missing from one of the two files for matching purposes

The processing mismatch risk self-assessment questions are listed in Exhibit 3-11.

File Out-of-Balance Risk

The detailed information processed by, or stored by, automated applications may not agree with control totals. For example, the detailed accounts receivable balances may not equal the accounts receivable fi-

EXHIBIT 3-11   Accounting Risks Self-Assessment Questionnaire

Risk Assessment Category	Processing Mismatch		

Item	Yes	No
1. Are timing rules defined so that the match process will not occur until the appropriate information is entered into the system?		
2. Are reasonable steps taken to ensure the accuracy of the keys used for matching?		
3. Are mismatches identified and promptly investigated?		
4. Are the causes of mismatches quantified and periodically evaluated?		
5. Are mismatch situations corrected within a reasonable time span?		

nancial total. This risk increases as the amount of time between reconciliations increases.

Out-of-balance conditions occur during processing and with data stored in computer files or data bases. The more common causes for out-of-balance conditions include:

Programming errors

Lack of balancing routines

Incomplete or inaccurate data and/or balances entered into the system

Timing differences between manual and automated processing

The most difficult situation to deal with is timing considerations when computers are balanced to manual totals. For example, in balancing cash deposited in the bank to cash recorded in the computer application, there may be delays in either function. In large, integrated systems the manual balancing control over computer applications may be complex.

Exhibit 3-12 lists out-of-balance risk self-assessment questions.

Inadequate Audit Trail Risk

Audit trails are needed to meet both organizational and regulatory requirements. Organizations need audit trails in order to substantiate proc-

EXHIBIT 3-12   Accounting Risks Self-Assessment Questionnaire

Risk Assessment Category   File Out-of-Balance

Item	Yes	No
1. Do computer files contain control totals?	✓	
2. Are the manual control totals maintained independently of the application system?	✓	
3. Are the detailed amounts reconciled to control totals on a regular basis?	✓	
4. Are out-of-balance conditions promptly reported to management so investigative action can be undertaken?	✓	
5. Are the balancing conditions tested in new computer applications or when changes are made to existing applications?	✓	

essing. Governmental regulations require organizations to maintain specified audit trail information for a variety of purposes.

Audit trails are used to both reconstruct and to substantiate processing. Reconstruction is needed in the event of problems. For example, if computer files are destroyed during processing, backup files, which are audit trail records, are used to reconstruct processing from a point of known integrity to the point of the problem. Substantiation is needed to ascertain how a problem occurred, to verify to a customer that processing is correct, and to permit auditors to verify the integrity of processing.

Various federal regulatory agencies require audit trail records. The Internal Revenue Service has decreed computer files are official records for tax purposes. As such, they require organizations to create an audit trail, which enables them to trace any and all transactions to the control totals, and to trace from a control total to all the supporting transactions. Agencies of the federal government are required to maintain audit trail records about individuals in fulfillment of the requirements of the Privacy Act of 1974.

The audit trail requirements need to be specified in the same manner as other user needs. These audit trail specifications should be defined by all the involved parties. The parties who can contribute to the content of an audit trail include lawyers, auditors, users, and senior management. Many audit trail decisions must be made on a cost-effectiveness basis, as the cost of preparing and retaining audit trail information can be costly.

EXHIBIT 3-13   Accounting Risks Self-Assessment Questionnaire

Risk Assessment Category   Inadequate Audit Trail

Item	Yes	No
1. Are audit trail requirements specified as part of the systems design?		
2. Has the organization developed an audit trail policy (this is commonly accomplished through a record retention program)?		
3. Are governmental audit trail requirements known?		
4. Is the retention period for all audit trail information specified?		
5. Is the adequacy and usefulness of the audit trail periodically evaluated?		

The inadequate audit trail risk self-assessment questions are listed in Exhibit 3-13.

Cascading of Errors Risk

The cascading of errors is the passing of errors from one program or system to another. The point of origin of the error is not the point of the problem. The problem can occur many programs or systems later. For example, a payroll calculation error may cause an error in the pension system. Alphabetic overtime hours may not cause a problem in the payroll system but may create some unexpected information and the passing of that unexpected information from system to system may eventually cause the pension system to do something erratic.

Cascading of errors can be caused by unrelated systems. For example, in a data base, system data may be entered by one system and used by many other systems. The use of common data can affect other data elements which, in turn, have a disastrous effect on an unrelated system. The cascading of errors risk is one that is difficult to prevent, and sometimes even to detect the cause of error. It is a risk unique to automated applications, and one growing in scope as more systems become interrelated.

Exhibit 3-14 presents the cascading of errors risk self-assessment questions.

EXHIBIT 3-14   Accounting Risks Self-Assessment Questionnaire

Risk Assessment Category ___Cascading of Errors_____

Item	Yes	No
1. Is processing divided into stand-alone units wherever practical?		
2. Are all the programs that use a data element identified?		
3. When one program is changed, are all the related programs tested to ensure there is no negative impact on these related applications?		
4. Are connected applications notified when a change has been made in an application that passes data to those applications?		
5. Is the frequency and result of cascading errors identified and monitored?		

Incomplete Accounting Entry Risk

Complete accounting entries require all the debits to equal all the credits. In many automated applications, it's not necessary to enter both sides of the accounting transaction; one side is entered and the other side automatically generated. In other instances, the partial entry of information creates additional accounting information.

Entering one half of an accounting transaction is a common practice in automated systems. For example, if a customer orders a product the sales order is entered, which automatically generates the accounting entry to reduce inventory, and charges the customer's receivable account.

One large organization found its book inventory continually out-of-balance with physical inventory. The cause was finally identified as product returns which were placed into actual inventory, but never recorded through the computer applications into book inventory. The systems analyst didn't know that debits had to equal credits.

The generation of many accounting transactions automatically can also cause problems. For example, a customer orders a product and the computer system automatically generates shipping charges, sales tax, salesman's commission, etc. Incomplete specifications, or untested changes to the computer system, can occasionally delete the program segment that generated part of the accounting transaction. The results are erroneous recordkeeping.

EXHIBIT 3-15   Accouting Risks Self-Assessment Questionnaire

Risk Assessment Category   Incomplete Accounting Entry

Item	Yes	No
1. Are the full accounting entries specified as part of the application requirements?		
2. Do accountants review systems to ensure that complete accounting entries are processed?		
3. Do accounting reconciliations ensure that the total debits produced by the automated applications equal the total credits produced?		
4. Are automated accounting transactions reviewed for assurance they are in compliance with generally accepted accounting procedures?		
5. Are differences between debits and credits reported to management so that they can investigate causes of the problem?		

The incomplete accounting entry risk self-assessment questions are listed in Exhibit 3-15.

Repetition of Errors Risk

The computer characteristic that provides consistency of processing also provides for the repetition of errors. This is a risk that is unique to automated applications. Not only does the computer repeat errors, but it can repeat hundreds of thousands of them within minutes.

The repetition of errors does not necessarily mean the repetition of the same erroneous transaction. Errors can be repeated for any of the following reasons:

Programming error

Multiple entry of the same transaction

Erroneous variable information in the automated application, such as a product price

Erroneous constant information in the application system, such as the wrong withholding tax rate or sales tax percentage

Hardware or software failure

EXHIBIT 3-16   Accounting Risks Self-Assessment Questionnaire

Risk Assessment Category   Repetition of Errors

Item	Yes	No
1. Do procedures and standards exist governing the scope of testing to be performed in application systems?		
2. Do people visually scan output after systems changes have been made to search for potential errors?		
3. When identified, are repetition of errors quantified and reported to management?		
4. Is output validated to ensure there are no significant repeating errors?		
5. Are adequate controls in place to ensure the reasonableness of constant information, such as sales tax percentages, in the application system?		

The repetition of errors may or may not be obvious. In some instances, such as putting alphabetic data in a numeric field, it is obvious, while in other cases, such as using the wrong product price, the repeated error may not be obvious. Large repeating errors tend to be caught more quickly than smaller repeating errors. For example, if payroll amounts were off $1,000 they would be caught more quickly than a $1 difference. In many organizations, many repetition of errors situations are considered a cost of doing business and neither identified nor reported to management.

Exhibit 3-16 lists the repetition of errors risk self-assessment questions.

Improper Cutoff Risk

On-line computer systems pose a threat to recording accounting transactions in the proper accounting period. For example, on-line banking systems permit withdrawal transactions to be entered into the system that are not to occur for up to thirty days in the future. Inventory systems have inventory committed for shipment but still in stock. As on-line data base systems continue to grow so will the accounting cutoff problems.

The on-line data base systems of many organizations run twenty-four hours a day, seven days a week. While cutoff is a business problem and not a computer problem, the continual operation of computer systems makes this business problem more difficult. Either the processing rules

EXHIBIT 3–17   Accounting Risks Self-Assessment Questionnaire

Risk Assessment Category ___Improper Cutoff___

Item	Yes	No
1. Have the business cutoff rules been defined?		
2. Can transactions be identified for placement in the proper accounting period?		
3. Are transactions held by the computer system awaiting processing identified by accounting periods?		
4. For continuously operating applications, have the accounting cutoff procedures been defined and implemented?		
5. Are cutoff problems identified and presented to management for appropriate action?		

must be definitive regarding cutoff, or the transactions must be identified by the accounting period to which they belong.

The improper cutoff risk self-assessment questions are listed in Exhibit 3-17.

Fraud Risk

Automated systems are susceptible to fraud, as is any other system. Experience has shown that the difference between manual and computer frauds is that computer frauds are usually for larger amounts. Thus, the risks in computer systems for fraud are greater than the risks in manual systems.

It's not necessary to have computer skills to defraud automated applications. Most of the frauds of computerized applications involve only manipulation of input. For example, frauds can occur by identifying and using valid passwords to defraud, or entering unauthorized transactions using valid forms and procedures.

Control-oriented personnel have just begun to develop fraud prevention and detection techniques. Just as control lagged behind technology, so does the auditor's ability to detect technological fraud. Only a small percentage of auditors have data processing skills, and only a small percentage of those are involved in fraud auditing.

Exhibit 3-18 lists the fraud risk self-assessment questions.

EXHIBIT 3-18   Accounting Risks Self-Assessment Questionnaire

Risk Assessment Category ___Fraud_____

Item	Yes	No
1. Is your organization's internal audit staff assigned the responsibility to audit for frauds?		
2. Are your control personnel trained in fraud prevention and detection techniques?		
3. Have the potential fraud points in your automated applications been identified and procedures taken to prevent those points from being used for fraudulent purposes?		
4. Are procedures established to document and report to management potential and actual frauds?		
5. Are fraud-reducing techniques, such as cryptography, evaluated and implemented where appropriate?		

EXHIBIT 3-19   Accounting Risks Self-Assessment Questionnaire

Risk Assessment Category ___Noncompliance With Regulations___

Item	Yes	No
1. Have the regulatory requirements been identified?		
2. Are the regulatory requirements included within the systems specifications?		
3. Has legal counsel reviewed the implementation method for regulations?		
4. Are changes in regulations monitored so that application systems can be updated accordingly?		
5. Are procedures taken to ensure the accuracy and completeness of information reported to regulatory agencies?		

Noncompliance With Regulations Risk

Organizations are required to comply with federal and state regulations. Some of these regulations address computerized applications, while others address the data processed by those applications. The satisfaction of these requirements is another type of application system requirement.

The computer, because of its many capabilities, has been addressed specifically by regulations. Privacy regulations govern many industries and cover the kinds of information that must be retained, destroyed, and made available to individuals. Pending regulations govern many aspects of computerized applications including computer crime.

The data produced by automated applications is governed by many regulations, depending upon the application. Payroll applications collect and supply information to the Internal Revenue Service, both federal and state. Pension programs are covered by pension laws; accounts receivable systems by interest rate legislation; and so on, according to the regulatory requirements. These regulatory requirements must be included within the systems specifications.

The noncompliance with regulations risk self-assessment questions are listed in Exhibit 3-19.

Noncompliance With Policies and Procedures Risk

Application systems should be constructed and designed to comply with the organization's policies and procedures. The policies and procedures should be incorporated into the specifications of computerized applications. For example, the controller's accounting procedures should be included in the specifications for all automated accounting applications.

Many data processing systems analysts are unfamiliar with the controller's accounting procedures. While the users of the application system may be aware of these procedures, they may neglect to inform the data processing systems personnel of those procedures. Thus, it is possible to design, implement, and operate computer systems that do not comply with the controller's accounting procedures.

The noncompliance with policies and procedures risk self-assessment questions are listed in Exhibit 3-20.

Inadequate Service Level Risk

Automated applications are designed to service users. If those systems cannot provide adequate service, then users must find alternative means to achieve their objectives. In some organizations, users maintain manual

EXHIBIT 3-20   Accounting Risks Self-Assessment Questionnaire

Risk Assessment Category	Noncompliance With Policies and Procedures		

Item	Yes	No
1. Are accounting policies and procedures documented?		
2. Have the accounting policies and procedures been given to the data processing department for incorporation into the development of financial applications?		
3. Do members of the accounting department advise on the implementation of accounting procedures in the automated applications that process financial data?		
4. Are automated financial applications reviewed to determine they are in compliance with accounting policies and procedures?		
5. When accounting policies and procedures are modified, extended, or deleted, is the data processing department notified of those changes?		

records because the computer systems cannot supply the needed information within the appropriate time frame, while in other organizations, users are purchasing minicomputers to satisfy needs which should be satisfied on the larger computer systems.

Service levels can be affected by the following conditions:

Insufficient computer capacity

Some users consume more than their fair share of resources

Inefficient computer systems or procedures

Improper assignment of work priorities

Obsolete hardware or software which makes special requests extremely costly and time-consuming

Miscommunication between users and data processing personnel

Inadequate service levels can be a very costly risk in many organizations. Large amounts of funds can be wasted because sufficient information is not available at decision points, or by users developing duplicate or alter-

EXHIBIT 3–21   Accounting Risks Self-Assessment Questionnaire

Risk Assessment Category ___Inadequate Service Level___

Item	Yes	No
1. Have the service levels been defined for all applications?		
2. Have priorities of work been defined?		
3. Are planning procedures established to ensure that capacity is sufficient to handle service levels?		
4. Are procedures established, such as multilevel billing rates, to discourage users from consuming too many computer resources?		
5. Are service levels monitored to determine user requirements are being satisfied?		

EXHIBIT 3–22   Accounting Risks Self-Assessment Questionnaire

Risk Assessment Category ___Improper Accounting___

Item	Yes	No
1. Do accounting manuals specify the proper accounting for information processed by automated applications?		
2. Are the accounting manuals in the hands of the appropriate data processing personnel?		
3. Do accountants participate in the specification of the accounting requirements for financial applications?		
4. Are procedures established to verify that the implemented accounting procedures are those intended by management?		
5. In instances where the accounting is specified by regulation, are the organization's lawyers involved in reviewing the specified accounting methods?		

native methods to get the information they need. The magnitude of the risk can only be measured when the service level requirements are specified and monitored.

Exhibit 3-21 lists the inadequate service level risk self-assessment questions.

Improper Accounting Risk

Accounting entries should be processed in accordance with generally accepted accounting procedures. These procedures are specified by accounting literature and governmental regulation. For example, the Foreign Corrupt Practices Act spells out certain kinds of improper accounting transactions.

Data processing personnel rarely have a knowledge of accounting procedures. Therefore, it is usually necessary for accountants to specify how financial applications should implement accounting functions. Unless this happens, improper accounting may occur.

The improper accounting risk self-assessment questions are listed in Exhibit 3-22.

DETERMINING THE MAGNITUDE OF A RISK

After the risk has been identified, the magnitude of that risk must be determined. Knowing that a risk exists is not enough. The organization must be able to determine the magnitude of the risk so that they can approach control from a businesslike perspective.

The determination of the magnitude of a risk should be future oriented. This is different from traditional control methods which look backward to determine what has happened in the past. Looking backward, one can obtain an assessment of the magnitude of the problem through historical experiences. Unfortunately, for many of the risks in automated systems there is no historical experience on which to estimate the future magnitude of the risk.

The accountant must learn to estimate the potential loss associated with a risk which has not yet happened. It is only through the identification of new risks and determining the magnitude of those risks that appropriate countermeasures can be designed. This type of approach is essential to the proper management and control over the use of advanced technologies.

The methods for determining the severity of the risk are covered in Chapter 4. Chapter 4 is designed to teach accountants risk-estimating procedures so that the proper resources can be allocated to controlling the new accounting risks.

RISK ASSESSMENT PROFILE

The risks that have been discussed in this chapter are the more common risks in computerized accounting applications. These risks can be used to provide an organization with a preliminary risk assessment of its automated accounting applications. The assessment is designed to show whether your organization's accounting applications are of high, average, or low risk.

The risk assessment is based upon the answers to the self-assessment questions associated with each of the nineteen accounting risks. In completing the self-assessment questions, two approaches can be taken. First, an individual can perform the assessment, in which case the result will be based on the assessment of one individual. Second, a group of people can answer the self-assessment questions. This will result in two or more assessments for each risk. One check mark should be put in the appropriate assessment column for each individual that assesses the risks.

After all of the self-assessment questions have been answered, the results should be posted to the Accounting Risk Profile form (Exhibit 3-23). The number of "no" answers should be accumulated for each risk self-assessment set of questions. The following table can be used to convert the "no" answers into a rating that can be posted to Exhibit 3-23 for that risk.

To use the "No" Answer Table, the assessor first determines the number of people that answered the self-assessment questions and uses that

"No" Answer Table

| | Number of "NO" Answers | | | |
Rating	One-Person Rating	Two-Person Rating	Three-Person Rating	Four-Person Rating
Very low risk	0	0–1	0–2	0–3
Low risk	1	2–3	3–4	4–6
Average risk	2	4–5	5–8	7–9
High risk	3	6–8	9–11	10–14
Very high risk	4–5	9–10	12–15	15–20

EXHIBIT 3-23 Accounting Risk Profile

Accounting Risk	Assessment					Risk Score	Rank
	Very High (5)	High (4)	Avg (3)	Low (2)	Very Low (1)		
Data entry error							
Improper code							
Unidentified data							
Unauthorized transaction							
Control level violation							
Lost transactions							
Erroneous output							
Processing mismatch							
File out-of-balance							
Inadequate audit trial							
Cascading of errors							
Incomplete accounting entry							
Repetition of errors							
Improper cutoff							
Fraud							
Noncompliance with regulations							
Noncompliance with policies/procedures							
Inadequate service level							
Improper accounting							
Totals							

column. All of the no answers are accumulated and found in the appropriate column to provide a rating. For example, if two people answered the
self-assessment questions and together had six no answers, their rating
would be a high-risk rating.

After all nineteen self-assessment ratings have been posted to the Accounting Risk Profile form (Exhibit 3-23), the evaluation process can begin. The value of the rating (1, 2, 3, 4, or 5 as indicated at the top of the
Assessment column) is posted to the Risk Score column. The rating value
(1-5) should also be added to produce a total for each column. The rank is
then determined. The risks are ranked as follows:

> Very high risk (5) = Rank 1
> High risk (4) = Rank 2
> Average risk (3) = Rank 3
> Low risk (2) = Rank 4
> Very low risk (1) = Rank 5

The evaluation of the accounting risk can be threefold. First, the scores
are ranked from one through five. The highest-ranking risks are ranked as
1, and the lowest-ranking risks are ranked as 5. Second, the nineteen risk
scores are combined to provide a total. This can be divided by nineteen to
develop an assessment for all of the accounting risks. The assessment for
all of the risks, or for the individual risks, can then be interpreted using
Exhibit 3-24, depending on where it falls on the assessment scale. Third,
totaling the number of rating for each assessment category illustrates the
number of risks falling in each of the categories. This can be helpful in
evaluating the risks to illustrate whether there is a normal assessment risk
curve or whether all of the risks have about the same level of control.

Accountants' Computer Guideline 2.   The starting point to improve the adequacy of computer controls is a knowledge of the magnitude of the existing risk.

EXHIBIT 3-24   Risk Assessment Interpretation Table

Risk Assessment	Interpretation
Very high risk	Organizations in this situation should be extremely concerned over the risks in their automated applications. The very-high-risk assessment is normally indicative of a lack of control skills within the organization. Organizations who assess their accounting applications in this category should hire outside consultants to conduct an in-depth study of the adequacy of the countermeasures in their application systems.
High risk	Organizations rating their accounting applications in this high-risk category should be concerned over the potential threat to the integrity of their accounting data. These organizations also should consider engaging an outside consultant to examine the adequacy of their countermeasures against risk.
Average risk	The installed countermeasures provide a reasonable degree of protection from loss associated with the risks. This category of risk should not provide great comfort to an organization. While many of the threats have probably been prevented, the remaining threats could still result in large losses.
Low risk	Installed countermeasures should prove effective against the types of risks existing in most automated accounting applications.
Very low risk	The installed countermeasures should be very effective against risk, even to the point where the organization may wish to determine if some of the controls are cost-effective, based on the extensiveness of the installed countermeasures.

part two

THE EFFECT
OF AUTOMATION

four

THE COMPUTER
AND THE ORGANIZATION

The structure of an organization and its automated systems should be synchronized. If the automated systems march to the beat of a different drum from the one building the organizational structure, a control gap will exist. The differences may grow so slowly that the problem is not realized.

When we first buy a house, it usually meets our expectations and needs. We eagerly await moving day so we can take advantage of the features of our home. The basement becomes our winter refuge, and the backyard pool our summer vacation retreat.

Slowly our needs and requirements change. A new child comes, which overcrowds our bedrooms, the pool becomes a hassle to keep clean, and the basement is cluttered with unwanted furniture and boxes. Satisfaction is turned to dissatisfaction, making the house more a source of irritation than pleasure.

Automated systems frequently exhibit the same characteristics as the older home. In the house, the stairs begin to creak with age, the paint starts to fade and peel, and the structure becomes too small to satisfy our requirements. As the systems maintenance becomes more difficult, fewer people understand or want to work with the older technology, and the system no longer conforms with standards.

Occasionally, we need to step back away from our home and analyze what it has done to our family structure. If the house no longer meets our requirements, it is time to make changes. The same concept applies to computer systems and organizational structure. When the two drift apart, changes need to be made to one or both.

This chapter examines the working of the computer and its effect on the organization. People make automated systems work, and people make automated systems fail. This chapter explains how the proper meshing of systems and organizational structure improves the probability of success, and how to achieve an organizational structure that complements the characteristics of the automated system.

KEEPING SYSTEMS AND STRUCTURE IN HARMONY

When an organization installs its first computer, the systems and the organizational structure are ordinarily in harmony. Like the new house, the systems were built to satisfy the requirements of the occupants. At that point, the systems move toward horizontal integration, while the organizational structure retains and often reinforces its vertical hierarchical structure.

Time moves systems further away from harmony with the organizational structure. This is illustrated in Figure 4-1. This movement is normal and should be expected. What is needed to rectify the disharmony is the continual modification of systems and organizational structure to keep the two in harmony. Figure 4-2 shows how the recommended continual modification permits systems and structure to come together and interact smoothly, versus the ever-increasing gap with its associated problems when the adjustments are not made regularly. For example, as systems become integrated, organizational structure must be established to oversee and direct that integration.

A self-assessment questionnaire (Exhibit 4-1) designed to identify

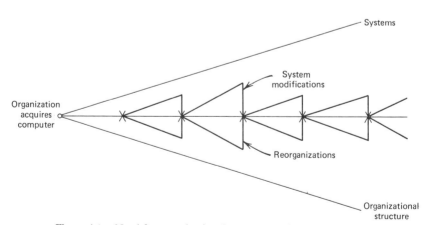

Figure 4-1. Need for organizational structure and systems changes.

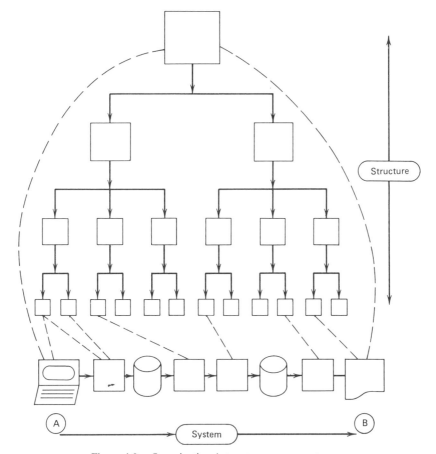

Figure 4-2. Organizational structure versus system.

the gap between your organizational structure and your systems follows. These self-assessment questions are designed to help the accountant determine how well the organization structure and systems are integrated. A "yes" answer indicates good integration between systems and organizational structure, while a "no" answer indicates a potential structural problem. The more "no" answers, the greater the concern.

Technological Rule of Thumb 4. People and the organizational structure are as important criteria to the success of automation as are the technocrats and computer programs.

EXHIBIT 4-1 Structure/Systems Integration Self-Assessment Questionnaire

Item	Yes	No
1. Does each system have a single manager responsible for that system who reports independently of the data processing function?		
2. Does that single manager have the responsibility for the movement of data between systems?		
3. Does that single manager have responsibility for the interface between that and other systems?		
4. Is one individual accountable for each data element?		
5. Is responsibility clearly established for common data elements such as zip code, employee number, product number, etc.?		
6. Does someone outside of data processing establish the priority for implementation of new systems?		
7. Does someone oversee the selection of hardware and software to ensure hardware and software compatibility throughout the entire organization?		
8. Is a single manager outside of data processing responsible for a chain of integrated systems?		
9. Is data managed as a resource of the organization as opposed to being managed by individual functions?		
10. Does a single manager have responsibility for information systems planning for the organization?		
11. Has a long-range data processing plan been established?		
12. Are all of the data processing costs consolidated so that the total resources expended for data processing is known?		
13. Are procedures established to identify, document, and report data processing problems to senior management?		
14. Have procedures been established for resolving disputes between users of data processing resources?		

HOW DOES AUTOMATION HAPPEN?

There is nothing magical about installing automated systems. It is the opposite of what most people think is the process. People see the results of automation and they can be very impressive. People see production schedules produced, inventory reordered in the proper amount, and savings account interest accumulated and compounded daily.

The automation challenge is not in accomplishing the tasks but, rather, breaking the tasks down into their component parts so that they are solvable. The change maker works with almost infinite detail as opposed to working with big problems. The complexities of the systems development process requires an organized approach.

The organized approach to systems development used by most organizations is called the systems development life cycle. The life cycle concept implies that systems are conceptualized and then continue through a period of time evolving into what is needed, then modified to meet changing needs, and when their useful life is completed the systems are terminated. A brief explanation of the life cycle phases is needed to provide an understanding of what happens during the developmental process. Most systems development life cycles contain the following five phases.

Requirements Phase. Defines what the system is expected to accomplish. Experience has shown that as systems become more complex and integrated additional resources need to be expended during the requirements phase to assure the proper integration into the network of systems. The tasks that should be accomplished during the requirements phase include:

Definition of data requirements

Definition of processing requirements

Definition of output requirements

Definition of timeliness and reliability of processed results

Development of criteria to measure the successful implementation of the requirements

Design Phase. Involves the transformation of the requirements into machine-accomplishable functions. The design process includes defining input into machine-readable characteristics, defining the processing rules and data file structures, and the output products. At the conclusion of the design phase, the specifications are in sufficient detail so that they can be transcribed into machine-understandable instructions. Using systems design languages, design specifications can be automatically translated into machine-readable instructions, eliminating much of the implementation phase.

Implementation Phase.   Includes the translation of systems specifications into machine instructions. This process is called programming, which translates system specifications into a programming language which can be translated through a compiler automatically into machine language. The language capabilities determine the resources available to the programmer for the translation process. The more powerful programming languages are called statement-level languages. The most used statement-level languages are COBOL, PL/1, FORTRAN, BASIC, and RPG. Lower-level languages require a better understanding of machine capabilities and are normally referred to as a macro- or assembler-level language. The end product of this phase is operational programs.

Operations/Maintenance Phase.   The implementation phase produces operational programs. The operations of these programs produce the results specified in the requirements phase. When conditions change, either in the user area or the operations area, the operational programs require modifications. The systems modification process is referred to as systems maintenance. Systems maintenance corrects deficiencies and errors in the operational programs as well as enhances the program's capabilities.

Termination Phase.   When the operational system no longer fulfills the user requirements, it should be removed from operation. The previous phases of the systems life cycle have been well defined, but the termination phase of systems causes many organizations management decision problems. The tendency is to let operational systems operate because they work. Even though the systems fail to fulfill many of the user's objectives, they operate and are a known quantity. The cost of developing new systems may appear to be prohibitive when compared to the operational cost of the existing system. Therefore, many systems are artificially resuscitated so that they may stay in operation even though they are inefficient and fail to fulfill many of the user objectives. Accountants need to develop guidelines for their organizations indicating when systems should be terminated. Some of the criteria they may wish to consider are:

Maintenance costs that are increasing over time

Systems which are slow responding to user requests for special listings of information

Systems using older hardware and software

Systems with no requests for changes (indicates users can attain needed information from alternate sources)

Systems which do not fit into the organization's long-range data processing plan

Technological Rule of Thumb 5. Without a methodical systems design process, the results may be a systems mess.

THE COMPUTER'S EFFECT ON THE ORGANIZATION

No family or organization can undergo a major change without affecting the style of living or doing business. Failure to consider and plan for change and the human resistance to change is an error made by many organizations. They underestimate the impact of the computer on all parts of the organization.

We will review the computer effects on the following four areas of an organization.

Decision making

People

Control

Security

The Computer's Impact on Decision Making

Managers need information as a basis for decision making. Better informed managers usually make better decisions. Computers can supply managers with the needed information. Information processed and stored by computer systems can be used by managers in the decision-making process.

The following three types of information are used by managers in making decisions:

Historical information

Future projections

Industrial and economic information

Information pertaining to events and activities outside the organization rarely can be provided by the organization's computer system. This would only be possible if the organization's computer had access to outside data bases. Thus, the information produced by the computer is restricted to historical information and estimates about future events.

The information produced by the computer may not be of value in the decision-making process because:

The information is received too late

The information is presented in the wrong format

The information is too voluminous

The decision maker doesn't understand the computer-produced reports

When systems are developed, it is important to identify the decisions that are made in the area covered by that system. Also, the characteristics describing when the decision should be made must be identified. Once the decisions have been identified, the information required to make those decisions can then be identified. The adequacy of the system can partially be determined by whether or not the information needed to make the decision is available to the decision maker at the time the decision is made.

Accountants' Computer Guideline 3. Identify accounting decisions as part of the systems requirements so that the information needed by accountants for decision making will be produced by the system.

Impact on People

The computer affects people, their jobs, their lives, their job performance. The importance of people in systems is often underestimated. We frequently think of systems as processes independent of people. We talk of "beating the system" and "getting around the system." People write letters to computers saying: "Dear Computer: Please correct a problem for me." The following is one of those letters which typifies the view that systems do not need people.

ABC Company
Big City, U.S.A.

Dear Computer:
Please help me. The people that work in your office don't believe me, but you know I sent in my payment because you cashed my check. Please tell the people where the money is or else my credit rating will be ruined.

A Frustrated Ex-Customer

People make systems work or not work. Machines only do what they are told. A major computer manufacturer says that one-half of all computer system problems are due to errors and omissions by people.

People interact with systems in four ways. They design systems; they implement and maintain systems; they operate systems; and they use the systems to perform their assigned tasks. The success of a system depends upon how well all these people perform their tasks. People can ''make'' or ''break'' systems because they tell the machines what to do, make sure they do it, and use the results produced. Keep this in mind as you analyze why computers are, or are not, effective.

An accounts receivable system in a large corporation proved to be ineffective. The accounts never seemed to be correct because of mispostings and other errors. The problem was eventually traced to the fact that two clerical people who had worked together side by side for a number of years were separated when the computer system was introduced into their department. They blamed the computer system for the separation, which had been an important source of their job satisfaction. Because of their unhappiness, the two clerks didn't care if the system failed and did the minimum needed to get by. When the people were reunited, they expended more effort and the system functioned properly.

A manufacturing plant in a large company wanted a production control system, but all of the proposed systems designs appeared unacceptable. The data processing department began to feel that they were wasting their effort in continually modifying the design based on negative comments. Finally they realized that there was one individual in the production department who was vetoing the design. They realized they had never consulted this individual on what was needed, and thus had alienated a person who, while not manager, was a kingpin in the department. The data processing department paid appropriate homage to that individual, and the next proposed design was enthusiastically approved, even though no significant change was made in the design.

Industrial psychologists tell us that when we change people's jobs, their responsibilities, and their authority, we meet resistance. Even change makers don't like their jobs changed. To ignore this fact in automated systems can substantially reduce the probability of the system's success.

Industrial psychologists recommend that the affected people be involved in the design process. These are the people who will be involved in the operation and management of the system, including clerical personnel. Early in the design process, the designers should present to the people affected by the new system how it will change their jobs. The designer should request input from those people on the practicality and usefulness of the system, but the primary objective is to gain support from the involved people.

The designers should interact with the users throughout the design process and again when the system becomes operational. During the first few days or weeks of operation, the designers should work very closely with the people using the system. After installation, the users should be given the opportunity to make suggestions and recommendations for system enhancements. Involvement of users in the design process tends to reduce problems.

Studies by one computer vendor indicated that people frequently sabotaged systems. Much of this sabotage was done to "get even with the company," as opposed to achieve personal gain. This makes it difficult to differentiate sabotage from errors and omissions.

One large insurance company experienced a periodic data file failure. The process of correction was costly and time-consuming. It wasn't until months after the problem began to occur that the cause was traced to an unhappy computer operator who deliberately caused the disk drive to "crash" the data file.

Another insurance company was harmed by an employee when policyholder dividends were sent out. The dividend notice offered the policyholders the following three options: (1) use dividend to buy more insurance, (2) apply dividend against future premiums, (3) get a check for the dividend. Options one and two were more favorable to the insurance company. An operator in the printing process was able to insert this message in all of the dividend notices: "If you select option three, we'll break your thumbs." The operator may have thought the message humorous, but many of the policyholders and company management did not.

Sabotage by disgruntled employees is increasing. College students who have spent four years in colleges attempting to "beat computers" do not stop when they become employed in industry. One of the methods of getting even with your company for poor raises, lack of promotions, lack of recognition for one's effort or being a person is to "punish" computer systems. Changing inputs, shuffling cards, failing to bring to the attention of management an obvious problem are all means of getting even with the company through the company's computer systems.

Some of the techniques that organizations are using to reduce and identify disgruntled employee sabotage include:

The inclusion of an industrial psychologist on the systems development team
Heavy involvement by all users in the design process

An easy-to-use procedure to correct problems in automated systems, such as a suggestion system (frequently with a reward structure)

Establishment of an error-tracking or SWAT team to trace the cause of problems

Assigning responsibility for each part of an automated system to a single individual

Recording and reporting of errors so that the types and frequency of errors can be monitored

Impact on Control

A $500,000 Systems Auditability and Control study, funded by the IBM Corporation and conducted by Stanford Research Institute, concluded that too little attention had been given to control in an automated environment.* This startling conclusion was the result of a two-year study. The study stated that the challenge of mastering technology had consumed so much of the resources of the data processing function that they had not had adequate time to design good control principles and guidelines.

The maturity of data processing has been described in many ways. However, most of these maturity cycles list the development of good controls as a sign of maturity of a data processing function. Because of the control requirements of the Foreign Corrupt Practices Act, many organizations have been pushed into the control phase of data processing maturity.

Few data processing organizations have a formalized methodology for designing controls in computer applications. The most common method is to not let the same mistake occur twice. Control design is often historically oriented, as opposed to addressing the new risks in an automated environment. Earlier the control dilemma faced by many organizations in their automated systems was discussed. Later chapters will cover some of the immediately implementable control solutions available to those organizations. Accountants having control responsibilities should be leaders in proposing control standards and guidelines.

Impact on Security

The concentration of data, and ready accessibility to the data, increases the importance of security in an automated business environment. Many

*Systems Auditability and Control Executive Report, Copyright 1977, The Institute of Internal Auditors, Altamonte Springs, Florida.

systems are accessible from any touch-tone telephone, enabling data to be manipulated thousands of miles away. These kinds of threats warrant the expenditure of time and effort on developing a good security program.

Individual documents were subject to security violations when the data were filed in various file cabinets throughout the organization. While paper documents were accessible, it was difficult to obtain and analyze a large quantity of these documents. In automated systems, data are centralized and large amounts of data can be reviewed quickly.

Another severe threat to security is the new analysis tools that permit complex analyses to be performed within a few minutes that only a few years ago might have taken several months to develop and execute. Using data base technology and query languages, perpetrators can restructure files within seconds, perform complex analyses, and obtain valuable data. For example, if someone was interested in obtaining a listing of employed engineers, that individual could do some comparisons between personnel data records, payroll records, pension records, and other information maintained about those individuals, do the comparisons and analyses needed to find the more valuable engineers, and then prepare for a headhunting firm a list of the most logical candidates to pirate away from that employer.

Data are as much an asset to an organization as cash. In addition, the manipulation of data records may be a much easier way to obtain cash than to actually attempt to withdraw from an organization's cash accounts. For example, deleting amounts due in accounts receivable, shipping product and not recording it as an amount due from a customer, or increasing the amount of interest paid on savings accounts can all be accomplished by manipulating data in a computerized application.

It is not necessary for an individual to take data to gain benefit from those data. A previous example explained the value of obtaining a list of an organization's key engineers, which could be sold to a headhunting firm. A list of an organization's better customers is also valuable, as are manufacturing trade secrets stored on computer file. All of these can be taken, but the original file remains intact, making detection very difficult.

Some security measures are costly and complex, such as cryptography, while others are relatively easy and cheap, like bait records. Cryptography is a means of translating information into unintelligible data through the use of a cipher. Bait records are records stored on automated files used to detect file compromises. For example, if the controller suspected that the organization's list of customers might be compromised, the controller could insert his or her name with a special middle initial on the customer file using a home address. If a contact was made with the controller using the bait middle initial, the controller would immediately know that information on that file had been compromised. The special name and address on the file comprise the bait record.

Some of the newer methods of ensuring security over automated systems include:

Appointment of a security officer (an individual who has primary responsibility for data security)

Development of a security policy

Use of cryptography

Use of bait records

User profiles (a document explaining which user can have access to which resource)

Accountants' Computer Guideline 4. For every known computer problem there is a solution, but until the accountants know the problem a solution is not possible.

SYSTEMS VERSUS ORGANIZATIONAL STRUCTURE

Most organizations can be characterized as having a hierarchical organizational structure. The chief executive officer sits at the top of the hierarchy, delegating responsibility and authority to lower and lower levels. While there are some organizations attempting new structures, such as the matrix structure, the hierarchical structure is the most common organizational structure.

This structure consolidates authority and responsibilities at the top of the structure and delegates authority and responsibility as the structure moves downward. Typical functions under a chief executive officer would be marketing, distribution, production, personnel, and finance. Each has been assigned a portion of the chief executive officer's responsibilities. The structure provides for checks on the other's scope of authority and responsibility. The hierarchical structure is illustrated in Figure 4-2 (Organizational Structure Versus System).

Many organizations begin automation by computing systems independently of each other. For example, the marketing function may automate order entry and invoicing, the personnel function may automate payroll, and the finance function may automate consolidation of financial statements. Each system operates as an independent system. These systems and the organizational structure operate in harmony because each system serves only one master.

As data processing matures, these stand-alone systems become integrated in networks of systems. As these systems become integrated, data flow from system to system to system. This is illustrated as the system flow portion of Figure 4-1. For example, the entry point of the system may be order entry by customers or marketing personnel. The final step in the system is a production schedule for the factory. The two ends of this chain of systems are the remnants of the old stand-alone system which distribute product, bill customers, record accounts receivable, determine inventory replenishment requirements, determine whether those requirements should be from purchases or the factory, develop factory schedules, and optimize the use of men and machines in the factory.

This chain of systems crosses many structural boundaries within the organization. The dotted lines in Figure 4-2 represent whose function in the organization has been automated. Many functions in the organizational structure have responsibility over part of a system, but no one except the chief executive officer has total responsibility over the entire system.

Let's examine what would happen if the production division is unhappy with some of the system outputs provided them (the report labeled "B" in Figure 4-2). The needed change requires a modification to the input provided by the order entry group (indicated by letter "A"). If it becomes necessary to resolve a difference of opinion, the parties involved must go up the organizational structure to the first person having jurisdiction, which may be the chief executive officer. In many organizations, the chief executive officer is the only one organizationally capable of resolving, or deciding on, the direction for large, integrated systems. Unfortunately, few chief executive officers either want to or will exercise that responsibility.

Lacking proper organizational structure to oversee systems, organizations look for informal means to accomplish those objectives. For example, many organizations establish steering committees to set system priorities and resolve differences of opinion in system direction and approach. Other organizations let that responsibility devolve to the data processing department. The systems analyst may need to act as a quasi-chief executive officer in making system decisions.

The disharmony between the organizational structure and the system cause the following conditions to happen in many organizations:

Informal System Structure. Lacking clear direction from senior management, organizations develop informal methods to overcome weaknesses in the organizational structure. These approaches include a strong data processing department, a strong user dictating direction, or a task force or steering committee appointed to debate and resolve organizational system differences.

Informal Systems. Users failing to achieve their objectives from the formal systems develop informal systems to achieve those objectives. Many divisions and departments install and use microcomputers to solve problems and provide information not readily available from the large computer systems. Rather than fight the organizational structure, they achieve their goals through alternate, but often expensive, means.

Extensive Systems Maintenance. When the original systems design fails to properly satisfy user requirements, users initiate requests for changes. In most organizations, the cost of systems maintenance exceeds the cost of developing new systems. While some of these systems maintenance costs are associated with changing business requirements, much of it may be associated with the failure of the organizational structure to provide the desired results. Some individuals believe that more than half of systems maintenance costs, a figure in the billions of dollars per year, are associated with the inability of the organizational structure to provide proper direction for systems.

Control Gaps. Many managers state that a system such as that illustrated in Figure 4-2 does not belong to them. It's somebody else's system. When managers take that attitude, what they are saying is, "I'm not responsible for the information placed into, processed by, or outputted from that system." In many organizations, it may be difficult to pinpoint responsibility and accountability for a system. When the data processing department assumes that responsibility by default, they then are accused of being power hungry.

PLANNING FOR AUTOMATION

Automation has had a greater impact on the methods of conducting work than any other single cause. The change in business methods is accelerating due to increasing automation of the business. Someone other than those implementing automation needs to oversee and plan the use of automation by the organization. Too frequently the direction of automation is centered in the acquisition and use of automated equipment.

The impetus to automate usually comes from one of the following three sources:

Senior Management. Senior management recognizes the need to improve productivity and capabilities. The solution often appears to be automation, and thus senior management establishes a function or a task force to oversee the acquisition, implementation, and operation of automated systems.

Data Processing.   Data processing management initiates studies and/ or requests new or enhanced capabilities to automate systems.

Users.   Those departments or divisions who can benefit from automation initiate the studies or requests to automate all or part of their function.

Much of the planning for automation centers around the equipment. This is because automation is not possible without automated equipment, and thus the equipment becomes the focal point for automation. Those people controlling the equipment often control automation.

Many organizations have designated a senior officer responsible for automation in the organization. Senior management looks to that individual to plan and propose changes in automation. The data processing function may or may not report to that individual.

Some organizations are appointing a member of senior management as data administrator for the organization. This is a high-level senior management position independent of acquisition and control of automated equipment. The data administrator has responsibility for data policy and definition within the organization. That individual administers data in the same way the personnel manager administers personnel and the treasurer manages cash and investments.

Most organizations recognize the importance of information as a resource to their organization. Information is comparable to people, machinery, and money as a resource that needs to be managed. Although, like people, it is not recorded on the books of the organization as an asset, in today's technological environment information may be as important as people in the continued success and growth of an organization.

The key to automation is information. The control over automation should be directed at information and not the equipment that processes that information. Direction needs to come from those responsible for the origination, processing, and use of information rather than the technical functions.

The administration of data defines the attributes, control over, and use of data in the organization. Most of the existing problems with automation are data problems. Automation magnifies the problems that exist within the organization. It rarely creates problems, but more frequently brings to the attention of management problems that have already existed. Unfortunately, many of these problems are associated with the use of automation and not with the organizational structure.

The data administrator is ordinarily assigned the following responsibilities:

Definition of data, its integrity, and timeliness
Definition of uses of data in the organization
Establishment of data access rules
Establishment of data security policies
Resolution of disputes between users
Establishment of data retention
Establishment of data audit trail requirements
Establishment of priority of implementation for new uses of data

Today's technology is a data-driven technology. Many of the application programs can be automatically created based upon data definition. The data attributes that, when documented using an automated tool called a data dictionary, can be used to generate a program include:

Data validation rules
Data access rules
Report output format
Data relationships

Large segments of the processing programs can be generated automatically from the data definition rules. Expected future capabilities will accelerate this trend. Thus, the individual who controls data may control automation in the organization.

THE CHANGE MAKERS

Organizations hire specialists to help them automate system functions. This is because most of their divisions and departments have full workloads and thus cannot undertake the automation process themselves. In addition, users of automation may not possess the skills necessary to redesign and automate their requirements to manage this new skill.
Organizations establish departments, which may be called:

Business systems department
Computer systems department
Data processing department
Computer operations
Systems analysis department

The real name should be *change makers* because that is their function. The name change maker would be more appropriate because it would recognize what they are attempting to do, and the human resistance to change. Systems analysis or development does not lead one to expect the drastic changes that are being made in people's lives, the methods of performing work, and the control over those new methods.

We need to look at these change makers to understand their motives, approaches, and the kinds of changes they are likely to make. Let's take a satirical look at the change makers as people and see what makes them tick:

Michael Manager—Chief of Data Processing

Michael is chief of the technocrats. It is his prima donnas that invade your sanctuary and rearrange your furniture because that's a better way to perform your job. In most organizations, Michael is a veteran employee and has lived through much of the technological change that has occurred in the organization. Michael understands integrated systems, but recognizes that the users may not. Thus, while Michael solicits and encourages users to participate, accept responsibility, and define requirements, deep down Michael knows that he knows more about what the company wants than anybody else. Michael's main problems are budget pressures from senior management and the continual string of changes requested by users. He hopes to eliminate these two impediments that keep him from advancing the "state of the art" in automated technology.

Sandy Systems Analyst

Sandy is the key change maker in the organization. Sandy is the architect who works with the user to reconstruct the methods of doing business. Unfortunately, Sandy knows little or nothing about the user's business, and a lot about technology. Sandy is frequently more concerned with the use and optimization of technology than with learning the user's business. Sandy is a computer science major who knows surprisingly little about business or people. Deep down, Sandy believes that all people can be replaced by machinery and that machinery can perform all functions better than people. Sandy also believes that data processing has no responsibility for data until it reaches the data processing department, and no responsibility for how or if the data is used after it leaves the data processing department. The hallowed sanctuary of data processing is where the action is, and it's where Sandy wants to be.

Penny Programmer

The whole world, to Penny, is programming. It doesn't matter whether Penny is programming a payroll system, inventory system, or creating another data processing library. The computer and the programming language are everything. Penny is similar to the clerk in the office who doesn't know or care about anything except what happens when the work arrives on her desk. Penny isn't interested in what the previous program has done or what the following program will do. What Penny has been told to do is what Penny will do regardless of the consequence to the organization. Penny's interest lies in learning new technology, new programming languages, and not in learning what the user does or does not want. Penny's, like Sandy's, allegiance is to technology and not the organization. When times are good, Penny and Sandy will leave an organization to gain a small pay raise, or to learn newer technology.

Oliver Operator

The operator of automated equipment is like a robot. People operate the computer in the same manner that a factory operator operates a drill press or production machine. The work is repetitive and frequently unchallenging. The job is often downgraded in the name of control. We feel it is a control risk if an operator understands programming, how the system works, or how to modify the system. In this environment, Oliver is usually present in body, but not always in mind.

Eunice User

This is the token representative from the user department to work with data processing personnel. Unfortunately, few users want to assign their best people to this translator role, so they often appoint a member of their department who has already joined the roles of the active retired (those people who have stopped working but are still on the payroll). Eunice is the individual to whom the data processing people look for answers and explanations of requirements. Eunice can play a major role in assuring successful systems or act as a bystander, letting the data processing personnel play a dominant role.

The above cast of characters is a stereotype of many of the bad traits found among the change makers. If you recognize these individuals as employees of your organization, you may have systems change problems.

On the other hand, if you can encourage these people to work for your competitors, not your organization, you may be well on the road to successfully automating your organization.

Change makers should be seen as translators. They translate user requirements into technological specifications. These change makers need to be multilingual. They must understand the language of technology and the language of the user. If they are not multilingual, they will err on the side of the language they know best.

When the change makers speak computerese better than userese, they will find that every problem can be solved on the computer, and most likely solved only by use of the latest technology. On the other hand, if the change makers speak userese better than computerese, then they may underutilize or misutilize technology. The ideal change maker can speak both languages fluently. Figure 4-3 shows the relationship between the players involved in automation.

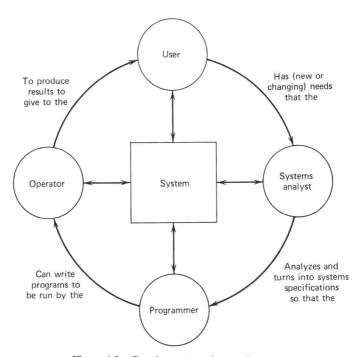

Figure 4-3. People–systems interaction.

Changes in Data Processing Responsibilities

Significant technological changes are occurring which will have an impact on the accountant and other users of technology. Many of the traditional data processing functions are disappearing, and are being replaced by new functions. For example, many of the tasks that have been performed by programmers are now being automated by the newer hardware and software. When data validation rules are defined with the data, the data validation programs can be automatically generated from the defined validation rules. It is no longer necessary for a programmer to translate those rules into programming languages. In addition, many of the functions performed by computer operators are being transferred to user areas and performed by user personnel at terminals.

System users are becoming more involved in the department, operation, and modification of systems that affect their area. Unfortunately, too many users still only speak userese and feel uncomfortable when the use of technology expands too rapidly. The solution is for the users to become more knowledgeable in computerese so that they understand what is available to them and how to get it.

Accountants' Computer Guideline 5. People are both the problem and the solution. Understand the strengths and weaknesses of computer people, and build on their strengths.

DOCUMENTING COMPUTER DECISIONS

A computer decision-making documentation form is illustrated in Exhibit 4-2. This form can be used to describe the types of decisions made in any computer system. The steps required to complete the form are:

1. Indicate the involved system and the date the form was completed.
2. Assign the decision number.
3. State the decision to be made.
4. Indicate for each decision the characteristic of when that decision must be made.
5. List the information needed to make the decision.

Let's review an example of the use of the form. Assume an inventory system, and that one of the decisions to be made is when to reorder prod-

EXHIBIT 4-2   Decision Description Form

System_____	Date_____	
Decision to be Made	Characteristics of When Decision Must be Made	Information Needed to Make Decision

uct. The decision characteristics are that the reorder is to be made within twenty-four hours after the on-hand inventory drops below a predetermined order point. The information needed to make the decision includes the identification of the product that has fallen below the reorder point, the economic order quantity for the product, and the suppliers that can provide the information. Providing this information to the decision maker from the automated system enables a logical decision to be made on how much product to order and from whom.

The above example could also have included a projection of sales for the next three, six, or twelve months. This type of information could be produced by a computer system using trend analysis. The trend could show whether sales of the product are going up or down and what expected sales may be in the future. Obviously, this doesn't take into account other events such as advertising promotions, the economy, and so on, but it is a source of information available in the decision-making process.

The accountant should look for this kind of decision-making documentation in financial systems. If decision-making requirements are not specified, then the type of information needed may not be collected and presented at the appropriate decision-making time. In our above example, a one-page report could be put out for each product that needed to be ordered. It is possible that the decision makers do not know what type of information could be provided to them by the computer, and thus may make many business decisions without using the power of the computer to help them in that process.

Accountants' Computer Guideline 6. The computer is a tool for processing administrative information and for decision making. Accountants should document the decisions they make and determine that the information needed for their decision is produced by the computerized systems.

TECHNOLOGY AND THE EXECUTIVE

The proponents of automated systems have proposed connecting senior executives directly to those systems. It has been suggested that senior executives place computer terminals on their desks and then interact with computer applications to gain needed information. These pictures of the modern executive with a computer terminal form an unrealistic image of the up-to-date, contemporary executive.

In practice, most senior executives do not want a computer terminal on their desk. First, most of these terminals operate by keyboard. Senior executives usually are neither trained nor proficient in the use of the keyboard. In addition, many of them relate the keyboard to a clerical operation as opposed to an executive operation.

Much of the information available from automated systems is operational, not planning information. Senior executives spend most of their time planning and, thus, the data they can obtain from the computer may not be the information needed or the data are not readily available in the format they need. Rarely do data processing personnel consult senior executives regarding the kinds of information or resources needed to perform their job.

The computer could provide capabilities to help senior executives perform their job better. Unfortunately, access to and use of that computer facility are difficult for most executives. They frequently do not understand how to use the computer as a planning tool. In addition, the type of software needed by senior executives is not available. The computer terminal on the senior executive's desk still appears to be years away.

INTEGRATING ORGANIZATIONS WITH AUTOMATION

A control weakness in many organizations is the intermeshing of the organizational structure with the use of technology. In too many organizations, the organization structure is out of synchronization with the automated applications. The solution to this dilemma is defining the needed functional responsibilities, and then determining that the organizational structure supports them.

There is no easy solution to this organizational dilemma. As technology advances and automated applications evolve, the organizational structure must continually be modified. The last chapter in this book predicts some of the technological changes that will be occurring within the next few years. If the organizational structure cannot complement these technological characteristics, there will be gaps in control due to missing or misplaced responsibilities.

Senior management needs to become more involved in the integration of automated systems into their organizations. It is only through the involvement of senior management that the proper assignment of responsibilities and changes to the organizational structure can occur. The integration of systems and structure requires the same study and planning that goes into other parts of the systems development function.

Accountants' Computer Guideline 7.   Ensure that responsibility and accountability are clearly defined in *every* computerized application.

five

ELECTRONIC EVIDENCE

You approach a cash dispensing terminal. You insert a magnetically encoded card, answer some queries about your password and your financial
requirements. A motor hums and $100 in cash is delivered to you by the
machine. You did not complete any negotiable instrument, you did not
sign any document, and yet the transaction was complete. What type of
evidence supports the validity of that transaction?

This section explores changing evidence in an automated environment
and its effect on the accounting function. It is the accountant's responsibility in an automated environment to ensure adequate evidence is produced and stored in that environment. The accountant bases decisions
upon the completeness and validity of evidence. Accounting procedures
involve the recording, use, and storage of evidence. The existence of evidence indicates an audit trail that can be used to substantiate processing
events.

OBJECTIVES OF ACCOUNTING EVIDENCE

The objectives of evidence are the same in both a manual and an automated business environment. Evidence is needed to verify and substantiate transactions and financial records. The objective of evidence is to
substantiate and verify the accuracy, completeness, and authorization of:

Events that begin a transaction

Results produced by processing and any updates made to the accounting system

Accumulated values in the accounting system used in financial statements and other financial documents

An audit team from a large CPA firm went into the office of one of their important clients to audit the accounts payable system. The accountants requested the kinds of evidence that had been used in previous audits to substantiate the accounts payable processing and balances. When the client informed them that all the evidence was now electronic, meaning that there were no hard-copy documents, the accountants were uncertain how to substantiate the accounts receivable processing. Auditing methods are based on certain forms of evidence. When those forms of evidence change, so must the audit methods.

Accountants and audit teams like the one described must keep in mind the objectives of evidence. While the forms of evidence change, the objectives do not change. Therefore, if the new forms of evidence satisfy the three objectives for evidence, those new forms of evidence should be acceptable to the accountant. On the other hand, if the new forms of evidence fail to meet the objectives of evidence, then accountants should require that additional evidence be provided.

ELECTRONIC EVIDENCE

Understanding evidence in an automated environment requires understanding the origination and collection of that evidence. Electronic evidence is a term used to define evidence which is not readable by people. Electronic evidence requires either special hardware or software to read it, or special knowledge about computer codes to interpret it.

Most of us carry electronic evidence with us every day. Many credit cards contain electronic evidence embedded within the card. We cannot see it with our eyes or read it, but machines can read the electronic information on the card. Our personal and business checks contain electronic evidence at the bottom of the check. Unused checks contain your account number and the identification number of the bank. After you have used the check and it has been processed through a bank clearing house, the amount of the check is also magnetically encoded at the bottom of the check. Telephones with special capabilities are available which can be coded with frequently called numbers requiring only one button to be pushed to dial a number. These coded numbers are another form of electronic evidence.

People are relying more and more on the accuracy, completeness, and authorization of electronically stored evidence. To ignore electronic evidence and rely only on hard-copy evidence can be misleading. The controls needed for electronic evidence should be in the repertoire of all accountants.

Many frauds have been committed by modifying electronic evidence without changing hard-copy evidence. Let's look at two electronic fraud examples:

1. The same magnetically encoded identification numbers that are electronically printed on your checks are also printed on your deposit tickets. Since machines debit and credit your account, it doesn't matter what's written on the deposit ticket; what matters is what is electronically encoded on that deposit ticket. Knowing this, individuals have placed deposit tickets in the racks at banks for people to use should they forget their own. Depositors come in and write their name, address, account number, and amount on the ticket, but ignore the fact that someone else's account number is magnetically encoded on the deposit ticket. When the deposit ticket is processed through the automated equipment, the deposit is made to the account indicated electronically on the deposit ticket, and not the account written on the deposit slip. Through this fraud, people have been able to get other people's funds deposited to their account and then withdraw those funds and flee.

2. Banks usually require a three-day waiting period before you can withdraw funds deposited by a check from another local bank. A defrauder in an East Coast city opened two checking accounts in the same city for a minimum amount. Then a check for a large amount from Account A was deposited in Account B, which required a three-day waiting period before the funds could be withdrawn. The defrauder had special checks printed showing the name of Bank A on the East Coast, but magnetically encoding the identification number of a bank on the West Coast. Since people usually establish the waiting period, the teller, noting that the bank was in the same city, indicated to the automated system the three-day wait to clear the check. The check was then put into the automatic clearing system, where it was magnetically sorted and shipped to the West Coast bank. When the check arrived, another clerk recognized that the check did not belong to them, thought the automated equipment had made an error, and sent the check back into the clearing house system. The cycle kept repeating. Meanwhile, the defrauder withdrew the funds from Bank B and fled. The fraud wasn't discovered until the check finally wore out going through the clearing house system sorting equipment. At that point, the misuse of electronic evidence was recognized.

Much of today's business is performed using electronic evidence. This evidence is not only a new means of recording information, but is a new means of conducting business. The change is much greater than just the changing method of recording information. As the above-described frauds illustrate, we are in a transitional period.

The electronic evidence transitional period is one in which many people rely upon hard-copy readable evidence, while the actual processing occurs using electronic evidence. Data processing people recognize the redundancy of much of the hard-copy evidence, but have not been able to do away with it because many people still rely upon it. The accountant needs to understand the new methods of producing evidence, as well as the new forms of electronic evidence.

Accounting Versus Automated Evidence

The evidence produced during the processing of an accounting transaction follows a logical flow from the source document to the general ledger (see Figure 5-1). The source document in the manual accounting system is transcribed to a journal. The information is then placed in a ledger and is eventually posted in total to the general ledger. For example, a check is received as a source document, resulting in a journal entry which will increase cash and reduce accounts receivable. The accounting information is posted into a cash receipts journal and then transcribed to an accounts receivable ledger. At the end of the accounting period, the summary information is posted to the general ledger from which the financial statements are prepared.

The same accounting transaction involving automated evidence follows a different processing path. The payment may or may not be received in the form of a check. Customers can have funds transferred electronically between banks, in which case there are no people involved. Assuming that a check is received, the information is entered into a terminal and into the automated system. This is the equivalent of the journal entry. The information flows into a transaction file, which in on-line systems may be an input queue (a temporary storage space to hold information until it can be processed). The transaction file is the equivalent of the journal. The transactions are posted to a recirculating file. In an accounts receivable system, this would be an accounts receivable recirculating file, which is the equivalent of a ledger. Periodically, that information is transferred electronically to a general ledger system from which financial statements are automatically prepared. Thus, in an automated system it is entirely possible for the cash to be received electronically from a bank and processed through the entire system and the financial statements produced without human intervention.

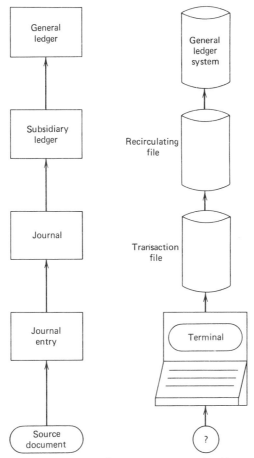

Figure 5-1. Accounting versus automated evidence.

Electronic Evidence Trails

The accountant is concerned with tracing transactions through processing. The audit trail, sometimes called a management trail, provides the ability to trace a transaction as it flows from a source document to the general ledger, or from the general ledger back to the supporting source documents. This trail is used to substantiate processing, answer questions, and correct problems.

The audit trail as illustrated in Figure 5-1 is a vertical trail of evidence. A vertical audit trail for an inventory system is illustrated in Figure 5-2.

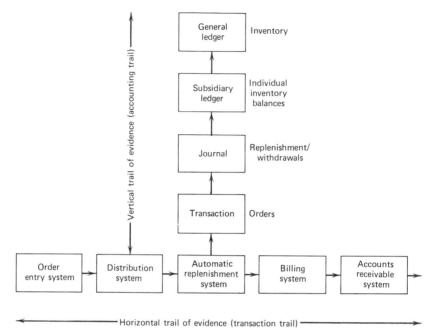

Figure 5-2.   Electronic evidence files.

This vertical trail of evidence begins with an order, which might be a customer order to buy products, or a purchase order to replenish stock. These orders are posted to the journals which provide listings of inventory replenishment and withdrawals. The information in the journal is posted to the subsidiary ledger which provides individual inventory balances. In other words, if you want to know the on-hand quantity of a particular item you go to the subsidiary ledger. This is summarized in the general ledger as an inventory account.

Most accountants can understand and visualize a vertical trail of evidence. Even when the processing is performed automatically and the evidence is electronic, the same vertical trail of evidence is visualized. Unfortunately, in actual practice most automated audit trails are horizontal. Let's look at a typical automated system, such as the one illustrated in Figure 5-2.

Technological Rule of Thumb 6.   Evidence produced by automated systems may be electronic, and therefore requires strong controls to ensure the integrity of the evidence.

The automated system illustrated in Figure 5-2 is an order entry billing receivable system. It is, in fact, many different systems all connected horizontally. The order from a customer goes into an order entry system which flows into a distribution system to disseminate product to the customer. That information goes into an automatic replenishment system which is connected to a billing system and an accounts receivable system. The automatic replenishment system generates an order to replenish inventory, and thus appears to flow upward in our vertical trail of evidence. As we saw in the previous chapter, systems flow horizontally, and so does evidence.

It is the interaction of automated systems and electronic evidence that produces the new risks of concern to the accountant. Those systems that do not yet rely upon electronic evidence pose fewer concerns than those with electronic evidence. However, the use of electronic evidence offers a system opportunity for increased user satisfaction and control, as well as the new risks.

RECORDING ELECTRONIC EVIDENCE

The methods of recording evidence and the forms of evidence are changing due to automation. Understanding these changes in evidential matter is important to the accountant in order to understand the impact on financial applications. The accountant's control responsibilities include assuring the evidence in automated systems is adequate.

The evidence produced by automated systems is affected by both the method of recording and the evidence media. In our previous examples about bank checks, the new form of evidence was magnetic ink characters at the bottom of the bank check. The method of recording this information was to have the depositor and bank identification numbers prerecorded on the check, and the dollar amount of the check typed onto the check with a special magnetic ink data entry machine.

This example illustrates that while some of the traditional evidence is still available, it is not used. The dollar amount on checks used for processing in a manual system was the handwritten dollar amount, and the method of recording was a pen. In automated banking systems, processing is based on the data recorded using magnetic ink characters; if these disagree from the handwritten amounts, the magnetic ink amounts will be the amounts used. The types of controls that were effective over manual recording of evidence are substantially different from controls needed for the newer forms of evidence.

We will examine the methods of recording evidence and the types of evidence recorded by those methods.

Methods of Recording Evidence

Technology has grown and continues to advance rapidly. The methods used for recording evidence a few years ago, such as keypunch machines, have been replaced by data entry terminals and key-to-disk machines. Therefore, discussing specific pieces of hardware and media only evaluates evidence at a particular point in time. As technology advances, the methods of recording evidence will continue to change.

We can divide the methods of recording evidence into the following categories as a means of understanding the new methods of recording evidence:

Recorded on media
Directly entered
Predetermined
Personal characteristics
Precoded

Recorded on Media. The recording of evidence is achieved by placing that evidence on computer media. For example, evidence can be recorded on punched cards, bank checks, computer tapes, and disks. The evidence is usually variable, such as hours worked by an employee, quantity of products ordered, and names and addresses of new vendors. The evidence is then available for use by computer processing whenever needed. The information is recorded using such equipment as:

Key-to-tape machine
Key-to-disk machine
Keypunch machine
Magnetic ink entry machine

Media-recorded evidence is performed by an individual whose primary function is the recording of evidence. For example, information is manually recorded on a form, and then given to a key entry operator, such as a key-to-disk operator. That individual then records the information via a key-to-disk machine onto a removable disk which can be read by computer and other automated equipment.

Directly Entered. During the 1970s, the primary method of recording data was to first record the data on media and then read them into a computer program. This has changed to directly entering data into processing programs. The media method involved an intermediary individual who either translated or transcribed information from one medium to another, for example, from an input paper form to a magnetic disk or tape.

The directly entered method records information so that it is directly readable by the computer program. For example, an individual such as an order entry clerk sits at a terminal and enters data into computer memory using a keyboard. Direct entry of information can be done by the individual who originates the transaction. For example, an order entry clerk can sit at a computer terminal and converse over telephone lines with customers and salespeople, while at the same time entering data into the automated system using a computer terminal. This eliminates the intermediate requirement that information be recorded on a form by the order entry clerk so that it could be transcribed by the intermediary, such as a keypunch operator, onto a medium like punched cards.

The directly entered method is ordinarily more economical and effective than media recording. Directly entering transactions into the computer system enables the system to converse with the individual entering the data about the correctness of the information. For example, if the order quantity were entered as alphabetic, the data would be in error. However, if the data were recorded on media that error would not be detected until the media, such as punched cards, had been entered into the system. On the other hand, if the information were entered directly, the system would challenge the correctness of the alphabetic quantity and it could be corrected immediately.

The equipment used to enter data directly includes:

Computer terminal
Process control devices
Cash dispensing terminals

Predetermined Method. Many forms of electronic evidence have been predetermined prior to processing. In these instances, the person entering the evidence merely confirms a condition which has been predetermined by the automated system. One of the more common types of predetermined evidence is the entry of some identifier which the automated system can recognize. Once that identifier has been recognized, the system accepts it as valid evidence. This evidence is frequently used as a means of authorizing a transaction, and will be discussed in a later part of this chapter.

Predetermined evidence is normally recorded by the individual responsible for a transaction. For example, an individual desiring to withdraw funds from an automatic cash dispensing machine needs to identify himself or herself through the entry of evidence which can be verified because it has been predetermined. In other words, if the individual enters the proper evidence the transaction will occur.

The equipment used to enter predetermined evidence includes:

Cash dispensing terminals

Computer terminals

Touch-tone telephones

Product dispensing equipment (such as gasoline)

Most of the predetermined evidence is in the form of codes and other identifiers. The computer is more efficient working with numbers; therefore, most predetermined evidence is numerical. While this may make it easy for machines, it frequently makes it difficult for people.

Industrial psychologists indicate that people's short-term memory is in the range of five to seven digits. If predetermined codes are longer than seven digits, they may be unworkable from a people viewpoint. Accountants involved in establishing these predetermined methods of recording evidence should discourage codes and identifiers that are longer than seven characters, if those codes are to be used by people.

Personal Characteristics. A new concept in evidence is to use individual characteristics as evidence. The technology for equipment to recognize personal characteristics has been developed. What is needed is advances in technology that make those methods more economical. While this method of recording evidence is relatively new, it appears to be the trend which will be utilized more fully during the 1980s.

Currently, there are three personal characteristics that are machine recognizable. Hardware can recognize voices, fingerprints, and signatures. A fourth characteristic that is workable is lip prints, but few people have been willing to kiss the computer good morning in order to be recognized.

Personal characteristics recognition is used principally for authorization. It has many advantages over the predetermined method of recording evidence. The predetermined method of recording evidence requires individuals to remember a sequence of characters and then provide personal security over those identifiers. In addition, the system must maintain security over those identifiers, which may require special hardware features to suppress the printing of identifiers on a terminal or printer. Because personal characteristics are unique and very difficult to copy, experience has shown that even forgers attempting to copy signatures cannot satisfy the identification criteria used by the equipment. This will be explained in the discussion of types of evidence.

Precoded Methods. Evidence can be prerecorded on media in order to improve accuracy of the information and to reduce the time required to record evidence. When the needed evidence is known, it can be precoded on documents. When the precoded documents are entered into the system, the needed evidence is there. Most precoded evidence is recorded on computer media and then entered into the automated systems through the media recorded method.

Precoded evidence is primarily used on turnaround documents. These are produced by the computer system. For example, many utility companies send a document to their customers containing both the billing data and the evidence regarding payment. When the customer returns this "turnaround document" with the payment, the utility company not only has the amount prerecorded, but the necessary identifiers to enter the evidence into the automated system to substantiate the payment.

TYPES OF ELECTRONIC EVIDENCE

The accountant is usually more concerned with the types of evidence produced, which are used daily, rather than the method of recording. It is helpful to understand the methods by which electronic evidence is recorded in order to understand how automated technology affects evidence.

The types of evidence available to the systems designer are extensive. Many systems designers are not aware of the variety, scope, and implications of the new forms of evidence. In many instances, they select evidence without understanding how it affects substantiating the transaction.

The criteria used by many systems designers in selecting evidence are:

Speed in Processing Evidence. The systems designer is concerned with systems performance because many designers are measured on systems performance.

Systems Designer's Experience. If systems designers are familiar with a certain type of evidence, they may wish to continue to use that type of evidence rather than trying some of the different types. This occurs even though that new evidence could be beneficial to the user. *Experimentation.* Some systems designers desire to use a new technology whether it is needed or not. Accountants should guard against this misuse of technology.

Easy to Use. The use of one form of evidence may simplify the systems designer's job, to the detriment of the user's evidential needs. For example, the systems designer may wish to use punched cards because the keypunch facility has been established, even though the application would be better suited by another type of evidence.

Examples of Electronic Evidence

The types of evidence will continue to change, and the accountant should be alert to new forms of evidence. The electronic evidence and methods for recording that evidence are listed in Exhibit 5-1. The more common types of electronic evidence include (note that there may be some transition before evidence becomes electronic):

Codes. A series of numbers, letters, or special characters which are understandable to a computer program. Codes can be recognized when printed using special type fonts such as that used by the Selectric typewriter, handwritten if the characters conform to recognition requirements, or even magnetically encoded on credit cards.

Microfilm/Microfiche. Information is recorded on film. The evidence can be recorded on microfilm from the computer or other means. Some devices permit the reading of the information on film back into computer memory. The technology is well developed for writing information from the computer onto microfilm; however, the technology to read that information back into the computer is just developing.

Magnetic Disk. A magnetized surface capable of recording large amounts of information. Current disk capacity can be billions of characters of information. The magnetic disk offers the advantage of evidence being directly accessible despite the billions of characters of evidence on the disk.

Magnetic Tape. A strip of magnetic tape, usually three-fourths of an inch wide and 2,400 feet long. One reel of magnetic tape can contain millions of characters of information—the amount of data that can be stored on a tape is dependent upon how closely the information is packed.

EXHIBIT 5-1   Recording Electronic Evidence

Method of Recording	Examples of Types of Evidence
Media recorded	Codes Punched cards Optical characters Microfilm/microfiche Diskette
Directly recorded	Magnetic disk Magnetic tape Magnetic ink Codes Logs
Predetermined	Passwords Codes Identifiers
Personal characteristics	Voiceprints Fingerprints Signature recognition
Precoded	Magnetic ink Magnetic coding Turnaround documents

Magnetic Ink.   A special ink with magnetic characteristics that can be read by machinery. The two common forms of magnetic ink are the special magnetic ink characters that are used by the banking industry, and mark sensing, which is used in many examinations as well as on forms used to indicate quantities of items ordered or shipped.

Diskettes.   A single disk surface, equivalent in size to a 45 rpm record, used to record input data. Diskettes are used on many microcomputers for input, processing, and storage purposes.

Logs.   Computer logs are like journals used to record a continuing series of information. For example, there is an operator log which records all of the events performed by the computer operator, a communication log which records all of the messages received and sent over communication lines, and so on. Logs in automated systems are one of the new and very powerful forms of evidence.

Passwords.   Secret identifiers used to recognize individuals or facilities requesting the use of resources. In sophisticated systems, passwords are generated automatically so only the system and the individual possessing the password know the password.

Identifiers. Special pieces of data used to identify some resource of the organization. Many identifiers are people-entered, such as product codes, social security numbers, and date codes. Other identifiers are built into the hardware so that one piece of hardware can recognize the origin of a signal or message.

Voiceprints. Voice characteristics that are decoded into electronic form. Voiceprints are usually used with a specific word(s) so that one person's voiceprint can be recorded and then matched when that individual reidentifies himself or herself. Frequently, several variations of the voiceprint for a particular word or group of words are recorded so that the match can be made against a series of voiceprints rather than a single voiceprint.

Fingerprints. The special scrolls on the tips of an individual's fingers can be placed on a cathode-ray tube, read, and identified. One current terminal uses the four fingers of both hands for purposes of identification.

Signature Recognition. An individual writes his or her signature on a cathode-ray tube using a light pen. The machine has prerecorded not only the signature, but the feed and speed in which the individual writes the signature. The signature is identified by both of these characteristics, which makes it extremely difficult to forge. Someone can forge the formation of the letters, but it is difficult to forge both that and the feed and speed in which the signature is written.

Magnetic Coding. Magnetic coding is ordinarily associated with credit-card-size cards in which identification information is encoded on a magnetic strip within the card. The information is not readable by people, but can be read by a machine when the card is inserted into a card reader.

Turnaround Documents. A document containing information which is sent to an individual or organization to be returned to the originating organization at a later date. All of the information needed may be included on the turnaround document, or some additional information may be needed. For example, a book club might send you a list of selections on a punched card. You return the punched card and it becomes the basis for sending or not sending a book to you.

The accountant should expect to find some other types of evidence, or variations of these types of evidence, in his or her organization. The examples are given to illustrate the wide variety of evidence used in automated systems. This evidence is replacing the more traditional hard-copy document, stamping, initialing, done to record the occurrence or authorization of an event.

Technological Rule of Thumb 7.   Advances in automated technology will continue to change both the types of evidence and the means of recording that evidence.

METHODS OF STORING EVIDENCE

Most electronic evidence is not readable by people. Therefore, it is impractical to store the electronic media in office work areas. Because the media are used by equipment, they are normally stored in close proximity to the equipment.

Electronic evidence may commence at the time of transaction origination, then be modified continually through the processing cycle. Evidence can be stored temporarily or permanently at its point of origin or use. For example, information may be stored on diskette or microfilm in the user area for inquiry and reference throughout the working day. In other instances, the evidence is transmitted and stored many miles from the originating office in order to protect it from disaster.

Most electronic evidence is stored on computer media. Examples of media include punched cards, magnetic tape, diskettes, magnetic ink documents, and so forth. As such, it is susceptible to both accidental and intentional modification. For example, most people are familiar with the legend printed on or supplied with punched cards, "Do not fold, deface, or mutilate."

The more susceptible the media are to damage, the more secure the storage area needs to be. For example, punched cards are difficult to read when they swell because of humidity. Therefore, the temperature and humidity in the punched card storage area are important. Magnetic disks are made to very small tolerances because a reading arm must be a few thousandths of an inch above the surface during use. If the disk is dropped or damaged, it only takes a very slight alteration of the surface to cause the reading head to destroy the magnetic surface. In addition, most magnetic media can be destroyed by a strong magnetic force, which requires still another type of protection.

The storage location for electronic media is normally suited and designed for the media. For example, there are special cabinets designed to store punched cards and magnetic ink coded documents. Reels of computer tape have special containers as do diskettes and disk packs. Due to the susceptibility of electronic media to damage, most organizations retain backup copies of electronic media. It is recommended that those backup sites be physically apart from the primary site. For example, a computer installation may store tapes and disks near the computer, but store backup tapes in another building or several miles away from the main site. If a disaster, such as a flood or fire, should occur in the primary site the data are still available in the backup site.

Some large organizations store computer media in vaults under mountains or in other very secure locations. These remote sites protect the organizations from large disasters which may wipe out a complete computer center or large part of a city, such as a tornado, hurricane, or earthquake. While there is a cost associated with transporting data between the primary and remote sites, that cost must be weighed against the risk associated with a major disaster.

ACCOUNTANTS' ELECTRONIC EVIDENTIAL CONCERNS

The day-to-day work of the accountant involves interacting with evidence. Use of electronic evidence should raise the following questions in the minds of the accountants:

1. Have the transactions represented by the electronic evidence been properly authorized?
2. Has the integrity of the electronic evidence been assured?
3. Is the scope of the electronic evidence sufficient?
4. Will the electronic evidence be available when it is needed?
5. Is the electronic evidential audit trail sufficient to permit easy access to the desired piece of electronic evidence?

The accountant needs to consider these five concerns when working with or designing evidence in automated systems (see Figure 5-3). We will examine these concerns individually and discuss specific accounting concerns.

Authorization Concern

Authorization has been indicated by a signature, initials, official form, time and date stamps, and so on. None of the traditional forms of authorization is included with electronic evidence. The signatures that were re-

Figure 5-3. Accountant evidential concerns.

lied upon no longer exist; they have been replaced by new forms of authorization evidence.

The concern this raises for the accountant is: How can one be sure that transactions represented by electronic evidence have been authorized? A forged check may look different from a legitimate check. An invalid request to provide a customer with credit may not have the proper authorization signature. However, an unauthorized transaction on electronic media may look identical to a valid transaction on electronic media. This poses the dilemma to an accountant of how to tell authorized from unauthorized automated transactions.

Several of the new types of evidence are ideally suited for substantiating authorization. For example, passwords, voiceprints, fingerprints, and signature recognition are all valid methods of authorization. The verification of those authorization methods is based upon the controls built into the automated systems. In other words, rather than relying upon a valid signature or valid form, the accountant must rely upon the adequacy of the controls to verify that the authorization method is correct.

Concerns the accountant should have over the authorization of electronic evidence include:

1. Have adequate methods been established to ensure transactions are properly authorized?

2. Has sufficient evidence been recorded to identify who authorized each transaction?

3. Are the system controls adequate to ensure the authorization rules are being complied with?

4. Is the system able to record and monitor the number of unauthorized transactions identified and rejected, as a basis for improving the system of control?

Integrity of Evidence

The accountant needs to be assured that all the evidence is valid, and that the accountant has access to the entire population of evidence. When records are electronically maintained, many of the manual controls that ensured the integrity of the evidence no longer exist. For example, accountants rely upon prenumbered forms to ensure that no transactions are lost. When the accountant works with data produced from computer files, there should be a concern about the completeness of the information.

The Equity Funding insurance fraud case was an example of the auditors receiving and relying upon electronic evidence, but that evidence was not representative of the entire population of evidence. The corporation created numerous fictitious policies which were identified by a unique code. When the Equity Funding auditors requested from the data processing personnel information about policyholders they were given only valid policies. The data processing personnel were able to eliminate all the invalid policies by using the unique code before letting the auditors use the information. The auditors did not validate the integrity of the electronic information, and thus failed to uncover the massive fraud. When the company went bankrupt the auditors were sued and convicted for improper auditing.

When the accountant receives the report developed from electronic evidence, the accountant should be concerned about the integrity of that information. Problems other than fraud can occur which would make the information invalid. There could be system problems which result in records being lost or changed, the hardware that produces the reports may be in improper working condition, or a simple problem could occur, such as several pages of the report being torn off and lost. The accountant needs some method of assuring the integrity of the electronic evidence received.

The concerns the accountant should have about the integrity of electronic evidence include:

1. What assurances are there that the evidence received is representative of the entire population of evidence?
2. What assurances are there that the information presented is valid?
3. What assurances are there that the evidence presented in the evidence requested (e.g., the accountant may wish to see records of products shipped, but receive a report on products committed for shipment)?
4. What assurances does the accountant have that all of the evidence produced by the automated system has been delivered to the accountant?

Scope of Evidence

The evidence about an automated transaction includes data on people, equipment, rules, and transaction values. All of these factors are involved in processing a transaction.

The amount of evidence produced in the execution of a transaction can be extremely voluminous. For example, several people may be involved, and numerous pieces of equipment may be used in the processing of the transaction. There are many rules, some of which affect the transaction processing, as well as numerous data values entered and/or produced during the processing of the transaction. The systems designers need to decide how much of this evidence should be saved to substantiate the transaction.

Let's look at an example of a transaction involving a pay raise to an employee. The company payroll policy indicates the frequency and timing for increases. The supervisor usually initiates the increase process. The employee's supervisor and the supervisor's supervisor interact in determining whether or not to give a raise and, if so, the amount of the raise. The raise information may be entered into the system using a keypunch machine and then processed by one or more computer systems. The rules that affect raises may state how frequently raises can be given and what percent of increase can be given. The rules may be cumulative, so that an individual cannot receive more than X% in a given year or two-year period. The data and forms involved in the raise can be numerous. The question the systems designer faces is: How much of this evidence should be recorded to substantiate the transaction? For example, is it necessary to know which equipment processed the evidence? These are important questions because they affect both the cost of evidence and the ability to substantiate processing at later dates.

The concerns that the accountant should have about the scope of evidence retained include:

1. Can the evidence identify the person responsible for making transaction decisions?
2. Does the evidence indicate the equipment used in recording the evidence so that problems can be traced to a specific piece of equipment?
3. Does the evidence substantiate which rules were used in determining transaction processing?
4. Does the evidence indicate which source documents and working documents were used in processing the transaction?
5. Has a cost-effectiveness decision been made regarding the amount of evidence retained to support transaction processing?

Time Frame for Review

Many organizations establish a record retention program. This program is frequently misunderstood in that people believe the only objective of the program is to retain evidence when, in fact, another objective is to limit the amount of evidence retained. Record retention programs are established for the purpose of destroying information as quickly as possible.

The retention period for evidence can be specified by numerous sources. The company retention program may decide how long each type of evidence needs to be retained. In addition, legal and regulatory requirements indicate the length of retention for many documents. For example, the Internal Revenue Service states that financial information needs to be retained for three full calendar years following the current year.

Many pieces of evidence are not essential to support transaction processing. In an automated environment, there is a lot of evidence produced during processing. Some of this is needed in the event processing is found to be inaccurate or incomplete, but is not needed to substantiate the integrity of processing. This type of information can be destroyed within a short time after transaction processing. For example, a communication log provides evidence of all the messages transmitted over communication facilities. This is necessary should problems occur, but as soon as processing appears to be reasonably correct the log can be destroyed.

The concerns the accountant should have about the time frame of retaining evidence for review include:

1. Has the retention period for each type of evidence been determined?

2. Does the evidence contain some indication of the period of time in which it should be retained?
3. Are procedures established to prevent electronic evidence from being destroyed prior to the fulfillment of the retention period?
4. Is the retention period in compliance with company policies and procedures?
5. Is the retention period in compliance with regulatory agency requirements and legal requirements?

Audit Trails

Having evidence is of little value if it cannot be retrieved. The objective of the audit trail is twofold: first, to locate evidence; and second, to substantiate processing. The audit trail shows the flow of processing so that it can be reconstructed.

Accountants have traditionally been concerned about the scope of the audit trail. However, in many automated environments the concern is that the audit trail is too extensive rather than not sufficient. For example, in an on-line data base environment it is not uncommon to produce several hundred thousand, or even millions of audit trail records in a week. The audit trail information could literally grow faster than people could read it.

A major fraud in a large bank involved a head teller manipulating dormant accounts. This is not an uncommon practice in banks, and most banks, including this one, had a procedure to produce a message whenever dormant accounts became active. As the teller removed funds from the dormant accounts, a message was produced. Unfortunately, the bank did not detect the fraud. It was detected when the head teller was caught in a raid in an illegal betting establishment. The police notified the bank that one of their tellers was placing very large bets, and from that information the fraud was quickly uncovered. When the individuals who should have been reviewing these messages were quizzed about it, they indicated that the messages seemed to be routine and did not appear worthy of investigation.

The lesson to be learned from this fraud is that much of the evidence produced by automated systems is never examined. A leading expert in computer fraud stated that in every fraud the expert had investigated there was an adequate trail of the fraud; the problem was that nobody took the time and effort to study and analyze the audit trail to discover the problem. This is a result of the computer producing too many audit trail records instead of too few.

The concerns the accountant should have about the evidential audit trail include:

1. Is the audit trail adequate to substantiate processing?
2. Have problems been prioritized so that when the audit trail uncovers a problem its importance will be recognized?

Accountants' Computer Guideline 8. The key to assuring adequate electronic evidence is building a sufficient system of controls to ensure the integrity of the electronic evidence.

EVIDENCE AND THE ACCOUNTING FUNCTION

Much of the change occurring in the accounting function can be attributed to changing evidence. Today, few accountants prepare journal entries, post data to journals, or maintain subsidiary ledgers. Most of the accounting information is recorded within the organization's automated systems. As these systems become more integrated, much of the remaining hardcopy evidence will also become electronic evidence.

In the following chapter, we will examine how the accounting function itself has changed because of automation.

Accountants' Computer Guideline 9. Accountants should participate in specifying the requirements and controls for the electronic evidence in financial systems.

six

AUTOMATING ACCOUNTING

The methods used to perform the accounting function in business have changed. Most of the manual accounting procedures have been automated. In many organizations even the general ledger and preparation of the financial statements have been automated. The tasks performed by the accountant have changed significantly during the past two decades.

This chapter explores those changes, showing the effect of automation on the accounting function. The chapter provides an overview of an integrated data processing system, and recaps how an automated system fits into the organizational structure. This discussion uses a marketing system as an example. The differences caused by automated accounting are discussed, again using a marketing system to illustrate the differences.

HOW DATA PROCESSING SYSTEMS WORK

Systems work by reading pieces of data, processing them, and producing results. No magic occurs, just a lot of planning, a lot of detail, which require some very specific rules and very well-defined data.

You may have wondered why documents used as input to computer systems require you to put each number and letter in a box instead of writing freehand. The reason is a computer system must know the length of each piece of data, such as the length of the price or quantity. For example, price may be a length of four, which permits a price in the range of $00.01 to $99.99. Note the zeros in the 1¢ amount. This is because to a computer a zero (0) is different from a blank space.

Once entered into a computer system, data may be used by several different computerized application systems. A basic concept of computer systems is to enter data in the computer only once. After that it should be available for all systems to use. For example, once a computer system has your address and phone number, it should not be reentered for another purpose but, rather, be retrieved from its location in the system whenever needed.

Let's study a computerized order entry/inventory/billing system at a university book store. Figure 6-1 illustrates the input form that might be used to order a book, which is the primary input into the system. The form includes the following data:

Student number

Book number

Quantity (of books to be ordered)

Amount per book

Charge (marked if the order is charged instead of paid)

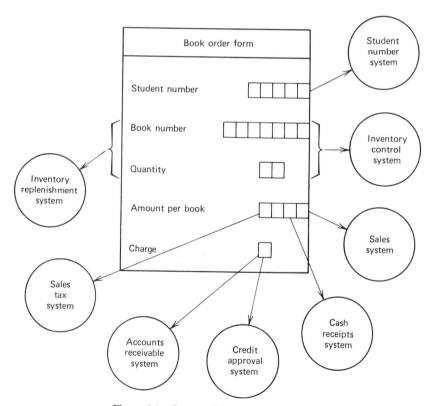

Figure 6-1. Input split to multiple systems.

The form contains all of the data needed to order a book. The amount per book may not be essential data because it could already be included in a computer program. However, it can be used as a control against the book number. If both the amount per book and the book number are used, the computer can cross-check them to be sure the right book has been ordered. It is unlikely that if the book number were wrong or two numbers were transposed, the erroneous number would be priced the same as the correct number.

Next, let's look at all the systems which use data from the input order form shown in Figure 6-1. Each of these systems uses the data for different purposes which are:

1. *Student Number (student numbering system).* Issues numbers to new students and acts as a control maintaining a list of active student numbers. Only students who have a student number are entitled to the student discount.

2. *Book Number and Quantity (inventory control system).* Reduces on-hand inventory by the number of books sold.

3. *Amount per Book Times Quantity (sales system).* Records the sale of books for both accounting and sales analysis.

4. *Student Number and Amount per Book Times Quantity on a Charge Sale (credit approval system).* If the student desires to charge the purchase of the books, this system determines whether credit may be granted to the student.

5. *Amount per Book Times Quantity (cash receipts system).* If this is a cash sale, cash will be recorded to reconcile with the deposit to the bank account.

6. *Amount per Book Times Quantity Times Tax Rate (sales tax system).* The sales tax will be automatically calculated on the amount of the sale and recorded in the proper account for later payment to the appropriate governmental unit.

7. *Amount per Book Times Quantity Plus Sales Tax (accounts receivable system).* If the student charges the book and the credit is granted, this system will record the charge in the accounts receivable ledger.

8. *Book Number and Quantity (inventory replenishment system).* When inventory reaches the reorder point, this system automatically places an order for more books based on anticipated sales volume.

From a single input form, transactions have been generated for eight different data processing systems. These systems interrelate as data flow from one system to another. One of the best features of the computer is its ability to feed data from system to system without human intervention.

However, it is not as easy as it sounds. We say processing is predetermined; by this we mean all possible conditions must be thought of and rules established. Within the example just cited there are numerous conditions which have not been discussed. This system must have provisions for the possibilities listed below:

Credit will not be granted

The book will not be in stock

After seeing the book, the student will decide not to buy it

The student will purchase the book but return it for a refund

The student will purchase the book but exchange it later for another book

The student will charge the book but not pay for it

The data on the book order form will be incorrect and the transaction rejected

The cash received will not agree with the cash owed

The purchaser of the book has a tax exemption certificate and should not be charged sales tax

The student orders more than one book and there are not enough books on hand to fill the order

Systems must handle standard procedures and also exceptions and unusual conditions such as those listed above. Special documents and forms may be required to handle these special processing situations.

If the system does not contain procedures to handle exceptions, chaos may result when they occur. In such cases, management must make on-the-spot decisions on how to handle the item manually. Later, data processing people have to work out the necessary procedures to handle exceptions. We often read in the newspapers about the poor results of inadequate planning.

The system must be able to determine readily what type of transaction is ready for processing, and then process that transaction according to predetermined rules. In computer systems, the rules which determine how to distinguish different types of transactions must be well defined because the computer does not have eyes and a brain to analyze situations as do people.

Input Transactions

In the previous example, we have seen how one input document provides data for eight systems. To do this, the data on the input document or transaction must be given to all eight systems. Computer systems use one transaction to create subtransactions for other systems. For instance, the book order causes replenishment of that book in inventory.

Transactions are records that contain a variety of information. These transactions must be uniquely identified so that the computer program can identify the type of transactions being processed. You must remember that computer hardware cannot read documents in the same sense as people do. Records going into a computer system must contain some kind of code to identify the record. This identification is frequently called a transaction code.

A payroll system provides a good example of the diversity of transactions in one system. This will show us how transactions can be uniquely identified. Listed below are eight transactions or records that exist in most payroll systems:

Records for new employees

Records indicating when employees get a rate change

Records indicating when someone transfers to a new department

Records indicating an employee is terminated

Records indicating the number of hours an employee worked during a pay period

Records stating the employee's pay rate, number of deductions, and other data related to producing the paycheck

Records containing the data needed to produce paychecks and other payroll information

Records indicating the amount of federal taxes, and so forth, withheld from the employee's wages

Figure 6-2 shows how transaction codes can be used in processing payroll data. The eight records described above are shown in this figure, together with their transaction code. For example, the record for a new employee has been given transaction code 01. When the computer reads 01 in the first part of a record, it can identify the record as that of a new employee. That record will then be given to the system that processes new employee records.

When an employee is given an increase, the payroll system must have a

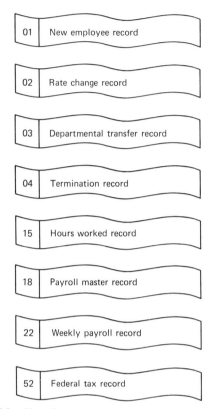

Figure 6-2.   Use of transaction codes processing payroll data.

record of that increase so the employee will be paid the higher rate. In Figure 6-2 that record is identified by transaction code 02. Therefore, when the computer program recognizes transaction code 02 in a record, it knows that an employee has had a pay rate change. The data in the record must indicate the name of the employee the new pay rate is for so this information can be recorded in the system that prepares the payroll. Now that we have established how a transaction can be identified, let's briefly examine how the data in that transaction can be processed.

HOW AUTOMATED SYSTEMS FIT INTO THE ORGANIZATIONAL STRUCTURE

Organizations need systems to operate. In systems, data flow horizontally between functions or departments on the same level in the organization.

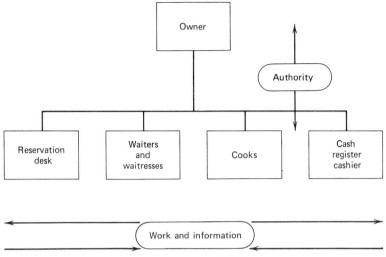

Figure 6-3.   Restaurant organizational structure.

However, lines of authority in organizations are vertical. Thus, while people take orders from people higher in the organizational structure (vertical movement), they accept work from a system which originated in other departments equal—or horizontal—on the organizational chart.

Let's see how this occurs in a restaurant. The organizational structure of the restaurant is illustrated in Figure 6-3. The owner has four departments and gives orders for (or directs) the responsibility, working hours, uniforms, pay, and so forth, of those four departments. This is a vertical organizational structure.

However, information and work flow horizontally. The reservation desk sends customers to the waiters and waitresses, they take food and beverage orders and give them to the cooks, the cooks give the prepared food to the waiters and waitresses to give to the customers. At the end of the meal the waiter or waitress gives a check to the customer, to be paid to the cashier. In the day-to-day running of the restaurant, the owner does not become involved unless problems occur. All the information flow—processed by the system—is on an equal work level.

Figure 6-4 illustrates the organization of a typical manufacturing company. The highest ranking individual is the president. Under the president are those in charge of the main functions of the organization, such as VP of marketing, VP of distribution, controller, VP of manufacturing, and treasurer. Under each of these individuals is a function or department. The size and complexity of the organization determine the number of levels within each function. The organization chart example is meant to be

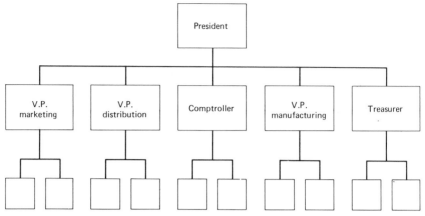

Figure 6-4. Typical organization of manufacturing company.

representative of a typical organization. To illustrate how a system relates to an organizational structure, we'll look at a system and then show how different functions in an organization have responsibility for different parts of the system.

Order Processing System

Most organizations have an order processing system. This system receives orders from customers, handles delivery of the product, and receives payment from the customer. In our previous example, we showed the student's system for buying a book. In this example, we will discuss the system that belongs to the book-selling business. Figure 6-5 is a flowchart of an order processing system. The flowchart begins with an order for a book, includes replenishment to inventory of books to replace the books sold, and continues in a never-ending cycle as long as orders continue to be received. The cycle is ordering, selling, ordering, selling, and so on.

After the order has been received, the processing part of the system begins. Before the recording and transmitting steps occur, the system must decide if the order is authorized (received from an accepted customer). This is especially true if credit or discounts are offered for special types of customers. For example, is the individual ordering a book authorized to receive a discount? If the order is on credit, is the customer's credit good? Once authorized, the order can be recorded and transmitted for processing. Processing of the order includes shipping and billing to the customer. The shipment reduces inventory. When inventory reaches a

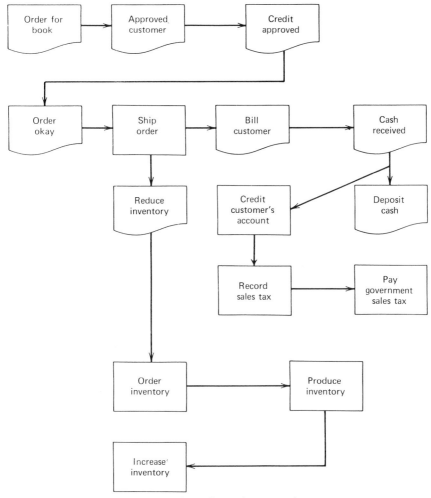

Figure 6-5. Flowchart of an order processing system.

certain level, the system initiates a replenishment order for more inventory. On credit purchases, the customer pays the amount on the invoice and the amount is posted to the customer's account. Cash must be deposited in the bank. If sales tax is involved, the sales tax is recorded and, at the appropriate time, collections are sent to the proper government agency. Obviously, in real life systems are much more complex than the example given. However, the example does explain the general processing necessary to fill an order for a single book. Now, let's see who is responsible organizationally for the various parts of this system.

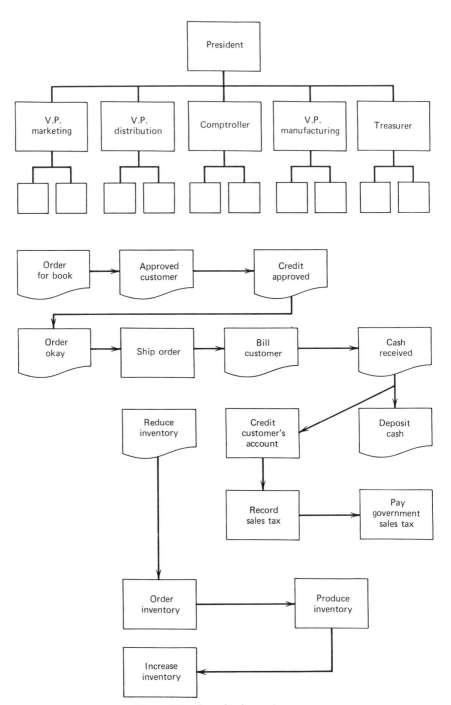

Figure 6-6. Organization and system.

Figure 6-4 shows a typical organization of a manufacturing company and Figure 6-5 shows the flowchart for an order processing system that would be used by a typical manufacturing company. Figure 6-6 shows the interrelationship of the system and the organization. By studying this figure, you can see how the various parts of an organization relate to the system.

The system functions are divided among several departments. The marketing organization is responsible for taking orders and determining if the customer is eligible to place the order under the terms specified. The controller's division approves credit. This means that the marketing organization cannot process the order until the controller's division has approved credit. Once the order has been authorized, it is transmitted to the distribution department for shipment. The distribution department has the responsibility to maintain sufficient inventory. When the inventory reaches the reorder point, the distribution department initiates an order to replenish the inventory. This replenishment order will be transmitted to the manufacturing division which will print more books. Once the customer's order has been shipped, the controller's division invoices the customer and records sales tax for later payment. The treasurer will receive the cash, deposit it in the bank, and tell the controller how much cash has been received. The controller sees that the customer's account is credited. When it is time to pay the sales tax, the treasurer will draw a check (authorized by the controller) to pay the appropriate government agency.

The data processing department which operates the system is not illustrated in Figure 6-6. This would complicate our understanding of the system because the data processing department is involved at numerous points within the system. For example, the data processing department would prepare the purchase order which goes to the controller for approval of credit. However, sometimes the system approves credit and forwards to the controller for approval only those orders which exceed the authorized credit limit. Later sections will explain the data processing function.

Each of the five departments illustrated in Figure 6-6 handles only a part of the system. The controller's division is not aware of what the distribution department is doing until a shipping notice is received from them indicating that a customer should be billed. The shipping clerk may have no idea how orders are obtained by the marketing department, and very few people in the organization will have an understanding of how the complete system works. One thread that weaves through all aspects of a system is accounting data. Accounting is the common denominator for all systems involving money.

HOW SYSTEMS RELATE TO ACCOUNTING

The recording and accumulation of accounting data follow a logical progression. When a financial transaction is originated, it is recorded on a supporting document. These documents are recorded in a transaction register. This register records the dollars involved in the transaction. The data in the transaction register is then summarized into journals. One or more journals comprise a subsidiary ledger. From these subsidiary ledgers general ledger accounts are developed. The general ledger accounts, either individual or combined, become the accounts listed in the organization's annual report.

The build-up of accounting information becomes more obvious in the following example. This is a manual accounting system. Let's look again at an invoicing system. When a sale is made, the amount is recorded on an invoice, then the amount is recorded in a transaction register. The transaction register can be a clerk's book of invoices. The day's transactions are totaled and posted into summary sales journals. Usually, each salesperson verifies daily sales against this summary total. The sales are recorded in the appropriate sales ledger. There may be several ledgers listing sales by type, by department, and by method of payment. The accumulation of all the sales ledgers becomes the amount shown for the general ledger accounts for sales. The sales amount from the general ledger account becomes the amount included in the annual report under "sales."

When this system is computerized, the ledgers, journals, and registers no longer exist in the familiar formats. They become punched cards, disk files, tape files, or a combination of these. No longer can you go to the ledger, open up a book, and look up an account in the familiar way. In the computerized system, this information is found on special printed reports or on the screens of on-line terminal machines.

The repetitive tasks of recording and accumulating sales information are performed by computer programs. Repetitive tasks include such things as accumulation of detail information and producing daily, weekly, and monthly sales amounts by type. In accounting EDP systems, there are three categories of computer programs: EDP systems that accept accounting data, EDP systems that process accounting data, and EDP systems that print accounting reports.

EDP programs that process accounting data take the place of the transaction register, summary journals, and subsidiary ledgers which are used in the manual accounting system. The information contained in manual systems is included in the EDP system in machine-readable format, such as computer tapes and disks. The comparison is illustrated in Figure 6-7.

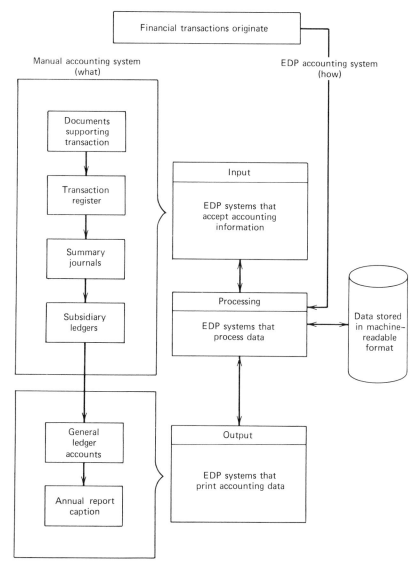

Figure 6-7. Comparison of the manual accounting system with the EDP accounting system.

An EDP system that prints accounting reports performs the same kind of function as the accountant preparing a report from the general ledger. A computer stores the data in approximately the same format and order as do general ledgers. From EDP systems, financial statements can be prepared in many formats including the annual report caption format. Figure 6-7 compares the manual accounting system with the EDP accounting system.

Viewing the EDP system as performing the accounting function brings us back to the "black box" concept. As an outsider, it may appear to you that financial transactions are being fed in one end of the computer and printed financial statements are coming out the other end. To understand EDP accounting systems, you should visualize the manual accounting system flow as *what* the system is supposed to accomplish. The EDP accounting systems flow shows *how* that accounting function is accomplished on a computer. We will learn in later chapters how this processing can be done within the computer.

Systems that process accounting data are usually separate from systems that process other parts of the business transaction. For example, an order entry system may carry only limited quantities of items and customer information. The accounting data associated with that order may be processed in a separate EDP system. Thus, problems in processing can occur when you realize the accounting data are processed separately from order data. Computers are machines with limited capabilities. Systems using computers are restricted by those limitations.

THE AUTOMATED ACCOUNTING PROCESS

In the past, the cornerstone of accounting control has been segregation of duties. This concept made sense not only from a control viewpoint but from the viewpoint of good work performance. As organizations grew in size, the number of different tasks increased.

Next, let's examine the marketing area of an organization in order to see how the various tasks become segmented. In a small organization the sales clerk can take the order, distribute the goods, and handle the cash or credit associated with the sale. The process is easy and readily understood. For example, if you were to hold a garage sale you could personally handle all aspects of the transactions.

Now, let's look at a large organization. In such an organization, we may have a sales force of several hundred people, thousands of customers, and millions of transactions in the course of the year. Now it begins to make sense to have specific personnel take orders and establish a distribution center to ship merchandise to the customers. A credit department of many people is needed to determine whether and how much credit will be offered to customers. A special group must prepare invoices and another group is responsible for handling cash receipts. Still another group is charged with the responsibility of maintaining accounts receivable.

This type of organization is common in most major corporations. Since tasks are separated, people in accounts receivable do not fully understand how orders are accepted and processed. One clerk knows only that sales increase accounts receivable and that credits or cash applied reduce them. If the customer pays on time, little action is necessary other than keeping the accounts up to date. Thus, different departments within an organization handle different segments of accounting associated with the marketing area. Figure 6-8 illustrates this.

Associated with the marketing area are a number of accounting entries. In the Fortune 500 companies, several different departments are concerned with these entries. In practice, we find one department creating half of an accounting entry and another department creating the other half of that entry. Exhibit 6-1 illustrates the accounting entries for the marketing area.

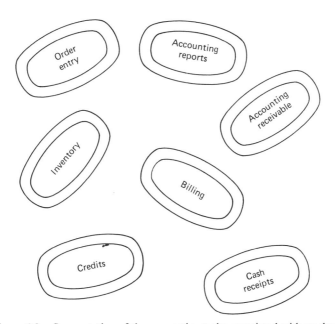

Figure 6-8. Segmentation of the accounting tasks associated with marketing.

EXHIBIT 6-1   Accounting Entries For The Marketing Area

Entry Objective	Accounting Entry		Responsible Department
Order	Inventory—Committed	$xx.xx	Distribution
Entry	Inventory—Open Stock	$xx.xx	Distribution
Accounts Receivable	Accounts Receivable	$xx.xx	Accounts Receivable
Billing	Sales	$xx.xx	Marketing (sales)
Inventory	Cost of Goods Sold	$xx.xx	Accounting
	Inventory—Committed	$xx.xx	Distribution
Credits	Sales—Returns	$xx.xx	Marketing (sales)
	Accounts Receivable	$xx.xx	Accounts Receivable
	Inventory—Returns	$xx.xx	Distribution
	Cost of Goods Sold	$xx.xx	Accounting
Cash Receipts	Cash	$xx.xx	Treasurer
	Accounts Receivable	$xx.xx	Accounts Receivable

Our first entry illustrates that when an order is accepted, inventory is committed to fill that order. The distribution department makes such inventory commitments. In manual systems, it is difficult to execute this type of entry. However, in automated systems, it is very easy to do.

Once the merchandise has changed hands, the accounting entry to record sales and accounts receivable can be executed. Note that the accounts receivable department is responsible for the accounts receivable half of this accounting entry, while the marketing or sales department assumes responsibility for the credit side of the accounting entry.

When goods are shipped to a customer, the cost of the product is transferred from ''committed inventory'' to ''goods sold.'' Note again in this case that one department is responsible for half of the accounting entry and another department is responsible for the other half. Students who leave school to begin work in a large organization find this concept difficult to comprehend. In thinking and comprehending how things work, it is a giant step from a garage sale to General Motors.

For example, handling credits is extremely complex in most organizations. Exhibit 6-1 illustrates but a few of the potential accounting entries.

The returned inventory can be sold for scrap, reworked, returned to open stock inventory, sold to employees at reduced rates, and so forth.

The cash receipts accounting entry is tightly controlled because both halves of this entry involve extremely liquid assets. Again, two departments develop this one accounting entry. The treasurer or cashier receives the cash coming into the organization and deposits it in the bank. The accounts receivable department is then notified and adjusts the accounts receivables accordingly.

Integrated Accounting

The advent of the computer brought a halt to the expanding universal theory of segregating duties. Large central computers reversed the trend by consolidating previously segregated functions into computerized applications. Figure 6-9 illustrates this segregation/integration conflict.

If we go back to our marketing area illustration (Figure 6-8), we see how the different tasks are segregated. This type of segregation works well in a manual environment. In our illustration, each task was performed by a different department. When data processing applications were designed, these tasks were consolidated into one interconnected computer application. As a result, there is a conflict wherein data processing causes tasks to be integrated while traditional accounting control and methodology tries to segregate tasks. Data processing is winning this conflict. While we still have accounts receivable departments, the *processing* of accounts receivable data has been moved to the data processing department. In actual practice, we find a restructuring of controls and organizations to complement the characteristics of computer systems. Handling of accounts receivable problems and controls still resides in the accounts receivable department, but the *performance* of these tasks is shared with data processing.

In small organizations, areas such as marketing are performed by one or two individuals. In this type of environment, the tasks are all closely interconnected. It is the formality and magnitude of the duties in large organizations that result in the segregation of these tasks. With the advent of data processing, an integration of tasks within large organizations has become practical.

We can call such integration a system chain. The chain is comprised of links, or accounting tasks, that, when connected, process the data associated with one area of an organization. Figure 6-10 illustrates how the accounting tasks associated with marketing are integrated into a system chain. The formal organizational structure in large organizations often

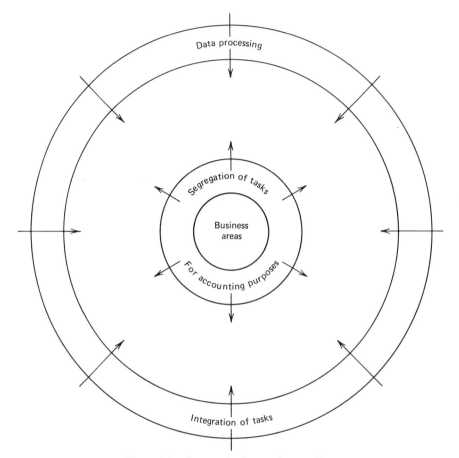

Figure 6-9.   Segregation/integration conflict.

conceals these system chains. In large organizations, we look at one link at a time. Most accounting courses teach one link at a time, practicing accountants work on one link at a time, and even auditors audit one link at a time. Yet, in reality, data flow from one link to another continuously to tie the links into a chain.

We need to visualize our system as a closed chain. The order entry link is the logical starting point in the marketing system chain. The entry of an order triggers the billing function, which feeds accounts receivable and the inventory systems. Most billing systems initiate a shipping document which authorizes the distribution area to ship the product. When product is returned, the credit link causes a backward flow: product is returned to

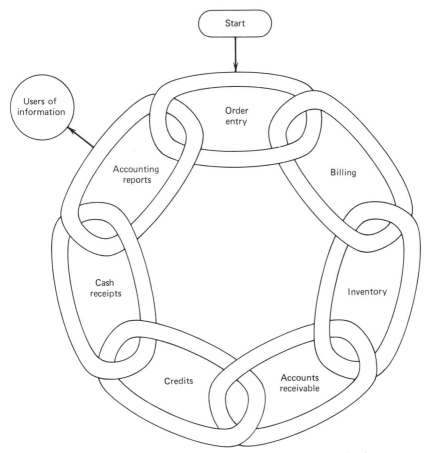

Figure 6-10. Integration of the accounting tasks associated with marketing into a system chain.

inventory and receivables and billing processing is reversed. The cash receipts link feeds into the accounts receivable link. Accounting reports are prepared using data contained in all the links in the chain. These accounting reports are used in many ways by people who need information from the marketing systems chain.

It is through reporting that data within these system chains become information. The system contains large amounts of data. Each piece of data or data element has little meaning until it is brought together with other data to become useful information through reports. For example, the fact that customer X bought product Y is good news for the organization. However, for the accounts receivable collections department, this is not significant information. But when that sale is reported with all other sales, management has vital information with which to make some decisions. For example, if product Y's sales have dropped off, management may decide on a promotional campaign for product Y. It is in this context that the accounting report link fits into the system chain. This action on behalf of management can stimulate more orders for product Y. Thus, the system becomes a closed chain.

HOW AUTOMATED ACCOUNTING WORKS

This chapter has explained the change in the accounting function when systems are automated and integrated. The impact of this change may be hard to comprehend for those who have not been heavily involved in EDP. The next chapter provides a marketing systems case study to illustrate the automation of accounting.

seven

AUTOMATED MARKETING SYSTEM EXAMPLE

We have discussed the accountants' computer concerns, and we have discussed how the computer affects the organization, the system of controls, and the accounting function. This chapter will illustrate these changes in action by discussion of an automated marketing system. The purpose of reading this case is to observe what happens in computerized organizations.

MEET THE MARKETING FUNCTION

To understand marketing, it is important to understand the major sections of marketing and the responsibilities of each section. In large organizations each section of the marketing function will be headed by a manager; in smaller organizations one individual may be responsible for two or more sections. The common titles of the heads of the major marketing sections and their responsibilities are:

Marketing Manager. The person responsible for planning, coordinating, and controlling the marketing function. Usually the marketing manager reports to the president of the organization. This manager participates with other executives of the organization in setting marketing policies.

Manager of Sales. This individual is responsible for directing the sales effort of the organization. This includes a determination of how the goods are sold, that is, through jobbers or directly to customers. This manager is responsible for establishing the standards and quotas for the sales force. This position involves dealing with customers, pre-

129

paring sales literature and sales promotion campaigns, as well as evaluating the effectiveness of the sales program. The accounting reports and analyses provided to the sales manager are tools in helping to develop effective sales programs.

Manager of Production Planning. This is the person who is responsible for determining the characteristics and adding or deleting items from the product line. This includes methods of packaging and styling the products. The manager of product planning also recommends the pricing structure.

Manager of Advertising. This is the individual responsible for planning and coordinating promotional activities. This manager often works with an advertising agency to plan advertising campaigns and other promotional strategies. The manager of advertising will work with other members of the marketing function to develop promotional campaigns to meet the sales quota. Up-to-date accounting and marketing information is extremely important if this function is to be performed properly.

Manager of Distribution. This person is responsible for maintaining the inventory and the shipping of products to customers. In larger organizations this may be organizationally separate from marketing. Distribution is responsible for storage, packing, shipping, and return of unacceptable merchandise as well as the security and protection of the products. Distribution centers may be located centrally or, depending on the volume of sales, regionally.

Manager of Customer Services. This is the person responsible for servicing customer needs after the sale. This function receives and responds to customer complaints. Customer services is usually charged with determining whether customer products will be replaced or repaired, or whether credit will be given if the customer feels the product does not meet specifications. The objective of this function is to keep customers satisfied.

Manager of Marketing Research. This manager is responsible for determining the type of products which should be produced and/or sold by the organization. Marketing research studies are conducted to determine the needs of customers and the likelihood of purchase of products.

The typical marketing function organization chart is illustrated below. This organization shows the relationship among the seven marketing managers. Later in this chapter we will discuss how the marketing function interrelates with the other major functions of the organization.

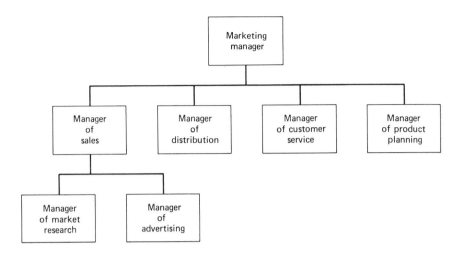

All these managers work together to produce revenue for the organization. Their functions and responsibilities are tied together in a series of related links, or steps, we call the marketing system chain.

Marketing System Chain

The marketing system chain has the responsibility for satisfying customer needs. This is accomplished by a chain of events comprised of many links; it begins when the customer initiates a purchase order and continues through the warranty/repair/replacement procedures. The chain also includes the replenishment of inventory. Figure 7-1 illustrates a marketing system chain for an organization that is selling a product. The chain is comprised of many links, or steps, such as credit approval, billing, and so on. If the organization deals in services, the same general framework would apply. However, in a service organization the steps relating to inventory would be replaced with service-oriented links.

The marketing system's chain normally includes a major segment of the organization's liquid assets. Unlike most other functions, in marketing there is a high turnover of assets. Marketing systems involve many transactions and are usually complex due to the intricacies of pricing and distribution. In a marketing system, there is a very close working relationship between accounting and marketing.

All the links in the marketing system revolve around the sale and movement of company product or service. The links involved in the marketing system chain are illustrated in Figure 7-1. Let's examine each link, trying to visualize how each link fits into the chain.

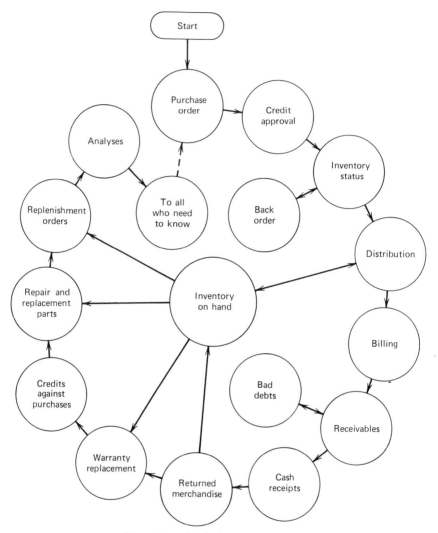

Figure 7-1. Marketing systems chain.

Purchase Order Link. This is the initiating action by a customer. It can result from a call by the salesman, be initiated directly by the customer, or be an automatic replenishment of product if previously agreed to by both parties. The formality of the purchase order depends upon the type of business, the previous relationship with the customer, and the funds involved. It can range from an oral agreement to a formal contract. The same holds for the acceptance procedure. In any case, the purchase order must be accepted by the selling organization before it is valid. Some organizations sell only to their dealer network, others will sell to the general public.

Credit Approval Link. When cash does not accompany the order, a credit approval procedure is needed. Generally, this is more formal for new customers than established ones. Most organizations establish dollar credit limits for customers. As long as the total of all previously unpaid purchases does not exceed this dollar limit, credit for new purchases will be approved automatically. A purchase which causes the credit limit to be exceeded must be reviewed and a determination made whether or not to grant additional credit to a customer.

Inventory Status Link. Before shipping a product, the inventory should be checked to see if there is enough product on hand to fill the order. When orders exceed available product, allocations must be made. If the product is in short supply or it cannot be replenished for some time, that product, too, may be shipped on an allocation basis long before orders exceed inventory. In automated systems, inventory status can be checked at the time purchase orders enter the system. In these systems, back orders and allocations can be handled automatically.

Back Orders Link. A file is maintained of orders for which product is not available. As soon as additional product is received, back orders are usually filled according to the date the order was received. When replenishment is not sufficient to cover all back orders, many organizations choose to make partial shipments in an effort to serve all customers fairly. It is practical for organizations to stock enough inventory so that out-of-stock conditions will never occur. However, the back order status must be continually monitored to avoid customer dissatisfaction.

Distribution Link. Approved orders, for which inventory is available, are given to the distribution section for shipping to the customer. The distribution section will determine the best way to ship the product unless the customer has specified shipping instructions. Distribution personnel pick the stock from inventory and package it for shipping. Occasionally, distribution personnel find some items depleted even though the perpetual records indicate the item is available. In this case, the distribution section will adjust the perpetual inventory records to reflect actual stock status. In manual systems, inventory status is usually maintained by the distribution personnel.

Billing Link. Invoices are prepared on the basis of information received from the distribution section. The information shows what products were shipped. Invoices may or may not accompany shipments.

Receivables Link. There are many different procedures for collecting billed amounts from customers. Some organizations state that invoices are payable upon receipt. Others summarize invoices on statements which are payable monthly. While the method varies from organization to organization, the invoice is usually the basis of posting to the customer's accounts receivable account. Statements, if used, are prepared by using data from the accounts receivable system.

Bad Debts Link. Accounts receivable not paid by customers result in bad debts. Since most organizations expect some of their receivables to be uncollectible, reserves are set up to cover this contingency. Accounts receivable are constantly analyzed to determine which customers may not be able to pay their accounts. If a customer has not kept his account current, many organizations still will deal with that customer, but only on a cash basis until the overdue amounts are paid. The object is to collect delinquent receivables while retaining the guilty customers.

Cash Receipts Link. Income cash is deposited by the cashier section with the supporting data going to the receivables section. In larger organizations, it may not be easy to match cash receipts with open items in the accounts receivables file. Customers may not indicate on payments which items they intend to pay for with the cash, or the amount paid may not match the open items because it is a partial payment. Occasionally, it is difficult to determine what account has been paid. For example, the customer may be listed under one name, but the payment is made under another name. This is why many organizations devise elaborate schemes to force the customer to return a portion of the invoice with the payment.

Returned Merchandise Link. Merchandise is returned for many reasons. We can learn a great deal about an organization and its products by examining why products are returned. Some of the more common reasons are:

Product was defective

Wrong product was shipped or ordered

Customer overstocked on a product and is returning the excess products

Product was shipped on trial basis or consignment and the customer did not find demand for the product so it is returned

Product is returned for correction of a defect

Product is returned because it failed to meet specifications

Organization recalled the product

Product was damaged by the carrier who returned it as part of an insurance claim

Customer failed to pay the amount due and the organization repossessed the product

Customers (retail customers) return the product for any of the above reasons and the organization must make good on the claim. It is important that the individual accepting the returned product clearly specifies the reason for the return so the reasons can be analyzed later. After the return, someone must determine whether the items returned can be entered back into inventory.

Warranties Link. Many organizations directly or indirectly warrant the use of their products. If the product fails to meet these warranty specifications, the customer can return the product for replacement or repair. After examining the returned merchandise, someone must decide whether the warranty should be honored. Some organizations will automatically replace or repair the product, not questioning the reason for return. Of course, if the number of warranty replacements becomes excessive, this policy needs to be reconsidered, as does quality control in the area producing the product.

Credits Link (against purchases). Credits are given to customers who are dissatisfied with their purchase. This credit represents a reduced purchase price. The reasons for dissatisfaction are as varied as the reasons for merchandise being returned. For example, if the customer buys a product today and a week later the company announces a price decrease, a customer who complains of unfair practices may be given a credit for the difference in price to maintain goodwill. Most organizations have a formalized method of giving and approving credits. The more money involved, the higher the granting authority must be in the organizational structure. In many organizations, very large credits must be approved by the president.

Repair Parts Link. Depending on the type of product, repair parts can be a large part of the business. For example, in the automobile industry, repairs and replacement parts are a very profitable part of the business. When a product is being manufactured, replacement parts are usually made at the same time. When model changes occur frequently, spare parts must be made while it is possible to do so. Availability of parts can become a serious problem for customers with older models. An organization may have its own repair department or it may make the parts and sell them to dealers who stock replacement parts and do the repair work.

Replenishment Orders Link. The replenishment of products in the warehouse is a very complex procedure. Under manual systems, when inventory reaches a certain point the pickers of the product in the distribution areas notify their supervisor that a product is in short supply. However, this is a poor method of stock replacement because there may or may not be more orders coming for that product. Using manual systems the quantity of items on unfilled orders is usually not known to the individual reordering stock. Computerized systems include orders on hand in the replenishment decision. A key link in the marketing systems chain is the analysis that indicates when inventory should be replenished.

Analysis Link. Many aspects of the marketing area are not identified in the marketing systems chain; for example, advertising, product research, and marketing research. These functions use information rather than supply it. They are not involved in the day-to-day process of marketing, but the people in those areas use the analysis of the marketing data to perform their tasks. These analyses can be presented in formats designed for the use of these functions.

Importance of the System's Chain

Accounting courses regularly discuss functions such as billing or accounts receivable. When accounts receivable are discussed, the entries which cause debits and credits to be made to receivables are explained in depth. The subject is treated as an entity and at the conclusion the student understands accounts receivable. However, what is really needed to understand accounts receivable is a discussion of the marketing systems chain. It is through an understanding of all the links in the chain (inventory status, returned merchandise, and so on) that the student comprehends how receivables fit into the business environment. The systems chain concept shows the interrelationships of the different links to one another.

    The full implementation of the last two links in the chain, replenishment orders and analyses, is only feasible on a computer. The computer has made these two links valuable tools in the business planning cycle. Without the computer, these two steps had to be done using sparse, and often out-of-date, information. With the computer, it is now possible to get the type of data needed for timely inventory replenishment and analyses. Some organizations are able to modify today's production based on yesterday's orders. Current replenishment information also enables organizations to have less inventory on hand. This means less carrying cost and less warehouse space to stock items. By providing timely information, computer systems give a large return on investment.

The cement that holds the chain together is information. Information is passed from step to step, much of it in the form of paper documents.

MARKETING PAPERWORK FLOW

The marketing systems chain produces numerous documents. Some are documents to be used later as input documents and others are solely output reports—all produced from the data within the system. As systems become more complex, there are fewer hard-copy documents generated from the system. On-line marketing systems operate with minimal input documents. The expression ''a paperless society'' reflects the small number of system documents, and the low volume of paper produced by systems. In many instances, the system functions without any paper output.

The purchase order, product return, and cash receipts are the documents that initiate action in the marketing systems chain. All other documents can be generated from data contained within the computerized application. Figure 7-2 shows the links in the chain and which links utilize those documents.

The key document is the one that initiates the purchase. To call this a document may be a misnomer because with on-line systems it may encompass only a few notes jotted on an old envelope which is destroyed immediately after the order is entered in the system. Once the information is entered in the marketing system, it can be reproduced on an in-house computer-prepared purchase order form. In many organizations, the in-house-produced purchase order serves as the shipping memo and invoice. This multipart document has three purposes. Part one serves as the purchase order; part two, as a shipping memo (an additional part may be a packing slip); and part three, an invoice. This multipart document is used heavily in organizations which ship their products within hours after the purchase order is received.

The purchase order can also be used as a credit approval document, and it may be used as the document to initiate back orders. In automated inventory status systems, the system itself can initiate back order documents when the on-hand status of inventory is insufficient to fill an order.

The shipping memo tells how many of what products are to be shipped and where they are to go. The distribution function uses the shipping

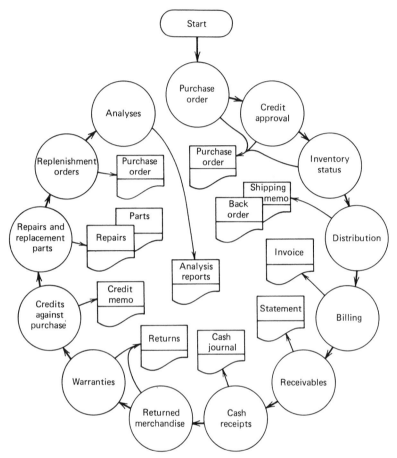

Figure 7-2.   Paperwork-marketing systems chain.

memo as authorization to ship stock. In some organizations, the invoice is attached to the shipping memo. Once the order has been shipped, the invoice can be mailed. The result is that the customer is both billed and notified that the order has been shipped.

On a periodic basis, statements will be issued from the accounts receivable system. These statements will show the accumulation of the invoices prepared since the last statement, less any payments and credits. One of the major problems in computerized systems is to include both the debit and credit side of the transactions in the correct accounting period. To ensure this, some means must be devised to properly record all invoices and shipments made during an accounting period. If the system is not well controlled, it is quite easy to get half of an entry recorded in one accounting period and half recorded in the following accounting period. For example, record a sale but don't reduce inventory until the following accounting period.

Once cash is received it should be recorded. In small organizations, this may be done by an adding machine tape or in a cash journal, while in larger organizations, computerized systems handle cash receipts. Usually, organizations separate the documentation from the cash when it is received. Mail room clerks may do this, or the checks and documents may be sent directly from the mail room to the cashier function to perform the step. The posting of cash to receivables can be automated using computer systems. However, even in automated systems, some individual posting to customer accounts may be necessary because of the problems of matching cash to open items in the accounts receivable.

Returned merchandise, warranty claims, and repairs all deal with products returned by customers. In some organizations, merchandise of this type is returned to a central location and then separated, depending on the reason for return. For example, items returned for repair go to the repair shop. The organization then decides on the disposition of the returned item. Most customers will accept the organization's decision, but some will not. In some cases, dissatisfaction has led to class action lawsuits against the organization. The defect may be something not thought of when the product was specified, but some aspect of the product has made it unsafe.

Not only do the financial aspects of the return need to be determined, but the disposition of the product itself. The product can be returned to inventory, repaired and returned to the customer, repaired and returned to inventory, or scrapped. The document on which the return is recorded must indicate which of the possible dispositions has been taken.

Most credits against purchases result from returned merchandise. Management will determine what type of credit, if any, is to be issued on the return. The condition of the product can affect the amount of credit given. However, credit can be issued for other than returned merchandise. For example, the customer may keep, but be given some credit for, merchandise arriving in a slightly damaged condition. It is important that the credit memo indicate the reason for the credit so that an analysis can be made of credits. Very valuable information for product planning and advertising and sales campaigns can be gained by analyzing the reasons why credit has been granted to customers. For example, a new product can be designed to overcome flaws shown to be extensive by the number of credits issued.

Many marketing systems automatically initiate purchase orders to buy replenishment stock. Also, based on the amount of purchases, the computer can initiate shipment of product from central to remote warehouses. People may or may not review automatic purchases from outside suppliers, or orders to manufacture more products.

A variety of analytical reports are produced from marketing systems. These reports are a valuable source of information for planning purposes. For example, the sales manager can anticipate buying trends based on the analysis of customers' buying habits. This can be very beneficial in ordering the right products. The real value of many computerized applications is that they reorient the data in different formats. For example, data kept by customer can be resequenced by salesman to show who's selling what and how much.

Sales Invoice Example

The invoice produced by the marketing system chain illustrates the basic information available from that source. The invoice reflects the information contained in the purchase order, supplemented with information available from the system itself.

Figure 7-3 illustrates a sales invoice. When customers order products they indicate the item, the quantity, the date wanted, and where it should be shipped. The "bill to" and "ship to" addresses may be within the system and all the customer needs to do is give the customer number. The system obtains the actual quantity shipped, the unit price for the quantity ordered, the total price, and any sales tax, freight charge, or discounts given the customer. Depending on the organization, the sales invoice may also show the salesperson who took the order and special customer information, such as the customer's own purchase order number. If this is a partial shipment, the sales invoice can show the amount on back order and the date on which it will be shipped.

All other parts of the marketing system chain amplify, use, or modify this basic information. This information will then be available in a readily accessible format. The two most common methods of accessing this information are by invoice number and customer number. Manual systems frequently have duplicate invoices and file one invoice by each method. Computerized systems maintain data in one sequence, but may have a cross-reference index so that by knowing one of these two pieces of information they will print access to the other. For example, if you know the customer's number, you can locate that customer's invoice, or if you know the invoice number, it will lead you to the correct customer information.

We have discussed the marketing managers and the system chain in

INVOICE

SUPER SALES COMPANY
NEW YORK, NEW YORK

BILL TO: ABC Company
Newark, New Jersey
July 4, 1976

SHIP TO: ABC Company
Stamford, Connecticut

DATE SHIPPED: July 2, 1976   TERMS OF SALE: 2/30, net 60

ITEM	DESCRIPTION	QUANTITY ORDERED	QUANTITY SHIPPED	UNIT PRICE	TOTAL
S325	Saw	500	500	$ 1.40	$ 700.00
X043	Hammer	300	200	2.20	440.00
N444	Nails — Box 300	1000	1000	.66	660.00
	Sales tax @ 7%				126.00
	Total invoice				$1,926.00

Page_____ of _____   INVOICE NUMBER___07325___

Figure 7-3.   Sales invoice example.

which they work. Next we will show the relationship of marketing and the other major functions of an organization to the links in the system chain.

ORGANIZATIONAL IMPLICATIONS

The marketing system provides input information into many of the organization's other functions. Most functions interrelate with marketing. Fig-

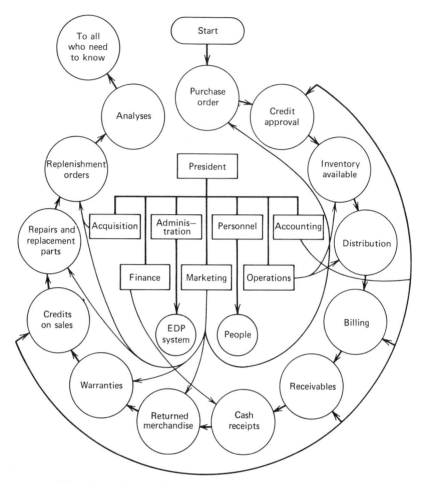

Figure 7-4.   Organization implications — marketing systems chain.

ure 7-4 shows the interrelationship between a marketing system chain and the organizational structure.

Figure 7-4 shows the seven major functions of an organization. Surrounding this organizational structure is the marketing system chain. The lines between the links of the marketing system chain and the organizational structure reflect the responsibility of the seven functions for each link in the chain. For example, the operation group has responsibility for maintaining an adequate inventory and distributing that inventory to customers.

The two elements not included in the marketing system chain are people and the EDP system. These were not shown on the chain because all systems include these two. The responsibility for obtaining personnel and maintaining personnel policies rests with the personnel function. The operation of the computerized segment of the system rests with the administration function. Administration may also be responsible for developing the organization's policies and procedures. While these procedures are generally developed in conjunction with the group they affect (marketing for marketing procedures, for example), the preparation and dissemination of the procedures would be the responsibility of administration.

Reports are produced by all computerized systems chains to assist the operating departments. These reports provide the work documents needed to operate, such as shipping notices and invoices. The analyses of operations produced by the system will be of interest to all groups affected by the system, including the president of the organization. Let's examine these documents from an organizational standpoint so we can fully comprehend the marketing system chain.

MARKETING SYSTEM CHAIN FLOW

Up to this point, you have studied the systems chain, the paperwork flow, and the organizational structure through which that paperwork flows. You have seen the interrelationships between the systems chain and the flow of documents. You have also examined the interrelationship between the systems chain and the organizational structure. In order to complete the understanding of the marketing system chain, you must put the three elements of a system in perspective. The three elements are the paperwork flow (the data), the organizational structure (the people), and the system (the rules).

The marketing system has been explained as a chain of links or steps to be performed. For purposes of showing the interrelationship among the three elements of a system, we will show the computerized aspect of the marketing system as a "black box." This black box will be organizationally located under the administration function. The application is representative of many computerized marketing data processing applications developed and operated by the data processing department. Figure 7-5 (Systems Flow—Marketing System Chain) shows the three elements of the marketing system in businesses which use computers.

In this illustration, we see six functions of the business organization identified, and the customer. The seventh function, personnel, is not shown, because it has no direct tie into the marketing system. In the marketing system illustrated, the customer is generally located outside the

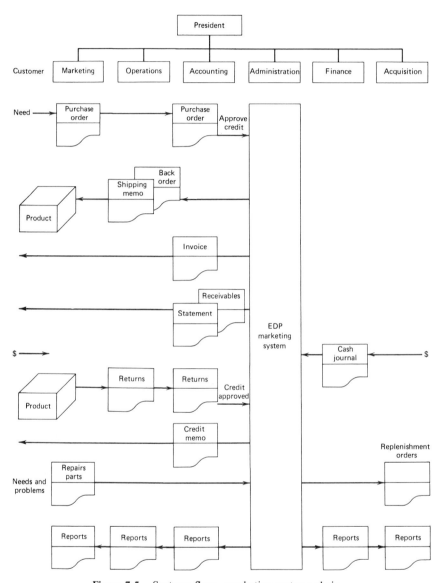

Figure 7-5. Systems flow—marketing systems chain.

business organization. For example, in a raw material system the customer is the production department operator.

Example Explained

Figure 7-5 shows the marketing system and its relationship to paperwork, the organization, and the system rules. As with any system, the initiation of a transaction (a need to be satisfied) begins with the customer of the system. In the marketing system, this is the customer's purchase order. The marketing department authorizes the transaction and requests approval of credit, if requested by the customer, from the accounting department. As previously stated, this credit approval can be built into the system, with the accounting department handling exceptions such as when credit limits have been exceeded. In some organizations the accounting department will handle every order, approving credit each time.

The purchase order is placed into the computer system. The computer system then prepares shipping memos and any back order documents required when sufficient product is not on hand to meet requirements. The operations department ships the product to the customer. Once the computer system is notified that the product has been shipped, an invoice can be prepared and sent to the customer. At this point, we can state that the objectives of the system have been satisfied. The need of the customer for a product has resulted in the product's being shipped to the customer.

In terms of system steps, the following has happened. The transaction has been *authorized, recorded,* and *transmitted* to the computer system for processing. *Processing* has occurred with the various documents and data *stored* for future reference. The results of the system (the product and associated paperwork) have been distributed (*output*) to the customer and the customer will make use of that product.

The concept of systems chains should become evident from this example. It has taken many links to accomplish all the steps. However, there are still many links of the marketing system chain yet to be completed.

Accountants tend to view each of these links as systems by themselves. For example, you can look at accounts receivable as an entire system. You may have studied accounts receivable as an entire system rather than as a link in the marketing system chain. It is incorrect to look at these as systems complete in themselves. We should consider them as links in the systems chain.

Let's examine why it is incorrect to view a link such as the accounts receivable link as a separate system. We will do this by discussing the steps in a system. The invoice is the initiating transaction into the accounts receivable system. Because the invoice comes from another part of the marketing system chain, the *authorization* and *recording* are complete before the accounts receivable link. *Transmission* can be accomplished through intermediary computer files. The accounts receivable link of the marketing system chain does *process* the invoice into the accounts receivable system. The data are *stored* in the accounts receivable file. *Output* is made through the preparation of statements to the customer and they are used in the payment of bills. Thus, not all system steps are accomplished in the accounts receivable link.

One of the unique features of the complex data processing systems is that the computer system itself becomes the initiator of transactions for other parts of the system chain once the customer initiates the original transaction. Because of this, it can become difficult to understand various functions such as accounts receivable in a computerized business environment. For example, if a customer is automatically replenished, the computer will initiate the transaction at the proper time.

After the customer has received product and been invoiced, the following steps in the marketing system chain must still be executed:

Cash Receipts.   Cash received from the customer is recorded and transmitted to the computerized marketing system. The customer's account is appropriately credited. Since this is performed completely within the computerized segment, no documents need to be issued.

Returned Merchandise.   If the customer returns a product, it is returned to the operations department. They will prepare the documents noting a return which must be approved by the accounting department before it is transmitted to the computer system. This results in a credit memo which is sent to the customer.

Repair and Replacement Parts.   A customer notifies the organization of a problem with one of their products. The organization must then initiate documents for repairs or to order parts. These documents are transmitted by the repair department to the computer system so billings can be prepared. If a large amount of money is involved, credit approval may be required before the repair is accomplished, but generally it is not required. This link in the marketing system results in a product's being returned, repaired and shipped, invoices being prepared, statements issued, and cash received. It may also generate returns, credits, and the need for additional parts or repairs.

Replenishment Orders. Based on predetermined rules, the computerized marketing system will initiate transactions to replenish diminishing stocks. Because replenishment of inventory for sale falls under the acquisition system, most of the rep!enishment processing will be handled by the acquisition system. The marketing system generates the initiating order.

Analyses. A major benefit of computerizing a system is the additional uses of the data generated by the system. These additional uses require additional programs in the systems chain. For example, the sales department will get a series of reports relating to the sales aspect of the system, the operations department will get reports on distribution of product, the accounting department will get reports on the financial aspects of the system, the finance department will get reports on cash receipts, and the acquisition department will get reports on inventory and replenishment status.

RESPONSIBILITY FOR DATA

Responsibility must be established for each data element in the system. The data elements belong to various functions in the organization. The functions have the responsibility of entering those data elements correctly. This responsibility also includes control over access and use of data. If a function fulfills its responsibility, it will oversee all the uses of the data for which it is responsible.

For example, the sales department would be responsible for entering correct customer information. Such data would include the customer number, customer name and address, and any other permanent data that the organization retains on its customers. The sales department would be responsible for the security of this information, and would make sure it has been used only by authorized personnel for authorized purposes.

The dollar amount of credit limits authorized for each customer is the responsibility of the controller. The controller would act on advice from the sales department but must also make credit checks on the customer through a credit bureau. Based on those credit checks, the controller would authorize a credit limit up to a certain dollar amount. This dollar amount is then entered into the computer system. If credit limits are exceeded, the controller has the responsibility to stop the sale or to authorize additional credit. Additional credit approval can be based on good payment records or a change in credit limit may be warranted. Conversely, if a customer were to fall behind on payments, it would be the responsibility of the controller to reduce credit or stipulate that sales to that customer are to be cash basis only until the account is in good standing again.

Many organizations take responsibility and control of data too lightly. This is a serious responsibility, deserving close attention on the part of management responsible for the data. Adequate controls inform those responsible for data who is trying to or has gained access to data so that they can then either approve or disapprove each request. Most *new* computer operating systems contain this type of control.

Accounting Data

Data elements of special interest to accountants are those which contain financial data. In marketing systems, these include credit limit and terms, balance due, payments, items' cost, discounts, credit given, and quantity on hand.

Some nonfinancial elements in the marketing system have financial implication. For example, "items purchased" has financial implications because when multiplied by "items' cost" it gives "balance due." While "items purchased" is not a specific piece of financial information, it is used in the calculation of financial data. The "items purchased" data element would be the responsibility of the marketing group, but would be of interest to the accounting group.

It is essential to maintain controls on financial information. Most accounting systems have such controls. A simple accounting proof (old balance plus additions minus subtractions equals new balance) if maintained on accounting data is an effective control. When these financial controls are maintained, detailed amounts should be regularly reconciled to control totals. When errors occur and the group responsible for the error is notified but they take no action, the organization is headed for trouble. Most computer problems could be corrected early if control information were properly utilized. Many potential problems are uncovered through data analysis.

RELATIONSHIP OF ACCOUNTING AND MARKETING INFORMATION

The marketing function has a major effect on the income data from the statement and balance sheet. What may not be readily apparent is in which captions on the income statement and balance sheet the various links of the marketing system chain end up. It is by understanding this relationship that accountants can put the marketing system chain into proper perspective with the financial statements of an organization.

Income Implications

The marketing system chain usually encompasses the majority of the income and expense dollars of an organization. Figure 7-6 shows this relationship. The income statement shown is simplified. The objective of the figure is to show how the various captions relate to the links in the marketing system chain. This is not to imply that the total amount in the

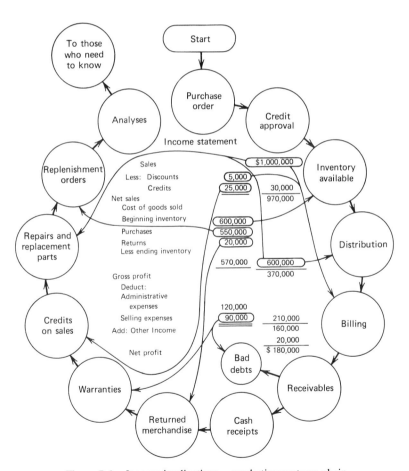

Figure 7-6. Income implications—marketing systems chain.

caption comes from the data in one link in the marketing system chain. For example, "bad debts" goes in selling expense but it is only a part—and, one hopes, a very small part—of selling expense.

Many of the items on the income statement come from two or more links in the marketing system chain. For example, the sales figures come both from regular sales and from selling repair work and replacement parts.

Balance Sheet Implications

The marketing system's major impact on the balance sheet is the contribution to profit and loss. The total income/loss is reflected in retained earnings on the balance sheet. Since profit is a reflection of all the links in the total marketing system chain, it cannot be readily illustrated in Figure 7-7. However, Figure 7-7 does illustrate which balance sheet captions are individually affected by the various links in the marketing system chain. For example, cash receipts will be reflected in the balance sheet cash caption at the end of an accounting period. Reserves for warranties would be reflected in the liabilities caption. Inventory and receivables are affected by many links in the marketing system chain. This is because a sale and the accompanying reduction in inventory affects receivables, returns, warranties, repairs, and all inventory-related links.

Importance of Accounting Implications

In actual practice, information from two or more computer system chains feeds into the same financial statement caption. For example, there may be several marketing system chains in an organization. This is especially true in a corporation with subsidiaries or special product lines. In addition, some parts of the marketing system chain may be manual while others are computerized. For instance, some organizations will sell advertising promotional material to customers on a special request basis. Because this is not a routine function of the organization, it is handled manually when it occurs. At other times sales to employees are specially handled because of special prices or other considerations.

The net result is that only a few people in an organization understand how the amount listed for a specific financial statement caption is accumulated. Dollar amounts can come from a variety of divisions of an organization, and the original figures are lost as they are accumulated at various levels of an organization.

Accountants who wish to understand the development of financial statements need to have a good understanding of systems. The implica-

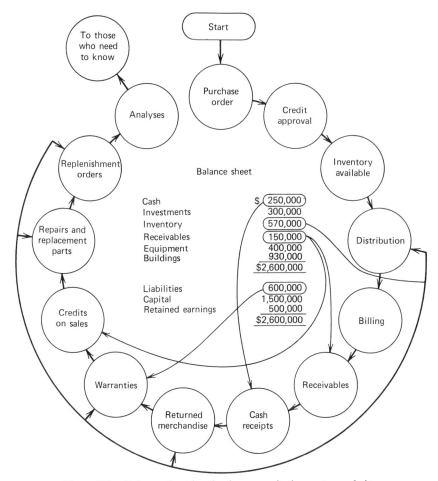

Figure 7-7. Balance sheet implications—marketing systems chain.

tions of a change in one system must be reflected in other systems to maintain continuity in a double-entry accounting system. Occasionally, a change will occur that affects only half of an accounting entry. For example, if returned merchandise is reflected only in a dollar credit to the customer and a reduction of sales, the inventory will be out of balance.

Few have the knowledge and skill to understand how accounting information from many different computer systems is consolidated into the financial statements of the organization. Figures 7-6 and 7-7 should prove helpful in illustrating that relationship. Accountants studying systems should try to develop charts such as these as a basis for understanding the relationship between systems and financial records. But because so few understand the control implications of computerized systems, problems can occur and go undetected.

AREAS OF CONTROL CONCERN IN AN AUTOMATED MARKETING SYSTEM

Each system chain has key control points which need to be monitored constantly. Profitable organizations have learned to implement controls at these points. The control information enables management to know when problems are occurring. Once they are aware of problems, management can act and correct them before they become serious.

The following is a list of some of the control points in the marketing system chain. This list is not meant to be comprehensive but, rather, to provide examples of these control points. Frequently the accountants are asked to monitor these control points in an effort to detect problems. Some typical control points are:

Credit Limit Policy Not Violated. Accounting departments authorize customers' reasonable credit limits up to a specific dollar amount. Conversely, salespersons are eager to see this limit set as high as possible. If the marketing division can exceed credit limits, it may try to do so in order to make a sale. Reports should be available indicating when credit limits have been exceeded.

Realistic Inventory Levels Are Maintained. A major drain on the resources of an organization is excessive inventory levels. This requires not only extra funds to purchase the inventory, but extra warehouse space, people, and resources to store and move the product. Every effort should be made to keep inventories at the minimum level possible to achieve optimal sales, with an acceptable level of stockouts.

Receivables Are Current. Receivables must be continually monitored so that the organization is aware when customers are late in making payments. This can indicate customers are getting into cash flow problems. Organizations should be ready to react quickly to this situation to avoid losses.

Selling Below Cost. Organizations frequently take a loss on the sale of products, but are unaware of it. This is often true in selling small items. For example, a 10¢ part may cost $5–8 to sell. Thus, a substantial service charge must be added to a small order or the company will lose money on each sale.

Customer Satisfaction Maintained. Organizations should continually monitor product returned, credits, and communications from customers who indicate their dissatisfaction. While only part of this information is provided by the computerized marketing system, all of the data should be monitored.

Pricing Policy Enforced. Salespeople may make concessions to customers to sell products. This is desirable providing it is not abused. Salespersons should be controlled to be sure their sales remain profitable.

Monitor Product on Trial. Sales personnel and customers obtain products on trial. This must be closely monitored to keep salespeople from "giving away the store."

Accounting and marketing are closely interrelated. Accountants perform many analyses of the marketing function because it is so important to the organization. For accountants to understand the full accounting implications of the marketing system chain, they must understand how marketing relates to the organization and to its financial statement. A high level of comprehension of these matters is necessary if accountants are to provide full service for their organizations.

part three

THE SOLUTION TO AUTOMATION

eight

COMPUTER RISK: IT MUST BE CONTROLLED

Controlling risk is the solution to most business problems. The failure to properly identify and control risks leads to frustration and unhappiness. Too many organizations install controls before identifying the risks which require control. This is not only a costly control design approach, but fails to satisfy people's systems objectives.

Not too long ago, I purchased a new automobile. My expectations paralleled the advertisement in which I saw the automobile driving through the clouds past beautifully clothed women, who were obviously pleased at the sight of the automobile. Reality set in on the day I drove the car home from the showroom.

As family, friends, and children raced out of the house to admire my new machine, they noticed oil leaking from underneath the car. I satisfactorily maneuvered the automobile back to the showroom without the engine being destroyed only to learn that what I thought was serious was just a common, everyday occurrence. The service manager assured me that many new cars leaked oil and that it could be fixed by that evening. Reality intruded into more dreams as new problems occurred regularly. Each trip to the automotive service department further shattered my expectations because each of my problems appeared routine to the service manager.

I was suffering from an expectation gap. I expected more than the automotive company planned to deliver. I expected an automobile that would drive through the clouds as women stood by admiringly. What I received was an automobile manufactured to certain tolerances and costs designed to achieve good but not perfect reliability. Neither the automotive advertisements nor the dealership sales personnel explained to me these tolerances and expected reliability.

Who or what caused this expectation gap? Did I unreasonably expect more than I should have? Did the manufacturer and dealership promise more than they knew they could deliver? These same expectation gap principles apply to automated accounting systems.

Accountants' Computer Guideline 10. Promise them anything, but be prepared to deliver on your promise.

This chapter outlines a step-by-step process for designing controls in automated systems. The process uses risks as the basis for control design. The process is based on the assumption that control is a design specification, and that the control specification process goes through the same steps as other parts of the automated application system development process.

CLOSING THE EXPECTATION GAP

Computer people have fostered the misbelief that computers are infallible. There is a mystique about the black box which causes people to believe that reports and data produced by the computer are correct. The fact that they are printed, that the numbers and letters are in neat rows and columns, encourages this mystique of accuracy.

When people sent you a handwritten note with information scrawled up one side, down the other, crossed out, erased, and sometimes unintelligible, you questioned the accuracy and reliability of the information. But don't those printed reports look authoritative?

The reason that information is unreliable, inaccurate, or incomplete, is due to the failure to adequately control risk. There is a risk that inaccurate or incomplete data will be entered into the system. There is a risk that information will be erroneously entered into the system or that the timing of the information will be wrong. These risks occur in all computer systems and to ignore the fact that they do exist is as unrealistic as to expect a new automobile to function properly all of the time.

Most accountants expect more from an automated application than that application can reasonably be expected to deliver. Computer personnel cannot build a perfect system. They know that the system will have problems and, like the service manager at the automotive dealership, will treat these problems as routine. Like the service manager, they cannot understand why people are so upset when problems occur. The reasons for the automated application expectation gap include:

People expect too much from automated systems

Data processing personnel do not explain in sufficient detail the types of problems that accountants should expect

Accountants fail to identify the accounting risk for data processing personnel

Data processing personnel do not require their users to define the error levels they can tolerate

Rarely do data processing personnel or users monitor and measure accounting system reliability

Because of these automated application characteristics, each problem comes as a surprise. I did not expect my automobile to leak oil and was surprised when it happened. If the dealership had told me that one out of every 872 automobiles would leak oil, I at least would have been aware that that problem could happen. If the data processing personnel were to tell you that there would be one data entry error for every 816 keystrokes, you would not be surprised when one happened. Unfortunately, the builders of systems do not explain this to the users of the systems, nor do the users of the systems ask the appropriate questions of the systems designers.

The expectation gap can be closed only by system expectation communication between the systems designers and the users. The users must help identify the risks, and then explain the reliability and tolerances acceptable to them for those risks. The systems designers must demand from their users this risk definition before building the automated application. It is only when both parties know what is expected, and that reliability can be measured, that both parties will be satisfied.

Accountants' Computer Guideline 11. Accountants should identify the gap between control expectations and control processes as the first step in closing that gap.

THE CONTROL DESIGN PROCESS

The systems development process begins by establishing requirements, and then designing and implementing those requirements. The process follows a logical pattern from start to finish. Unfortunately, it costs many millions of dollars and several years to develop an effective systems design process.

Most controls are designed by using the "horses out of the barn" technique. This technique states that problems should not occur twice. If the horse gets out of the barn, lock the door; if the horse escapes through the window, put bars on the window; and so forth. The process is neither methodical nor effective against many of the new computer risks.

Control has not been considered to be a high priority systems responsibility. Management accepts responsibility for organizing, planning, directing, and controlling. Management isolates control as a special responsibility, but data processing personnel do not. It is this lack of attention to control that has caused many of the data processing problems.

A suggested control design process is illustrated as a pyramid in Figure 8-1. The pyramid illustration is used because the steps at the base must be performed before the next higher steps can be performed. In too many systems, controls are implemented without building the proper base for those controls. Thus, it should not be a surprise to anyone when the controls fail to satisfy users' expectations and/or needs.

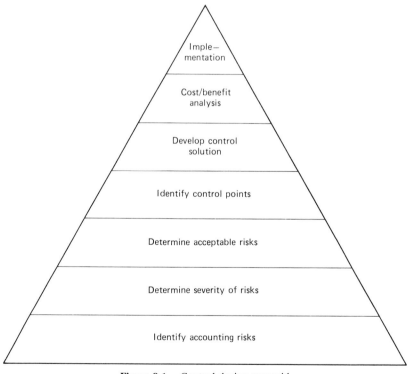

Figure 8-1.   Control design pyramid.

The control design process involves the following seven steps:

1. *Identify Accounting Risks.* An analysis to determine all of the events which could cause problems.
2. *Determine Severity of Risk.* Ascertain the seriousness of the risk to the organization.
3. *Determine Acceptable Risk.* Ascertain how much of a risk the user is willing to live with.
4. *Identify Control Points.* Determine those points within the automated application where the risk is most likely to occur.
5. *Develop Control Solution.* Determine the controls that can reduce the risk to the acceptable level.
6. *Cost/Benefit Analysis.* Determine the economics of installing the control.
7. *Implementation.* Install the controls that will reduce the identified risks to the acceptable level.

Accountants should not expect to find this control design process in operation in their organization. Very few data processing functions use this methodology for implementing controls. The process is ordinarily not used because data processing personnel are positive rather than negative thinkers. As positive thinkers, their main concern is satisfying user needs as opposed to determining all of the reasons why those needs may not be satisfied.

The accountant, even though possessing minimal data processing skills, should understand the control design methodology. Accountants understand risk, and understand why things do not succeed. As such, they may have to fulfill the role of teacher and counsellor to the data processing professional in explaining risk and control design. This seven-step control design process need not be a time-consuming process. The amount of effort that should be expended on control design will become readily apparent as the risks and severity of those risks are identified. If the risks are low, the amount of effort should be low; likewise, when the risks are high, the amount of effort may need to be correspondingly high. The considerations and methods used for each of these seven steps are individually explained.

Technological Rule of Thumb 8. System designers are not taught control design principles and processes and, thus, should not be expected to build well-controlled systems.

Step 1: Identify Accounting Risks

The control design process commences with risk identification. If there are no risks, there is no need for controls. These identified risks become the control requirements.

Chapter 3 explained the types of accounting risks found in most automated financial applications. Obviously, these generalized risks do not explain the more specific risks related to the individual application. For example, a payroll system would include the risks outlined in Chapter 3 and all of the following specific application payroll risks:

Unauthorized employees will be paid

Compensation will not be at authorized rates

Payroll deductions and adjustments to payroll accounts will not be properly authorized

Employee benefits and perquisites will not be properly authorized

Recorded payroll will not be for work actually performed

Payroll and related withholdings will not be correctly computed and remitted when due

Payroll costs will not be reported at the appropriate amounts and in the appropriate period

Payroll costs will not be properly classified in the accounts

Access to personnel and payroll records will not be suitably controlled to prevent or detect within a timely period duplicate or improper payments

Coupled with these are the nineteen general accounting risks also outlined in Chapter 3. The systems development team must determine which risks are applicable to the system under development. Thus, the end product from this step is a list of risks that must be addressed during the systems design process.

The most common method for identifying risks is a risk analysis scenario. This is a think session, or brainstorming session, designed to synergistically identify the risks.

The risk analysis scenario is a multidisciplined exercise. The participants in the exercise should have various backgrounds, such as:

Accounting
Data processing
Security

Application experience
Systems design experience

The risk analysis team is organized and spends several hours brain-storming in an effort to identify the potential risks.* The tasks to be performed by the risk analysis team, under the direction of the task force leader, are:

Statement of the task force responsibility by the chairman

Explanation or dissemination of the resources outlining common risks

Open period, usually between two to eight hours, for brainstorming to list as many potential risks as possible

Summarization and agreement by the task force of the applicable risks from those identified by the task force

Documentation of the applicable risks

Step 2: Determine Severity of Risk

We all live with risk every day of our lives. Some risks are highly probable, such as falling or burning ourselves, so we are very careful about where we walk and how we handle fire. Other risks have a very low probability, such as the risk of earthquake or flood, and to those we pay little attention. Still other risks, such as automobile accidents or theft, may be a higher probability risk than we think, and perhaps we should give them more attention than we do.

The severity or magnitude of a risk tells us how much attention we need to give to that risk. It forces us to spend our time on high-magnitude risks, while not devoting much time and effort to the low-magnitude risks. Without determining the severity of the risks, we may use our time ineffectively.

---

*Some of the sources that are helpful as input to this exercise include *Guideline for Automatic Data Processing Risk Analysis,* published by the National Bureau of Standards as Federal Information Processing Systems Publication No. 65, U.S. Department of Commerce, Washington, D.C., 1979; *Computer Control & Audit,* by William C. Mair, Donald L. Wood, Keagle W. Davis, published by The Institute of Internal Auditors, Altamonte Springs, FL, 1976. Accounting risk documents are published by most of the large certified public accounting firms: for example, *A Guide for Studying and Evaluating Internal Accounting Control,* Arthur Andersen & Co., 1978; Report of the Special Advisory Committee on Internal Accounting Control, issued by the American Institute of Certified Public Accountants, New York, 1978; and *Computer Control and Security,* by William E. Perry, John Wiley & Sons, New York, 1981.

The two most common methods for expressing the severity of risk are:

1. *Stratification.* The magnitude of the risk is divided into strata, such as high, medium, or low risk. The strata used can be as simple as the previous three-category example, or as complex as necessary to explain the potential impact of the risk. For example, severity of the risk can be divided into five or even ten strata, as well as considering the impact on such factors as people, resources, competitiveness, and so forth.

2. *Annual Loss Expectation.* The magnitude of the risk can be expressed in terms of dollars, such as a $500,000 risk. When risks are quantified, they are also ordinarily annualized. For example, the $500,000 may be the expected annual loss due to a specific risk. The annualizing process is used because it coincides with budgets and other planning procedures.

The severity of the risk can be determined by the risk analysis task force or it can be determined by the systems design team. The determination should be made by individuals knowledgeable in both the risk area and the risk assessment process. In most cases, the determination is an estimate or projection, because the risk situation has yet to occur.

The severity of a risk can be determined using one of the following four methods:

Historic approach
Formula approach
Subjective estimate approach
Scenario approach

Historic Approach.   The historic approach is based upon a future projection of events that have occurred in the past. The approach normally involves the collection of information about past problems. This experience is then used to project the severity of the risk in the future. For example, if experience has shown that one out of twenty-five invoices will be inaccurately priced, then that experience can be applied to X invoices over the next month, year, or several years.

The historical method is effective only for known risks. For example, risks such as keystroke errors, inaccurate processing, or equipment failures have a track record of reliability. This track record can be used in predicting the probability of future risk for those events.

If the organization has had no experience with a risk, then the historic method is not effective. For example, if the organization is trying to project data lost due to improper control of data base technology, there may be no historic basis on which to make that projection if the organization is not using data base technology.

The historic approach involves the collection, analysis, and summarization of large amounts of data. For example, if communications problems were being projected, then it would be necessary to analyze communications logs. In medium- to large-sized installations, it is not uncommon for these logs to accumulate several million records in a month. Thus, the collection and analysis process can be both time-consuming and costly.

The historic approach can usually project losses in quantitative terms. The terms may not always be in monetary units, but may be in terms of events such as errors or equipment downtime. Unfortunately, many installations do not save historical data relating to risks, or do not save it long enough to permit valid projections to be made.

Risk projection using historical data is acceptable to most people. The method uses the experience of the organizations to project future losses. Because the historical information is factual, it is difficult to dispute the accuracy of the projection.

The major disadvantage with the historical approach is that it assumes that those events that have happened in the past will continue to happen in the future. This assumption may be invalid for many different reasons. People cannot expect conditions to be unchanging. This is particularly true in a highly automated and rapidly changing environment.

Formula Method. Risks have two variables. These are the frequency of occurrence and the loss per occurrence. These two variables become the basis of projecting loss using the following formula:

$$annual\ loss\ expectation = \text{frequency of occurrence} \times \\ \text{value of the loss}$$

The formula is quite simple to work. For example, if we were determining the annual expected loss due to mispriced invoices we would plug our variables into the formula. If the expected loss due to mispricing was $25 and the frequency of mispricing was 100 invoices per year, then our expected annual loss would be $2,500 ($25 loss times 100 frequency equals $2,500).

The formula method has two failings to its use. These are the estimation of the loss per occurrence and the estimation of the expected frequency of loss. Outside of these disadvantages, the formula approach produces a quantified risk. The mathematics are easy.

Insurance companies use actuaries to calculate the expected frequencies and the expected losses. The actuaries use both historic information and any other information that they can gather which may have an effect on the projection.

Accountants do not have a staff of actuaries available to project the losses due to business risks. However, they are not placing money into an insurance pool and drawing it out to pay expected losses. Accountants are determining the severity of risk to help them plan the control design program. This means that the decision of the estimate does not have to be nearly as accurate as the insurance actuary.

In many projections of loss due to risk, great precision is not needed. The amount of precision required is dependent upon the variance between the control solution and the projected loss. For example, if the loss is projected to be very high and the cost of controls very low, or the projected loss to be low and the cost of controls very high, there is little need for great precision in either the expected loss or the cost of controls. It is only when the two are close in value that precision needs to increase.

The National Bureau of Standards recommends the following approach be undertaken to calculate the annual loss expectation:

Step 1: Preliminary Considerations. Have top management make a commitment to, set objectives for, select a team for, delegate responsibility to the team for, and review results of a risk management program.

Step 2: Asset Identification. Identify resources such as hardware, software, data, personnel, supplies, communications, facility, procedures.

Step 3: Asset Valuation. Determine sensitivity and dollar value of assets to an owner, an abuser, and a subject.

Step 4: Vulnerability Analysis. Identify weaknesses within the organization (including its computer systems).

Step 5: Threat Analysis. Identify external menaces or abusive forces that can destroy or misuse resources.

Step 6: Threat/Vulnerability Pairing. Determine which threats can combine with which vulnerabilities to cause loss or damage.

Step 7: Loss Exposure Value. Use a methodology where loss exposure is calculated or estimated for each threat/vulnerability pair attacking an asset.

Step 8: Predictive Analysis. Identify frequency of threat/vulnerability materialization with respect to an asset (frequency of loss exposure).

Step 9: Exposure (Risk) Assessment. Use a method for combining loss exposure frequency and loss exposure values to obtain annual loss expectancy in dollars or other unit of measure for each damaging event and then for all possible damaging events.

Step 10: Safeguard Identification. Identify safeguards/controls/countermeasures that will reduce vulnerabilities.

Step 11: Safeguard Cost. Identify costs to acquire, implement, and maintain these safeguards.

Step 12: Cost/Benefit Tradeoff Analysis. Select a safeguard or a combination of safeguards whose cost is less than the total loss exposure before implementing the safeguard or safeguards.

Step 13: Feasibility Analysis. Assign priority to safeguards considering operational, economic, and technical tests in addition to the cost/benefit analysis.

Step 14: Implementation Plan. Include time frame and approach for adding selected safeguards.

Step 15: Test/Evaluation. Determine new level of risk with a new exposure assessment; use for accreditation purposes.

The major advantage of the formula method is that it can produce a quantified loss estimate with minimal factual data available. A quantified expected annual loss attracts more attention than a categorized loss, such as high, medium, or low. In addition, the formula method is recognized and used extensively. The formula method forces those involved in the control process to quantify risk situations.

The disadvantage of the formula method is primarily misunderstandings which can result regarding the reliability of the results. The formula can produce a precise mathematical number which is not precise. This can be overcome partially by rounding expected loss into the nearest thousand or five thousand dollars. Another disadvantage is that the expected loss is annualized. This may be misleading on infrequent losses, such as those that might occur every fifty or one hundred years. In those instances, when the loss occurs it can be devastating, but the loss projected through the formula method may be acceptable.

Subjective Estimate Method. The subjective estimate approach uses the experience of the systems design team to estimate the severity of the risk. The team draws upon their individual or combined experiences to project a loss situation. Frequently, this is done by comparing a specific risk situation to previous experiences with which the designer has familiarity. For example, if the systems designer has experienced X errors per thousand keystrokes in previous systems, the designer may assume that it is a good subjective estimate to use for a future system.

The results produced by the subjective estimate are as good as the estimator. In some instances, the subjective estimate is more precise than that calculated by other methods. While this is not a scientific approach, it has proved effective in many systems design situations.

Advantages of the subjective estimate method are that it is quick and that it draws on and utilizes the experience of the systems design team. The disadvantages are that it is not supportable and that it is subject to the biases and previous experiences of the systems designer. If it is a situation in which the systems designer has had no previous experience, the estimate may be poor, which could lead to erroneous decisions.

Scenario Method. The scenario method is used when there is insufficient information or experience to use one of the previous methods. The scenario method tends to draw inferences from other similar situations. The method may only provide partial information because there are insufficient facts to develop a true loss estimate.

The scenario can take one of the following three forms:

Cost Estimate Scenario. This method attempts to determine the cost to correct the risk situation. For example, the systems designer may not be able to estimate risk associated with an improperly priced invoice, but can estimate the cost to fix an improperly priced invoice. This would be the minimum benefit from control, as well as maybe the only calculable loss.

Probability Scenario. This method estimates the probability of an event occurring or not occurring. For example, the designer might estimate that there is a 2 percent probability that an order would be lost. However, the method does not estimate the value of the order or how the loss of an order would affect the organization.

Situation Scenario. The results of the scenario would be the probable situation produced as a result of the threat. For example, if the system is not able to prepare and submit a required report on time to a regulatory agency, then the result may be a statutory sanction. The sanction could be avoided by anticipating the most likely outcome for the situation.

The scenario method can be effective in situations where neither the frequency nor probable loss can be estimated. The approach provides the advantage of developing valuable planning information. The disadvantage of the scenario method is the incompleteness of the planning information. Having only partial loss information may cause the manager to make the wrong decision.

Step 3: Determine Acceptable Risk

Most user requirements define what the system is supposed to do, while risk requirements define what the system is not supposed to do. However, just as normal systems specifications must be specific, so must risk specifications. For example, if a report is to contain fifteen pieces of information, those pieces of information must be described in detail; and if that report is due at 4:00 p.m. each day the user must also specify the tolerances or reliability of producing that report. The user may specify that the report can be produced within plus or minus one hour from the due time, or that it must be produced on time at least 90 percent of the time.

The concept of ''acceptable level of risk'' will be new to most users. Most are accustomed to defining their requirements, but not defining the tolerances or reliability of those requirements. This has led to many of the problems in data processing.

If users were told, for example: (1) Your report will be on time 90 percent of the time; (2) The data entered will have an average of twenty-five errors per day; (3) Products will be mispriced 1 percent of the time; or (4) Quantity shown will be accurate within plus or minus 2 percent, risk would be defined as a requirement by these types of reliability and tolerance statements. They also define to the user the degree of reliability the user can expect out of the system. As we will see in later steps, if users want a higher degree of reliability they may have to pay more for it.

In discussing the acceptable level of risk, cost will be an important factor. First requirements are stated, which is the acceptable level of risk. The control designer then estimates what it costs to achieve that requirement. If it is too high, then the user may wish to adjust the acceptable level of risk higher or lower.

The end products of this step are control requirement statements to the systems analyst. It is from these control requirements that controls will be designed.

Step 4: Identify Control Points

Controls are placed in automated systems at the point where a risk can be turned into a loss. This point can be called the risk point or the control point. It is the point where controls will be most effective, and the least costly.

Risks per se cannot be controlled. For example, one accounting risk is fraud. If we were attempting to control the risk of fraud, all we could do is develop a corporate policy which says the company is against fraud. This would have little impact on whether people commit a fraud or not.

Risks are controlled within activities which are subdivisions of the operations performed in the data processing function. For example, programming is an activity, and placing controls over that activity can help reduce fraud by restricting program development and modification to authorized individuals.

The recommended method for identifying control points is a three-part process as follows:

Part 1. Identify Control Area. Select which area in the data processing system or function is the best place to reduce the risk

Part 2. Select Activity. Determine which activity at that place is best suited to reduce the risk

Part 3. Determine Point. Select the specific point within the activity where the risk can best be reduced

Let's look at an example of this three-part control point identification process. Let us assume that the risk we are concerned about is the inability to recover operations after a problem. The computer operations area is the place where the risk can be controlled. The activity in computer operations in which the risk can be controlled is the recovery activity, and the specific point within the recovery activity is the development of recovery procedures.

There are four areas within the data processing function to control risks. These areas and the applicable controls are discussed individually in the following chapters. The four areas for the placement of control are:

Systems Design Area. The methods, tools, and techniques used to convert user requirements into operational systems

Automated Applications. The systems that process user data to achieve the desired results

Computer Operations. The hardware, software, and people needed to operate the automated application

Computer Security. The procedures and methods needed to ensure the integrity of the previous three areas

EXHIBIT 8-1   Primary Accounting Risk Location Points

Areas of data processing Accounting risks	Design Process	Automated Application	Computer Operations	Security
1. Data entry error		✔	✔	
2. Improper code		✔		
3. Unidentified data		✔	✔	
4. Unauthorized transactions				✔
5. Control level violation				✔
6. Lost transactions			✔	
7. Erroneous output			✔	
8. Processing mismatch			✔	
9. File out-of-balance			✔	
10. Inadequate audit trail	✔		✔	
11. Cascading of errors			✔	
12. Incomplete accounting entry	✔			
13. Repetition of errors			✔	
14. Improper cutoff	✔			
15. Fraud				✔
16. Noncompliance with regulations	✔			
17. Noncompliance with policies/procedures	✔			
18. Inadequate service level			✔	
19. Improper accounting	✔			

The identified accounting risks can be associated with one of the four areas of data processing. Exhibit 8-1 shows in which area the nineteen identified accounting risks are located. For example, the data entry error accounting risk is located in the computer operations area.

The primary accounting risk location point figure identifies the primary area for controlling the risk. However, controls may also be installed in the other data processing areas in support of the primary area. For example, while the people entering data into computer operations are the main risk for error, both the design process and the automated application can contribute to the reduction of error through good design procedures and data validation routines in the automated application. While these are effective, they cannot stop people from entering a quantity of sixty when they mean six.

Step 5: Develop Control Solution

The previous four steps have identified what needs to be controlled and where those controls should be placed. In one of the previous examples, we identified continuity of operation as the risk that needs to be controlled, and the recovery procedures as the point where the controls should be located. This step explains how to build the control solution.

The control solution is the systems of control that will reduce the risk to the acceptable level. The term systems of control is given because rarely will one single control achieve the control objectives.

Systems of control are very complex. Control is divided into both environmental and application controls. Environmental controls are the general or administrative controls, while the application controls are the specific controls designed for a specific application.

It is frequently the interaction between the environmental and application controls that determines the effectiveness of controls. The AICPA Special Advisory Committee on Internal Accounting Control stated in their report

> A poor control environment would make some accounting controls inoperative for all intents and purposes because, for example, individuals would hesitate to challenge a management override of a specific control procedure. On the other hand, a strong control environment, for example, one with tight budgetary controls and an effective internal audit function, can have an important bearing on the selection and effectiveness of specific accounting control procedures and techniques.*

Few data processing systems designers understand environmental and application controls, and even fewer understand the interrelationship between the two. In fact, many systems designers may not be familiar with which environmental controls are used by their organization.

*Tentative Report of the Special Advisory Committee on Internal Accounting Control, issued by the American Institute of Certified Public Accountants, September 15, 1978 (not copyrighted).

The control solution is also a combination of manual and automated controls. For example, manual controls may oversee the preparation of input going into the automated systems, or they may verify the accuracy of processing by the automated segments of the system. On the other hand, the automated controls may challenge the input provided by individuals, as well as perform many other control functions.

The specific controls that can be used by the systems designer number into the hundreds. The methods and variation of those controls comprise a much greater number. It has been estimated that in the United States there are 50,000 different payroll applications. This means that organizations have developed 50,000 different ways to perform the common function of payroll. If data processing ingenuity can produce 50,000 permutations from a single requirement, it would unsettle the mind to estimate the number of combinations and permutations of the approximately 1,000 identified controls.

The development of the control solution requires an individual who understands the following characteristics of control:

Risk and risk analysis procedures
Environmental controls
Application controls
Interrelationship between environmental and application controls
Available controls
Function of controls
Feedback data (for monitoring controls)

Controls can be divided into the following categories:

Preventive. Controls which stop an event from occurring

Detective. Controls which uncover that an undesirable event has occurred

Corrective. Controls which provide the evidence needed to understand and/or remedy the problem

Discretionary. Controls whose execution is optional

Nondiscretionary. Controls whose execution is not optional

Most automated controls are nondiscretionary, while most manual controls are discretionary. For example, a manual control would be a guard monitoring who enters the plant. If the guard is lax, or away from the guard post, unauthorized people can enter the restricted area. On the other hand, if data validation routines have been built into a program that accepts input, that input cannot enter the system unless those data validation routines have been executed.

The next four chapters provide guidance on developing control solutions in a data processing environment as follows: chapter 9, Controlling the Design Process; chapter 10, Controlling the Automated Application; chapter 11, Controlling Computer Operations; chapter 12, Providing Computer Security.

Step 6: Cost/Benefit Analysis

Controls are designed to reduce risk. If the cost of controls exceeds the risk, then it makes little sense to install the controls. Without a cost/benefit analysis, an organization may not be aware if they are under or overcontrolled.

The cost of risk includes:

Loss due to the realization of a threat
Cost of controls to reduce that risk

Many organizations only consider a single factor in the control determination. If the control seems costly, they may decide not to use it, while on the other hand, if the risk seems great, there are few questions over installing controls. Both may result in poor control decisions.

The cost of risk is illustrated in Figure 8-2. This figure shows that the

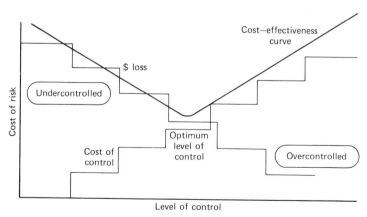

Figure 8-2. Cost of risk.

dollar loss due to a risk drops as the number of controls is increased. The cost of the risk is the total of the dollar loss plus the cost of control. For example, if the expected loss is $1,000 and the cost of controls to keep the loss at that level is $200, then the cost of risk is $1,200 (the dollar loss of $1,000 plus the cost of $200 worth of controls equals $1,200 risk).

As the controls are increased, it can be expected that the dollar loss will decrease. At some point, the cost of controls will exceed the dollar loss due to the risk. This results in a cost-effectiveness curve. The left side of the curve represents an undercontrolled situation, while the right side of the curve represents an overcontrolled situation. The low point in the curve is the optimum level of control, which should be the target for control design.

Let's look at an example of this cost-effectiveness curve for controls. Let us assume that we are a credit card company and that our risk is nonpayment of accounts charged. If we issue cards without controls, we can expect a loss of, say, $500,000. This loss is unacceptable, so we decide to install controls. Our first control is to issue a book of invalid credit cards, which costs us $50,000 per year to print and disseminate, but it will reduce our losses to $350,000. The cost of risk is now $400,000, which is the $350,000 loss plus the $50,000 cost of controls. Next we install a control to have our merchants call us for approval for charges over $100. This costs us $100,000 but reduces our losses to $125,000. The cost of risk is now $275,000 which is the $125,000 loss plus the $50,000 to issue the book of bad cards, plus the $100,000 to service the merchants' telephone calls. We now decide to increase our controls and make the merchant call in at $50. This costs us an additional $50,000, and reduces our expected losses to $100,000. This makes the cost of risk $300,000 which shows we have now passed the optimum level of control and are moving into our overcontrolled portion of the cost-effectiveness curve.

The cost/benefit analysis provides the advantage of identifying both undercontrolled and overcontrolled situations. It is equally as important to reduce controls when they are not cost-effective as it is to add controls when they are needed.

The reluctance on the part of management and data processing personnel to control has been a cost/benefit concern. Many feel that the accountants and auditors prefer to err on the side of too many controls which, unfortunately, has frequently been true. What is needed is a sound economic argument for controls.

The arguments and counterarguments about controls are more frequently emotional than factual. Accountants have been accused of "crying wolf" too often on controls, while data processing personnel have been considered poorly controlled because they seem to be continually fighting controls. Most arguments disappear when control is approached from a cost perspective.

One impediment to control implementation has been that data processing personnel are not judged on controls. They frequently are judged on getting systems completed on time, within budget, and satisfying the users. If these requirements are met, management has been reluctant to require either more or less controls in the system. In addition, many managers do not feel qualified to comment on the adequacy or inadequacy of control in automated systems.

If user satisfaction is a primary criterion for evaluating the systems design, then they will install controls that help assure the continued satisfaction. For example, if the user doesn't want input errors, then the systems designer may install some very expensive controls to reduce those errors so that they have a minimal impact on the user area. The fact that the systems designer has overcontrolled input, which is a common practice in data processing, rarely receives much attention. If the user knew the cost/benefit of those controls, they might choose fewer controls.

Step 7: Implementation

The last step in the control design process is to install the controls that are cost-effective in reducing the risk to an acceptable level. The controls may be installed in either or both the manual and automated segment of the accounting application.

The implementation of control in an automated application will be performed by the individual responsible for the area of the application in which the control is installed. For example, environmental controls may be installed by computer operations personnel, data processing management, or even senior management of the organization. Application controls may be installed by the user if the control is operational in their area, or by the data processing systems personnel if the control is implemented within the automated application.

The implementation process involves the following five tasks:

1. *Build Control.*   Perform those procedures necessary to build the required control.
2. *Test.*   Verify that the control functions as specified.
3. *Document.*   Create documentation that explains what the control is and how it works. This is necessary for both understanding and maintenance.

4. *Train.* Teach the people that will be using the control how it works and the steps they must perform based on the predetermined control actions.

5. *Implement.* Place the control into an operational status.

The implementation of a control should be a routine procedure *if* the previous five steps have been performed and the proposed control implementation methodology has been defined and taught to the systems analysts/programmers. The less standardized the control design process, the more difficult the implementation step becomes. In some instances, programmers must control a situation which has not been defined, and cannot find a control decision maker. Too frequently, the control decisions made under these circumstances are poor because of the time constraints and lack of control requirements. For example, the programmer may be told that the sex of an individual will be indicated with an M or F. Unfortunately, the programmer realizes that for numerous reasons a code other than M or F might be entered. Here is a risk situation and a control point. The programmer may decide that if an F hasn't been entered it will be considered an M. This may be a poor control choice and may result in embarrassment and loss of business for the organization.

Accountants' Computer Guideline 12. Knowing how to control computer systems is of little value until that knowledge is put into practice.

CONTROL PLAN OF ACTION

Accountants can no longer afford to sit by and watch under- or overcontrolled automated applications designed. The accountant needs to become a participant in developing control procedures, and designing controls for financial applications. Accountants should develop a plan of action for their organization to ensure adequacy of control in automated applications.

At a minimum, the control design plan of action should include the following steps:

1. *Develop a Control Design Methodology.* Develop and implement a methodology for control design in automated applications (a suggested seven-step procedure has been outlined in this chapter).

2. *Assign Control Responsibility.* Develop the necessary procedures to ensure that a single individual has been assigned the re-

sponsibility for the adequacy of control in each automated application.

3. *Document the Control Process.* Require documentation in each automated application that identifies the risks within that application, the severity of those risks, and the control procedures installed to reduce those risks to an acceptable level.

4. *Continually Evaluate the Effectiveness of Controls.* Monitor the effectiveness of the controls to ensure they have achieved the system control requirements.

Accountants' Computer Guideline 13.   If the accountant doesn't carry the control banner, no one may—and then who is to blame?

nine

CONTROLLING THE DESIGN PROCESS

The computer is a tool used to solve business problems. It is also a complex tool frequently requiring months or even years of experience to use effectively. The solution to business problems requires the translation of requirements into computer languages by people having data processing skills.

The design process for a computer system is similar to being chauffeured to a new location. The chauffeur understands the automobile, how to drive, and how to take directions. What the chauffeur doesn't understand is the location where you desire to go. You must painstakingly explain to the chauffeur where you want to go, and if the chauffeur is not familiar with that location you may have to provide continuous directions.

The systems designer is familiar with the computer, how to accomplish work on the computer, and how to take directions. What the user must do is explain in great detail exactly what needs to be accomplished on the computer. The more explicitly the user can explain those requirements the higher the probability of the system satisfying those needs. The systems designer, like the chauffeur, can easily get lost if the directions are unclear. In addition, a simple wrong turn can take the passenger miles from the desired location and consume extra time and effort, as can poor directions to the systems designer.

The systems design process is the method for instructing the computer what is needed. The process assumes that the person with the requirements is unskilled in data processing technology and, therefore, must work with a skilled data processing professional to accomplish the desired results. The rationale for having a data processing function is that the cost of this interface and translation with the data processing function is less than the cost of having all the users learn how to use the automated equipment effectively.

This chapter provides immediately implementable solutions to the problem of controlling the design process. The process is briefly explained, together with the accounting risks inherent in that process. A series of key controls for controlling the design process are explained in detail. Accountants should encourage the use of these controls. In addition, recommendations are given for controlling each phase of the design process in order to improve the probability that the desired results will be achieved at the end of the process.

OBJECTIVES OF THE DESIGN PROCESS

The primary objective of the design process is to translate user requirements into machine-executable instructions. The process is considerably more complex than translating two people languages, such as translating English to Spanish. The computer design process must first break down user requirements into sufficient detail so that they can be translated into machine-executable instructions.

The definition of systems requirements is usually a long and tedious process. Many of the actions that we take for granted in the performance of a manual task must be painstakingly described for a computer. Thus, the process is not so much one doing complex tasks but, rather, breaking simple tasks into their component parts.

If our shoelace becomes untied, we reach down, make a few swift moves, and our shoelace is retied. We think of this as a simple task, one not requiring much experience, time, or effort. At least, we don't think it's complex until we try to explain it to a four-year-old child. Suddenly, the task becomes complex. Now imagine trying to explain it to a two-year-old child and the task becomes even more complex.

Computers provide only very simplistic capabilities. In fact, when broken down into its component parts a computer can do only the following three tasks:

Move Data.   The computer can move data in and out of the computer, and within the computer.

Mathematics.   The computer can perform additions and subtractions. All other mathematics are variations of these two capabilities, such as division being multiple subtractions, and multiplication being multiple additions.

Comparison.   The computer can differentiate between information to determine if two pieces of data are equal, or if one is higher or lower than the other. The computer hardware predetermines the sequence of all characters so that, for example, it knows that a letter A is higher than a letter B, which enables the computer to arrange alphabetic as well as numeric data.

With these simple instructions, the computer can perform such magnificent tasks as sending a man to the moon, operating an inventory replenishment system for a large corporation, transferring billions of dollars over electronic networks, or fouling up your personal charge account records.

The design process must break down user requirements so that they can be performed using these three instructional capabilities. Obviously, there are many variations of each type of instruction, but the basic objective is to break down requirements into component tasks that can be accomplished using these three instructions. These requirements are translated into a machine-executable instruction which enables the computer to perform the system tasks.

In addition to meeting the needs of the user, the design process has the following additional objectives:

Optimize Technology.   Properly utilized, computer technology provides almost limitless benefits to organizations. Misused, that same technology can inhibit progress, cost far more than it is worth, and sour people on the use of computers. The optimization of technology involves not only the proper use of the computer software and hardware, but the proper interaction between people and technology.

Meet Constraints.   Systems designers must operate within the constraints placed on them by the organization. Among these operational constraints are:

System design standards
Organizational policies and procedures
Hardware/software capabilities
Budgets
Schedules
Capabilities of system team personnel
Data processing operations standards

Frequently these restraints may cause the system design team not to fulfill all of the user requirements. For example, if the team is not allocated sufficient budget, schedule, or resources, the team is forced to compromise user requirements or have the constraints changed. Unfortunately, senior management may require the team to finish the project within the constraints and still meet the requirements. This is an impossible task which causes the systems design team to make their own compromises, many of which will cause user dissatisfaction when the system becomes operational.

Integration.   Rarely does a single computer system operate independently of other systems. At a minimum, systems operate concurrently and vie for computer resources. More commonly, systems obtain data from other systems and feed data to still other systems. Systems designers are responsible for the integration of their system with all other connected systems.

Technological Rule of Thumb 9.   The number of tasks involved in building an automated application exceeds people's ability to remember and evaluate. It requires a formal documented design process to effectively and economically build an automated application.

SYSTEMS DESIGN ACTIVITIES

In the early days of data processing, the systems analyst was given a job to do and told to do it. It was similar to the early days of aviation when pilots flew in open cockpits with leather helmets and a scarf around their neck. It was a romantic era and one fondly remembered by data processing pioneers.

The unstructured systems design process was also a costly and unreliable process. A typical controller's joke when presented with an estimate to design a computer system during the 1960s was what factor to select to multiply the estimate by. Many controllers would determine the expected cost of a system by multiplying the data processing estimate by a factor such as three or four, in order to produce a realistic estimate. Unfortunately for data processing, many of these controllers were more accurate in their estimates than the data processing personnel.

In time, the data processing systems development process achieved maturity. Structure has been brought to an unstructured process. Using the new systems design principles, analysts can develop systems that meet user needs within the time and budget constraints.

The systems design processes are known by many different names including:

Systems Development Life Cycle (SDLC). A phased approach to computer systems design, outlining the steps and procedures to be undertaken in each phase.

Hierarchical Input Process Output (HIPO). A procedure that defines and structures functions into a hierarchy like an organizational structure. The top function is related to lower and lower functions which produce a hierarchical definition of requirements.

Top-Down Design. A process similar to HIPO which begins with the definition of objectives and then works downward through the satisfaction of those objectives.

Structured Design. A horizontal design showing the flow of data through automated systems. The structure indicates how results produced by a system are created backward through the processing of data to the origination of data.

All of these design processes provide structure to the design process. The methodologies restrict the systems analyst/programmer's ability to innovate in the design process. However, the systems designer is not restricted in innovating and meeting user needs. The objective of the structured approach is for analysts to use time-proven design processes so that they are free to use their creativity in solving user requirements instead of devoting their effort to mastering technology.

The activities performed during a design process are defined differently by different methods. Some design processes include as many as sixteen activities, while others include as few as five. The systems design activities described in this chapter are representative of the major design methodologies. The activities presented were selected because they emphasize the activities that should be subject to control.

Controllable Design Activities. From the time a need is defined until that need is satisfied, a series of design activities occur. Accountants wishing to reduce accounting risk in automated applications need to be assured that adequate control exists in the performance of these design activities. The activities can be individually controlled if the activity deliverables are defined; for example, if the expected results of each activity are predetermined, such as report formats, data definition, and so forth.

The activities requiring control in the systems design process are:

Requirements
Resource selection
Design

Program
Acceptance test
Implementation

The activities and deliverables are listed in Exhibit 9-1 and discussed individually below.

Accountants' Computer Guideline 14. The systems design process needs the accountants' control experience and participation.

Requirements Activity

The requirements activity drives the design process. The more explicitly the requirements are stated, the easier the design process becomes. As systems become more integrated and complex, the tasks to be performed within the requirements activity increase.

In explaining the entire design process, we will use the analogy of building a house. While there are differences, there are also numerous similarities between the two activities. If we look at the owner as the user of the house and the builder as the systems designer, we will see many parallels.

Let's look at how an individual might define the requirements for a house. The individual would meet with the builder, just as the user would meet with the systems analyst. The objective of this activity is for the homeowner and the builder to come to terms about the homeowner's requirements and the builder's capabilities.

The potential homeowner can state requirements in generalized terms such as, "I would like a four-bedroom house, with living room, dining room, kitchen, and family room, of approximately 2,000 square feet, and at a price not to exceed $100,000." The builder can take these require-

EXHIBIT 9-1   Systems Design Process Deliverables

Design Activities	Deliverables
Requirements	Description of needs to be satisfied
Resource Selection	Hardware/software specifications
Design	Program specifications
Program	Data processing debugged system
Acceptance Test	User okay
Implement	Operable system

ments and build a house the builder believes will satisfy those requirements, but that end product may or may not satisfy the homeowner because of the nearly infinite styles of homes that could meet those general requirements.

When a homeowner gives a builder very general specifications, then the requirements activity is short and the builder can go and do his or her thing. Many computer systems begin with requirements that are vague, such as, "I would like a new accounts receivable system" or "I would like an automatic inventory replenishment system."

If, however, the potential homeowner defines the requirements in great detail, then the builder can quickly commence the work and the final product has a high probability of satisfying the homeowner. For example, the user might specify not only four bedrooms, but the size of each bedroom, the amount of window space and closet space, as well as the bedroom layout. The house can be described as two-story or ranch or split-level, the dimensions of the house can be specified, as well as the type of construction material desired. The schedules and costs can be specified, as well as the types of subcontractors that the homeowner would like to build the house.

Having detailed requirements does not necessarily mean that all those requirements will be implemented because of the external constraints. What it does provide is a starting point for detailed discussions. As the homeowner begins discussing the requirements with the builder and architect, the interaction most likely produces a slightly different home from that thought of by the homeowner at the beginning of the requirements phase. It is to be hoped the changes will increase the homeowner's satisfaction, just as the ideas and recommendations presented by the systems designer should make the systems more effective, efficient, and economical from a user perspective.

The requirements phase of the design process is the least structured of any phase. It is in this phase that much of the systems creativity should occur. Therefore, it's not a phase that should be rushed, and it is not a phase which can conclude without all the necessary decisions being made.

The deliverables to be produced from the requirements phase are the descriptions of the needs to be satisfied by the system. The specific deliverables to be produced during the requirements phase normally include:

Data requirements
Cost/benefit calculation for the proposed system
System satisfactions

Output requirements

Processing requirements

System integrity requirements

Staffing requirements

Budget and schedule requirements

Agreement that sufficient resources exist to successfully complete the project

Systems acceptance criteria

Training requirements

Effect on other automated applications

Effect on people

The requirements are then combined into a request to management for approval to implement the system. Some organizations have predetermined formats and content for those system proposals, while others permit the project team to develop an appropriate proposal. If approved, the requirements become the basis for not only building the system, but measuring the system's performance.

Resource Selection Activity

The resource selection activity is a technical activity and one of only minimal interest to the accountant. However, the activity has been frequently abused and thus requires some attention from the accountant. The resource selection activity is the selection of the hardware and software used in support of the accounting application.

The "keeping up with the Joneses" philosophy is regularly applied to the selection of computer hardware and software. As soon as new technology is introduced, many data processing personnel want to obtain that technology for technology's sake. Once obtained, the data processing function has a solution looking for a problem.

It is necessary to understand how many data processing personnel think in order to understand the resource selection activity abuse. Data processing personnel judge one another by the currentness of their skills. For example, data base technology is now "in." No red-blooded systems analysts or programmers would dare admit that they didn't understand and aren't experienced in data base technology. Few organizations would want to hire a data processing systems analyst/programmer who was not experienced in the use of data base technology. Thus, there is a strong need to keep technology current in an organization.

The following excerpt on the use of advanced technology is from a report by the Comptroller General to the Congress:

> Data base management systems are computer software packages—computer programs, documentation, users' manuals, etc.—which can help organizations manage, manipulate, and retrieve data from computer-based systems. If properly planned and controlled, the systems can provide federal agencies with an effective and efficient management tool to better organize and access data and to improve the accuracy and timeliness of information available for decision making. If not properly planned and controlled, the systems can be complicated and costly, providing management with more problems than solutions or benefits.
>
> Most agencies the U.S. General Accounting Office (GAO) visited did not adequately plan before acquiring a data base management system; consequently, they may have spent substantial amounts for automatic data processing resources that they did not need.
>
> The costs of acquiring data base management systems are generally insignificant compared with the costs involved in using them in what is technically known as a "true data base environment." This requires a long-term management commitment to application software, computer hardware, communications, procedures, training, and support which will cost far more than the system itself. In most instances, organizations do not save data processing dollars by integrating files and implementing a data base management system, primarily because of increased costs associated with a more complex system.*

The accountant does not possess the necessary skills to determine whether or not recommended hardware and/or software is required. What the accountant can do is first determine that the expected benefits have been adequately defined and are measurable. Second, the accountant can confirm the value of that technology with outside sources. For example, the above-cited GAO report on data base should raise some questions in the minds of many over the value of installing data base technology unless sufficient planning has occurred. An organization should not be caught in the trap of using technology just because it is the latest technology.

When people purchase a house, they go through a resource selection process. This can be left to the builder, but most homeowners, aware of the cost of materials, become involved in the process. While the homeowner does not understand the grades of wood, thickness of pipes, wires, and so forth, the advantages and disadvantages of the different materials

*Data Base Management Systems—Without Careful Planning There Can Be Problems, U.S. General Accounting Office, Washington, D.C. (June 29, 1979).

can be explained so that the homeowner can make intelligent decisions based upon his or her funds and needs.

The resource selection activity may be a separate activity, or it may be embedded in either the requirements activity or the design activity. However, it can be a costly activity both in terms of current and future dollars. It is important that the accountant have sufficient information in hand to measure the success of the hardware and software so that appropriate action can be taken should the resources fail to achieve the projected results.

The deliverables produced from the resource selection activity include:

Hardware requirements

Operating software requirements (data base management system)

Recommended hardware

Recommended software

Long-term hardware/software requirement projections

Criteria to measure the effectiveness of the hardware and software

Design Activity

The systems design activity breaks down the requirements into accomplishable tasks for processing by the computer. During the design activity, the project team attempts to achieve the requirements utilizing the available resources. The system is not built during this activity, but at the end of the activity it is known whether or not the requirements can be accomplished within the project constraints.

In the building of a home, this activity is frequently performed by an architect. The architect has the requirements of the homeowner, including the resources available to build that home. The architect must then break down those requirements into blueprints from which the home can be built. The architect, like the systems designer, works within certain constraints such as zoning requirements, building requirements, and available resources.

The design activity includes a close interchange between the user and the project team. The design is variable, as our previous example of the development of 50,000 different payroll systems illustrates. There are many different ways to solve the same problem, many of which are approximately equal in capabilities. What may be different between the design alternatives are the ease of making future changes and the ability to interact with other automated applications.

The requirements activity is usually a user-dominated activity, while the resource selection activity is a data processing-dominated activity. The word dominated is used to mean who is responsible for the activity, and who provides direction. The design process need not be dominated by either party. It should be accomplished through a close working relationship in which the project team attempts to match user requirements to available resources.

As the systems design process continues, the formality of each phase increases. The design activity, for example, is more structured than the requirements activity, and the activities following design will be more structured than the design activity.

The deliverables produced from the systems design activity include:

Data definitions
Record definitions
File definitions
Program processing specifications
Report formats
Input formats
Systems data flowcharts
Control procedures
People procedures

Program Activity

Programming is an activity which translates specifications into machine-executable code. It is usually performed using programming languages such as BASIC, RPG, COBOL, PL/1, or FORTRAN. The individual performing the function does not have to understand what the user is attempting to accomplish. It closely parallels any language translation such as English to French.

Much of the programming function has been automated over the past twenty years. When computers were first introduced, the programmer performed all of the functions necessary to perform a task on a computer. Now, many of the functions have been automated so that the programmer performs fewer and fewer of the overall tasks, but still performs the valuable function of overseeing that the automated programming performs properly.

To the homeowner, programming is the building of the home. If the home blueprint is well done, and easily understood by the contractors, the house is built without problems. However, if the blueprint fails to show specifically where the heating ducts, pipes, and electrical circuits go, all three subcontractors may attempt to use the same space for their own purposes. When this happens, it requires a lot of on-the-site adjustment. Programmers fall into the same trap. If the design specifications are not clear, the programmer may have to make a lot of on-the-spot programming adjustments to compensate for design weaknesses.

The deliverables to be produced at the conclusion of the programming stage include:

Tested programs

Operator instructions

Systems documentation

User documentation

Operational interfaces (called "job control language" by several computer hardware vendors)

Acceptance Test Activity

The acceptance test activity is a verification by the user that the system performs to the user specifications. During the program activity, the data processing department has the opportunity to verify that the system performs according to what they believe is the user specification. Unfortunately, if they misunderstood the user they both have built and tested the system erroneously.

Acceptance testing is a time-consuming and costly process disliked by many users. It requires the user to prepare extensive amounts of test data, and then run the test data to ensure that user personnel can operate the system and that it produces the desired results.

Acceptance testing may consume between 10 and 20 percent of the total system expense. There is a direct relationship between the effort expended in acceptance testing and the degree of assurance that the system performs as specified. The data processing personnel test the mainline processing, but may not test some of the other conditions important to the user.

Acceptance testing should perform the following types of testing:

Stress Testing. A determination of whether the system can process the maximum expected volume of data

Performance Testing. A determination that the system achieved the specified level of performance

Regression Testing. Determination that the system does not cause problems with existing systems and functions that currently work correctly

Error Testing. Determination that the system will reject erroneous conditions so that they will not adversely affect normal processing

Error Handling. Determination that errors uncovered in the system can be corrected and reentered on a timely basis

Operator Testing. Determination that the computer operators can adequately operate the system using operator documentation

Documentation Testing. Determination that there is sufficient written documentation to assure that the system is understandable and maintainable

User Training. Determination that user personnel understand the system and can use it in the performance of their day-to-day activities

Acceptance testing to the homeowner is walking through the home examining the completed product. If the homeowner specified certain appliances and fixtures to be installed, the homeowner will make sure that they have, in fact, been installed, and that they work. For example, the homeowner might turn on faucets, turn on lights, use appliances, and so forth, to test that the items work.

At the completion of the acceptance test, the deliverables include:

A list of defects noted during testing

A list of problems which, although the system performed as specified, caused difficulty in using the system in practice

User concurrence to put the system into production, or identify modifications that need to be made prior to putting the system into production

Implementation Activity

The last activity is to put the application system into use. This is the equivalent of the homeowner moving into the new house. However, just as moving is a difficult and time-consuming task so is the process of placing an automated application into a production status.

An important concern during the implementation phase is that the integrity of data will be preserved. For the homeowner this is the equivalent of moving furniture without having it damaged or lost. Unless steps are taken to ensure the integrity of data, unforeseen problems may result.

Many organizations develop a fail-safe implementation process. They determine that if the systems cannot be successfully installed by a certain time on a certain date, they revert back to the old system. This assures that when a system must be operational something will be working.

DESIGN PROCESS ACCOUNTING RISKS

Six of the identified accounting risks require special attention during the design process. These accounting risks, which have been described in Chapter 3, are:

Inadequate audit trail
Incomplete accounting entry
Improper cutoff
Noncompliance with regulations
Noncompliance with policies/procedures
Improper accounting

The design activity in which controls should be placed to reduce the accounting risks are identified in Exhibit 9-2 (Design Risks/Activities Matrix). The matrix can also be used to explain some of the tasks that need to be performed in each activity. For example, the requirements activity should specify the audit trail, cutoff, regulations, procedures requiring compliance, and the required accounting methods.

The control of the design process should be based on the use of key controls governing the design process. These key controls reduce the design process accounting risks and also help reduce many of the risks associated with other data processing activities. The controls for each activity are individually discussed, explaining the type of controls which, if implemented within those activities, would reduce the design process accounting risks.

DESIGN PROCESS KEY CONTROLS

A system of controls over the design process encompasses numerous controls. Some of these are more effective than others. Key controls are defined as those controls which provide the greatest deterrent to the systems design threats.

The key controls that accountants should establish for control over the systems design process are briefly described in Exhibit 9-3 (Design Process Key Controls) and explained below.

EXHIBIT 9-2   Design Risks/Activities Matrix

Design Process Accounting Risks \ Design Activities	Requirements	Resource Selection	Design	Program	Acceptance Test	Implement
Inadequate audit trail	✔		✔	✔	✔	✔
Incomplete accounting entry			✔	✔	✔	
Improper cutoff	✔		✔		✔	
Noncompliance with regulations	✔		✔		✔	
Noncompliance with policies/procedures	✔	✔	✔	✔	✔	✔
Improper accounting	✔		✔		✔	

Steering Committee. A steering committee is a committee of key user and management personnel who have been given the responsibility to oversee the data processing function. This group functions independently of the data processing organization in order to establish data processing priorities and monitor data processing activities. Normally a steering committee is not a line function but, rather, a staff function. The steering

EXHIBIT 9-3   Design Process Key Controls

Key Control	Purpose of Control
1. Steering Committee	User-directed data processing
2. Data Administrator	Manage data as a resource of the organization
3. Quality Assurance Function	Provide an independent assessment of the quality of automated applications
4. Formal Design Process	Ensure proven design process steps are followed
5. User Acceptance	Make user responsible for the system
6. Budget	Monitor costs
7. Schedule	Monitor time frame

committee is comprised of senior management, user management, and normally includes one or more members of data processing management. The steering committee can be chaired by a member of executive management or the data processing manager. Among the tasks frequently performed by steering committees are:

Establish priorities for implementing systems
Approve new hardware/software
Approve data processing budgets
Resolve data processing disputes
Approve data processing policies and procedures

Data Administrator.   A data administrator is a member of senior management designated responsible for managing the organization's data. The data administrator concept implies the organization will manage data as a resource, much as it manages people, money, and plant. The data administrator is not a data processing specialist. The data administrator defines the organization's data policy, reliability, definition, and integrity. Much of this individual's time may be spent resolving data definition disputes between users.

Quality Assurance Function.   The quality assurance function is an independent function assigned the responsibility to assess quality in automated applications. The function is designed to improve quality throughout the data processing organization, as opposed to just reviewing individual applications. In many organizations, the quality assurance function develops standards, approves developmental and maintenance procedures, oversees the installation of new hardware and software, establishes data processing standards, establishes testing standards, and certifies systems acceptable to be placed into production.*

Formal Design Process.   A formal design process is a standardized systems design methodology for building and maintaining automated applications. The formal design process normally divides design into segments, much as has been explained in this chapter. An integral part of most formal design processes is the type and scope of required documentation.

User Acceptance.   The user makes a decision on whether or not the sys-

---

*Information on the quality assurance function is available from the Quality Assurance Institute, 9222 Bay Point Drive, Orlando, FL 32811.

tem can be placed into operation. In many organizations, the user must formally sign a statement that indicates the system has met the user requirements. The objective of user acceptance is to force the user into accepting responsibility for the proper functioning of an automated system. Once the user has accepted the system, then the user assumes the responsibility, in terms of both work and budget, to make changes to the system to correct deficiencies.

Budget. The project team is allocated a specified amount of resources to complete the project. Some organizations allocate the entire amount needed to complete the project, while other organizations only allocate sufficient funds to complete the project through the next management checkpoint. Budgets, and budgetary monitoring, enable management to ensure that the project is being completed within allocated resources. Budgeting is only effective when it is coupled with the formal design process, so that management is assured that the required deliverables are prepared within the allocated budget.

Schedule. The project team is provided a time frame for completion of the project. This is usually expressed in terms of calendar checkpoints at which time predetermined deliverables are to be completed. The schedule, and the budget, enables management to ensure that the project is being completed in accordance with the project plan.

Requirements Activity Control Solution

The requirements phase controls pay dividends in later phases. Not only are the control requirements well defined, but their implementation can be monitored during the following systems design phases. The accountant should determine that the requirements procedures include the following control tasks:

Cost/Benefit Analysis. A detailed analysis of the cost to develop a system, both tangible and intangible, and the benefits to be derived from the installed system. Using calculations such as return on investment or cash flow rate of return, a determination can be made of the economics of installing the system.

Requirements Definition. All the requirements should be spelled out in writing.

User Involvement. The user should provide sufficient support to the requirements activity so that the user is sufficiently represented to direct and monitor the specification of the requirements.

Evaluate Alternatives. The recommended system solution should be chosen from among a set of solution alternatives. At least one of the alternatives presented should be a manual alternative.

Data Requirements. The needed elements of data should be defined as well as the timing for receiving those elements of data. Experience has proven that if the data requirements are adequately defined, the effort and cost of obtaining and using that data are also well defined.

Regulations Defined. Compliance to regulatory requirements should be defined so that their effect on the design can be measured during the requirements phase.

Volume and Service Requirements. The expected volume including future projections should be determined, as well as the service level requirements expected from data processing.

Quality Requirements. The level of expected quality should be specified so that a determination can be made at various checkpoints as to whether or not the desired level of quality has been achieved.

These requirements activity controls are representative of what the accountant should expect within a well-controlled systems design process. The more of these controls the accountant finds, the greater the assurance that the product produced from the design process will meet user requirements and be well controlled.

Exhibit 9-4 is designed to help the accountant assess the adequacy of control in the requirements activity. A yes answer on the checklist indicates a good control practice, while a no answer indicates a potential control weakness. The accountant concerned over the requirements activity should review these questions with the data processing personnel. Areas of potential control weakness should be discussed with the data processing personnel as a basis for improving the requirements activity controls. A similar checklist will be provided for all of the data processing activities discussed in this book.

Resource Selection Activity Control Solution

The resource selection process should be based upon a long-range data processing plan. Obtaining hardware and software that does not fit into that plan may end up as a costly venture for the organization. Many organizations estimate that it costs two to three times the cost of hardware and software to make it operational in the organization.

EXHIBIT 9-4   Requirement Activity Checklist

Item	Yes	No
1. Does the requirements activity conclude with a formal management checkpoint?		
2. Does the requirements phase prepare a report requesting management's approval to implement the designated automated system?		
3. Has the proposed solution been selected from among a reasonable set of alternative solutions?		
4. Has a cost/benefit study been made?		
5. Is the source of required data known?		
6. Has the user area accepted responsibility for the defined requirements?		
7. Have the volume of transactions and expected service level requirements been stated?		
8. Have regulatory requirements been identified?		
9. Have the organization's policies and procedures governing the application system been identified?		
10. Have the system control requirements been specified?		
11. Has the expected level of quality been identified?		
12. Have criteria been defined to measure the implemented system against the requirements?		
13. Has the manual segment of the automated application been specified?		

Most large organizations have specialists who work in the hardware and software selection area. The data processing function is complex and is a difficult task for the novice to do effectively. Even the marketing representatives of many of the large computer vendors are frequently uncertain about the advantages and disadvantages of certain hardware/software configurations. In some instances, the representatives are not even sure if certain configurations will work.

In this highly technical environment, it is important that procedures be established to avoid the misuse of resources. Some of the controls used in reducing improper resource selection activities include:

Hardware Selection Group.   Individual(s) specializing in the procurement of hardware and software. These individuals are trained in the selection process and are generally familiar with the types of hardware/software available in the market.

Hardware/Software Selection Criteria. A procedure for identifying the important characteristics of hardware/software so that the selection process can be limited to those products which meet the selection requirements.

Competitive Bidding. Giving the resource specifications to multiple vendors so that they can offer bids to satisfy those requirements.

Consultants. Using hardware and software experts to supplement data processing personnel skills where necessary.

Hardware/Software Manuals. Subscribing to the major reference services, such as AUERBACH and DATAPRO, which evaluate and rate hardware and software.

Experience Logs. Maintaining records on the reliability and performance of hardware and software in order to determine whether or not performance levels are achieved. This can be used to select future hardware and software.

Exhibit 9-5 is designed to help accountants assess the adequacy of resource activity controls.

Design Activity Control Solution

The design activity determines how the requirements will be achieved. It is during the design process that the systems design constraints may affect satisfying user requirements. The lack of sufficient talent on the project team, hardware/software limitations, or schedule constraints can result in the requirement specifications being changed. The accountant should look for controls that provide the greatest assurance that the user needs will be satisfied.

The kinds of controls the accountant should look for in the design process include:

Report Formats. The reports produced by the system should be illustrated in the format in which they will be prepared, explaining the information included in the report and the reliability of that information.

Record Definitions. The data contained in the system records should be defined.

File Specifications. The information in the file should be defined.

Processing Specifications. The rules to be implemented during processing should be defined.

Error Listing and Error Handling. The method of resolving problems should be defined.

Control Procedures. The methods that assure the system integrity is preserved should be defined.

Checkpoint Reports. The project leader should periodically report the status of the system.

Management Checkpoints. The status should be independently reviewed periodically by management, auditors, or a quality assurance function.

EXHIBIT 9-5   Resource Selection Activity Checklist

Item	Yes	No
1. Does the resource selection activity conclude with a management checkpoint?		
2. Do the hardware and software requirements fit into the organization's long-range hardware and software plan?		
3. Has the hardware and software been selected by individuals qualified to make that selection?		
4. Were selection criteria established before the hardware and software were selected?		
5. Has a reasonable bidding process been implemented to obtain hardware and software at the lowest possible cost?		
6. Were outside consultants and services used where needed?		
7. Are procedures established to monitor hardware and software performance so that vendors whose hardware and software does not achieve requirements will not be eligible to bid on future projects?		
8. Have criteria been established to measure the hardware and software performance?		
9. Does the hardware and software include sufficient capacity to handle big loads?		
10. Are the system resource requirements specified sufficiently in advance to facilitate the selection of hardware and software?		

EXHIBIT 9-6   Design Activity Checklist

Item	Yes	No
1. Does the design activity conclude with the management check-point to enable management to adopt or reject the design recommendations?		
2. Have the desired output results been defined?		
3. Have the records used in the system been defined?		
4. Have the files to be used in the system been specified?		
5. Have the processing specifications been determined?		
6. Has the method of handling errors been specified?		
7. Has the system of control been designed?		
8. Are the systems specifications documented?		
9. Has the system audit trail been defined?		
10. Have the methods of recovering the system in the event of problems been specified?		
11. Is the design in conformance with the system requirements?		

Exhibit 9-6 is designed to help the accountant assess the adequacy of the systems design activity controls.

Program Activity Control Solution

The programming activity translates the design specifications into machine-executable instructions by using a programming language. Well-defined specifications minimize the programming effort. The accountant needs to be concerned about both the adequacy of the specifications and the implementation of those specifications by the programmer.

The programmer is limited by both the programming language capabilities and the skill of the individual programmer. Programming may involve the preparation of hundreds or even thousands of programming statements.

The controls that an accountant should look for in the programming activity include:

Programming Standards.   Required methods for writing programs
Structured Programming.   A methodical approach to the design of programs that helps ensure that the specifications have been achieved

EXHIBIT 9-7   Program Activity Checklist

Item	Yes	No
1. Have the programs been specified before coding commences?		
2. Have programming standards been established and followed in designing programs?		
3. Is a formal process such as structured programming used in the design and coding of programs?		
4. Have program testing standards been established and followed?		
5. Have program documentation standards been defined and followed?		
6. Are programs tested to ensure that they conform with system performance criteria?		
7. Are programs reviewed to ensure that they achieve system specifications and comply with programming standards?		

Testing Standards.   Minimum levels of testing that must be performed to ensure the program meets design specifications

Quality Assurance Review.   An independent review to ensure that the programs achieve systems specifications and comply with programming standards

Documentation Standards.   Minimum levels of documenting what the program does and how it performs the task

Naming Conventions.   Standardized ways of identifying segments of programs for ease of maintenance

Exhibit 9-7 is designed to help the accountant assess the adequacy of the program activity controls.

Acceptance Testing Activity Control Solution

Acceptance testing provides the user with the assurance that the system measures up to the design specifications. It provides an opportunity for the user to verify the correctness of operations. The user has the responsibility for the design and execution of the acceptance testing process.

Many users design acceptance testing criteria in conjunction with the systems design process. Acceptance testing can begin as early as the requirements activities. This activity should be performed independently of the systems design activity so that it tests what the user believes the system should do, and not the project team's interpretation of what the user wants.

Acceptance testing tests both the manual and automated segments of the system. The data processing test performed during the programming activity rarely tests the manual aspects of the system. Thus, a true systems test may not occur until the acceptance test activity.

Adequate time should be allowed for acceptance testing. Part of the acceptance test process might include training of user personnel. However, until the data processing people are convinced the system functions properly, it may be too early to train user personnel in new methods.

The controls the accountant should look for to ensure that the acceptance testing activity is performed properly include:

> *User Training Procedures.* The documentation and methods used to train user personnel in the functioning of the system
>
> *Base Case Test Package.* An exhaustive set of test data that tests not only what the system is supposed to do, but verifies that the system can perform properly when invalid data is entered into the system
>
> *Error Reentry Procedures.* Tests the function that receives error listings, makes the necessary adjustments, and reenters the corrected data into the automated system
>
> *Acceptance Test Criteria.* The standards by which the system will be measured to determine whether or not it passes acceptance testing
>
> *Acceptance Testing Responsibility.* The assignment of the responsibility to make the decision as to whether or not the acceptance testing has been successful

Exhibit 9-8 is designed to help the accountant assess the adequacy of the acceptance testing activity controls.

Implementation Activity Control Solution

The implementation activity involves those tasks necessary to place an acceptable system into production. This not only involves placing the proper programs into production, but assures that the necessary data are available and that the people and instructions for use of the new system have been distributed and understood.

The implementation process may be a minisystem in itself. The tasks may include file conversion, movement of programs to new programming libraries, as well as the understanding and implementation of various

EXHIBIT 9-8   Acceptance Testing Activity Checklist

Item	Yes	No
1. Is the user responsible for acceptance testing the application system?		
2. Must the user make a positive statement that the system achieves user specification prior to it being placed into production?		
3. Does acceptance testing include evaluating the manual parts of the application system?		
4. Does acceptance testing involve evaluating the ability of people to use the application system?		
5. Are the system controls tested?		
6. Is the systems audit trail tested?		
7. Is compliance to regulations and the organization's policies and procedures tested?		
8. Are error conditions tested?		
9. Is user acceptance test data prepared independently of the data processing system's data?		

manual procedures. Organizations should allow for the option that all of the steps necessary cannot be performed. This option should permit them the capability to revert to the previous system should the implementation activity prove unsuccessful.

The kinds of controls that the accountant should look for in the implementation process include:

Fail-Safe Procedures.   A methodology for reverting to the previous system in the event the new system cannot be successfully implemented

Implementation Criteria.   The yardsticks that must be achieved to ensure the implementation has been successful

Data Integrity Controls.   The procedures and methods used to ensure the integrity of data during the implementation process

Backup Files.   Procedures should ensure that there is always sufficient backup of data during the implementation process to permit the implementation to be retried as many times as necessary

EXHIBIT 9-9   **Implementation Activity Checklist**

Item	Yes	No
1. Is the implementation activity established as an independent controllable activity?		
2. Are the steps required to implement an application system documented and followed?		
3. Are controls established to ascertain whether or not the application system has been successfully installed?		
4. Are fail-safe procedures established to revert to the old system in the event the new system is unsuccessfully installed?		
5. Has the integrity of data moved from the old system to the new system been ensured?		
6. Have adequate procedures to ensure the integrity of backup been implemented?		
7. Will the integrity of the old system be assured for a reasonable period following the implementation of the new system in case it is necessary to revert processing to the old system?		

Previous System Integrity.   The integrity of the old system should be retained in the event that problems occur shortly after the new system is implemented and it becomes necessary to revert back to or to reference the old system

Exhibit 9-9 is designed to help the accountant assess the adequacy of the implementation activity controls.

DESIGN PROCESS CONTROL PLAN OF ACTION

The design process produces automated applications. Weaknesses in the design process can cause control weaknesses in the automated systems. Accountants should take the necessary actions to ensure that the design process in their organization is adequately controlled. The following plan of action is recommended to accountants to ensure the adequacy of control in their design process:

     1. *Implement a Formal System Design Process.*   Install a systems design methodology that requires designers to follow a series of predetermined steps in the design process.

2. *Use Key Controls.* Install the recommended key controls described in this chapter to ensure that the design process will achieve user requirements.

3. *Establish and Evaluate Acceptance Criteria.* Ensure that systems cannot be designed until the acceptance criteria have been established to ensure whether or not the system has been successfully installed.

4. *Establish Computer Resource Justification Procedures.* Require that the procedures to acquire new automated technology follow the same justification procedures as required to implement new automated applications.

Accountants' Computer Guideline 15. Time spent in the design process may be the most fruitful use of an accountant's time.

ten

CONTROLLING THE AUTOMATED APPLICATION

To paraphrase the jargon of the tire industry, "The application operation is where the rubber meets the road." The results produced by the automated application are used in the decision-making process and operations of the organization. Problems in the system quickly become organizational problems.

The accountant has a vested interest in automated financial applications. Any application that processes financial data produces accounting information. The accountant is a secondary user for most of the organization's automated applications. As a user, the accountant should ensure that controls are adequate for accurate, complete, and authorized financial information.

AUTOMATED APPLICATION CONTROL OBJECTIVE

The accountant's control objectives for application systems are the same whether the application is manual or automated. The implementation of the controls is different if the application is automated. Let's examine the application control objective for the purpose of clarifying the accountant's concerns.

All Recorded Transactions Are Valid. The validity of transactions may be more difficult to verify because transactions are automatically generated, are entered into the system without supporting source documents, and the system is more accessible for intentional and unintentional entry of invalid transactions.

All Valid Transactions Are Recorded. Problems that can cause a transaction not to be recorded include hardware and software malfunction, incomplete error tracking, and the failure to pass proper parameters between the systems.

All Transactions Are Properly Valued. Transactions can be improperly valued due to incomplete or inaccurate information on master files such as product and services, plus programming errors.

All Transactions Are Recorded in the Proper Period. The 24-hours-a-day operation of many on-line applications creates a system where there are always transactions awaiting processing. This, coupled with the lack of a physical cutoff point, shifts the responsibility for recording transactions in the proper cutoff period from operations to an application programming responsibility.

All Transactions Are Classified in the Appropriate Account. Transactions may be classified in the wrong account due to the incorrect recording of the account number, errors in the system and programs, and the miscoding of financial accounts used to allocate accounting information among several financial accounts.

All Transactions Are Properly Summarized. The information from transactions may not be properly summarized because transactions are lost, modified, or duplicated due to operating errors such as failure to include a day's operation, system and programming errors, and the posting of a transaction to the wrong total.

All Transactions Are Posted to the General Ledger. Errors may occur in posting accounting information to the general ledger because of the failure to include all the sources of accounting data, duplicate or erroneous postings, as well as systems and programming errors.

All Transactions Are Authorized by Management. Unauthorized transactions may be recorded if management fails to definitively specify the authorization rules and then to enforce those rules in the processing environment, or if misunderstandings arise about the intents of management.

All Inputs/Updates/Outputs Are Accurate and Complete. Inaccurate and incomplete transactions can occur due to incorrect entry of transactions, hardware and software failures, systems and programming failures, and intentional or unintentional modification.

The accountant should ensure that the automated applications adequately address the above accounting issues. The automated application concerns are primarily data concerns. The accountant uses his or her understanding of the risks to help design control solutions.

CONTROLLABLE APPLICATION SEGMENTS

An automated application is comprised of both manual and automated segments. The amount of data processed manually and automatically varies between applications. In a typical application, the transaction originates in the manual segment, is authorized there, and then is entered into the automated processing segment which, in turn, is followed by a manual segment where people use the results of processing.

The coupling of automated systems reduces the amount of processing performed in the manual segments. For example, system B may be located between automated system A and system C. The input to system B comes from system A, and the output from system B goes to C. Thus, for system B there is no apparent manual processing. The original transaction going into system B originated in system A.

The situation is further complicated by the definition of an application system. The data processing system definition is done primarily for the convenience of implementation or the segregation of functions. However, the definition of an application system for an accountant should be based on processing financial transactions. For example, to an accountant a system is the function that processes orders, maintains the accounts receivable records, or pays employees.

The accountant should maintain an inventory of application systems. This inventory of systems provides the accountant with a basis for identifying the flow of accounting information through the automated applications. This inventory is the starting point for controlling automated applications.

Dividing Applications into Controllable Segments

Computerized applications, because of their size and complexity, may appear impervious to understanding. However, application systems, like many other facets of life, are understandable once they are broken into component parts. For example, a 2,000-part jigsaw puzzle offers the same challenge as the computer system. It appears impossible to understand and complete.

Let's look at how many people approach understanding and assembling a jigsaw puzzle. First they find all of the outside pieces. These are easy to identify because of the straight edges. Next they select the corner pieces, again easy to identify. With the four corners in place, the smaller population of outside pieces seems workable. After a short time, the outer edge of the jigsaw puzzle is complete and the individual's confidence begins to grow. Now pieces of the same color are identified and those can be put together. The subpieces fit into the total, and within a short period of time what appeared to be an insurmountable challenge has turned into a completed jigsaw puzzle.

The computer system is no different from the jigsaw puzzle. We need to select from the total system those pieces that can be dealt with individually. When we have mastered all the pieces individually, we can then see how they fit together and function as an operational unit.

An application system can be divided into the following six controllable segments:

Origination (authorization)   Storage
Data entry   Output
Processing   Use

Technological Rule of Thumb 10.   Controls need to be placed into activities. The division of technology into controllable activities aids in the control design process.

These segments are illustrated in Figure 10-1 and described individually below.

Origination (authorization).   Manually originated transactions drive automated applications. However, there are approximately nine transactions automatically generated for each manually generated transaction. Let's look at the process in a retail organization.

A customer enters the store and buys a product using a credit card. The sales clerk records that transaction on a point-of-sale terminal. The customer gets the merchandise and a copy of a sales slip and that ends the manual processing. During the manual entry of data at the point-of-sale terminal, the information is fed into a series of automated applications and may perform any or all of the following steps:

Change the customer's available credit balance

Charge the customer's account for the purchase, which will eventually result in a monthly statement

Reduce the inventory account of each item purchased

Automatically generate a purchase order for any item ordered whose quantity on hand has fallen below the reorder point

Generate a sales commission for the salesperson

Generate a commission for a buyer or department manager

Update sales by salesperson and other accounting classifications

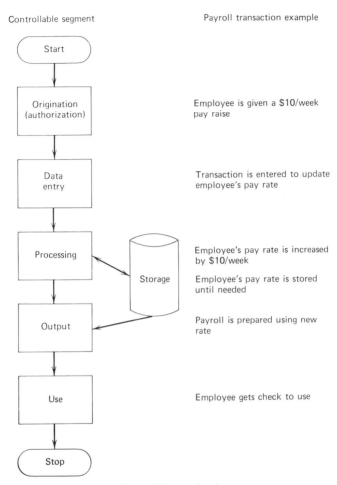

Controllable segment   Payroll transaction example

Figure 10-1. Controllable application segments.

The transaction origination segment creates a transaction but may not enter it into the automated system. In some applications, this requires the preparation of an input form. In other applications, the origination is merely a thought process which will be used as the basis for entering data into the automated segment (entering a sale through a point-of-sale cash register). The type of evidence retained about origination is an application system decision. It is a decision in which the accountant should participate.

The origination process usually includes the authorization of the transaction. In many instances, the entry of the transaction constitutes authorization. For example, when a salesclerk enters a customer order, the system assumes the order is authorized because it came from an authorized source. In other instances, authorization is automated using system rules. For example, when a customer wishes to withdraw funds from a cash dispensing terminal, the transaction is authorized by the customer entering a magnetically encoded card and a password, which are validated by the system to provide the necessary authorization. The methods and evidence retained about authorization are systems decisions. The accountant should participate in determining how the authorization process will be accomplished and the authorization evidence retained.

Data Entry Segment.   Data entry is the conversion of information into a machine-readable format. The process takes information that is understandable to people and converts it into a format that is understandable to machines. In some instances, the two formats are identical. Let's look quickly at some of the data entry methods:

Keypunch.   Convert information to holes in punched cards

Key-to-Disk.   Convert information to electronic codes on a disk surface

Magnetic Ink Characters.   Typing characters onto paper using special fonts and magnetic ink—this is most common on bank checks

Mark Sensing.   Darkening predetermined areas on a form, usually with a special pencil—used frequently to record examination answers

Optical Scanning.   The recognition of numbers and characters optically when they conform to standard character structures

The entry process can be performed by the data entry clerk, such as the keypunch operator, or performed by the person who originates the transaction. The data entered normally conform to a predetermined format. This explains why much of the information going into the computer must be written into boxes.

The accountant is concerned that the data are transcribed correctly. The data entry process is a step that does not need to occur in a manual system and thus provides another opportunity for error. The risk of error is higher when data entry clerks are used. For example, they can misinterpret the letter "O" for the number "0" or the number "1" for the letter "I", and so on.

Processing Segment.   The processing rules must be predetermined. The computer can make decisions during processing, but only those decisions which have been predetermined. For example, if the rules for granting credit for a pending sale are that the value of the sale plus the amount due from the customer must be less than the credit limit, then the processing segment can apply those rules and make a decision. However, if the decision required has not been predetermined and included within the processing segment, the decision cannot be made.

Processing is the segment that controls the automated portion of the system. Many of the controls are incorporated into processing, which not only verifies the integrity of processing, but can also verify the correctness of the other segments. Adequate controls in the processing segment can reduce many of the computer risks.

Storage Segment. One of the capabilities of an automated system is the ability to store and quickly retrieve large amounts of data. The information is not in hard-copy format, and thus can be rearranged and modified quickly. This provides both processing advantages and control risks.

Newer systems separate the file management and storage segment from the control of the people who develop the application system. The new concept for this segregation of functions is called data base. When utilized, the data administration segment is under the control of an individual called the data base administrator. This individual has the responsibility for the integrity of the organization's data.

Output Segment. The end product of an application system is the results produced from that system. The system is no better than the data produced by the system. It is of little value to perform all other segments correctly and then produce erroneous results.

The accountant should be concerned about both the data produced and the format in which it is presented. Poorly presented or described information can lead to poor management decisions. Reports produced from automated applications should be accompanied by instructions on how to use those reports.

Use Segment. People need to be trained in how to interpret and use reports. Many computer reports are poorly constructed and do not provide instructions on how to use the information. Thus, either the information is used erroneously or not used at all.

Studies of computer problems indicate that in most systems computer-produced reports provide the necessary information to correct most of the system's problems. What happens is that people do not use those reports for some of the following reasons:

Voluminous Reports. The quantity of paper produced is beyond human ability to absorb. When systems produce 300- and 400-page reports, people cannot be expected to read, analyze, and act on those data.

Quality of Actions. Reports fail to specify the items requiring immediate attention from those requiring attention when time is available. The users of the report may not have sufficient insight and knowledge about the application to make those decisions, and thus may spend time working on routine conditions while urgent conditions remain unattended.

Scope Unknown. Users of reports may not know the types of data or calendar periods covered by the report. For example, the caption "sales" may mean book sales, tentative sales, committed sales, or some other designation. Other reports indicating "for the period ended November 18" may mean a day, a week, a half-month, or a month, or some other time period. Reports need to be specific.

Action Responsibility Unspecified. People may not know they need to take action on certain items. If the instructions are not specific, individuals may think that other people are taking action.

Application Processing Example

A payroll transaction example is included on Figure 10-1, parallel with the controllable application segments. The processing of the payroll transaction illustrates the processing of an employee pay raise from its origination through the spending of the money by the employee. The illustration shows how automated applications are divided.

An employee's supervisor makes the decision to increase an employee's pay by $10 a week. This decision process by an individual begins the transaction. It's not necessary for the supervisor to write down that transaction, although it is advisable, especially when a large number of transactions are originated.

The payroll system is automated, requiring the pay raise information to be entered into the system. Because pay rates are usually batched and entered in a group, the information is probably transcribed onto a hardcopy form, and then entered into a computer by a data entry operation. The form with the employee's number and increase is given to a data entry clerk, who enters it onto a disk following data entry instructions.

The information is transmitted to the processing segment. This segment obtains the employee's master record from the payroll file, and then adds $10 to the employee's pay rate. The new information is then placed into the storage segment for retention until needed for the processing of payroll.

The processing segment upon command produces the payroll checks for the next pay period. The processing involves the calculation of both gross and net for the preparation of the check. The check is printed by the output segment onto the bank check. The automated segment of the process is now complete.

The completed product, the paycheck, is delivered to the employee's supervisor. At this point, the results of processing are used in the satisfaction of the obligation to pay employees for their work. Once the employee receives the check for his or her use, the application function is commenced. However, it should be noted that there are other applications in the chain still to be performed. These applications include the forwarding of withheld taxes and employer taxes to regulatory agencies, transferring funds to the bank to cover the payroll checks, and an independent reconciliation of the payroll account.

Accountants' Computer Guideline 16. Identify which risks occur in which segment and then ensure controls in that segment are adequate to reduce the risks.

AUTOMATED APPLICATION RISKS

Six accounting risks can best be controlled by the automated applications. An Application Risks/Segment Matrix (see Exhibit 10-1) shows in which segment(s) of the application the risks are most prevalent. The matrix is provided as a tool for the accountant in locating the most cost-effective segment in which to place controls. The matrix is not meant to imply that these are the only risks but, rather, the risks that need to be addressed in the application segment. For example, erroneous input is a constant risk, but only needs to be addressed at the entry point, and not in each application in a series of interconnected applications.

APPLICATION KEY CONTROLS

A system of internal control is comprised of many controls. Some of the controls will be strong and others weak. Visualize two boards nailed together with many nails, a few very large and many medium and small nails. The small- and medium-sized nails can rust and break, but the wood will stay together as long as the large nails remain firm. A few key controls, like the large nails, can hold the integrity of an automated system together.

The key controls that an accountant should look for in all automated applications are listed in Exhibit 10-2.

EXHIBIT 10-1 Application Risks/Segments Matrix

Automated Application Accounting Risk	Origination	Data Entry	Processing	Storage	Output	Use
Data Entry Error	✓	✓				
Improper Code	✓	✓				
Unidentified Data		✓				
Lost Transactions	✓	✓	✓	✓	✓	✓
Erroneous Output					✓	✓
Processing Mismatch		✓				
File Out-Of-Balance			✓	✓		
Cascading of Errors		✓	✓			✓
Repetition of Errors	✓		✓		✓	

EXHIBIT 10-2 Accounting Application Key Controls

Key Controls	Purpose of Control
1. Control coordinator	Individual assigned application control responsibility
2. Change control	Order implementation of application changes
3. Error control	Timely correction of errors
4. File simple accounting proof	Ensure integrity of application files
5. Externally maintained control totals	Redundant control outside automated segment of application
6. Access control	Restrict access to authorized individuals
7. Processing accountability	Make people accountable for their acts
8. Application audit trail	Provide capability to reconstruct processing
9. User documentation	Instruct user on how to optimize the use of the application
10. Application testing	Independent testing to assure application conforms to specifications

Control Coordinator. The control coordinator is an individual independent of the application system project team, the user, and computer operators assigned the responsibility to ensure the proper functioning of the application. The control coordinator normally reports within computer operations or to an administrative officer of the organization. The tasks typically performed by a control coordinator include:

Verify that all inputs are received
Verify that inputs are received on a timely basis
Verify that the application is run in accordance with the schedule
Maintain and verify independent control totals
Monitor the reprocessing of error messages
Monitor the availability of special forms
Verify the accuracy and completeness of output
Verify the timeliness of output
Verify the functioning of security procedures
Maintain logs on application processing

Change Control. More funds are expended on maintaining existing systems than building new systems. Change is a way of life in data processing and needs to be controlled. Many of the problems associated with applications are problems that occur when changes are made to that application system. Change control is a process to monitor change from the point where the change is initiated through the successful implementation of the change. At a minimum, the process includes:

Change identification (usually a change numbering system)
Change approval procedure
Change implementation schedule
Documentation update after the change
Modify operator and user documentation after a change
Inform operational personnel when a change will be installed
Inform control coordination personnel when a change will be installed so they can be alert for potential change problems
Prioritize change backlog requests

Error Control. Computer systems have thousands of instructions specifying numerous rules, conditions, and procedures that must be followed. Failure to follow the rules can result in modification or rejection of transactions. These actions usually result in an error or warning message. The individual responsible for those transactions should confirm automatic corrective actions, then correct and reenter error conditions. To ensure that errors are properly corrected and reentered on a timely basis, the error correction and reentry procedures should include:

Error identification (usually an error numbering system)
Error tracking to ensure no errors are lost
Prioritization of errors so that high priority errors get first attention
Document error correction procedures

File Simple Accounting Proof. The integrity of the file is a major application responsibility. Maintaining a simple accounting proof on file control fields provides reasonable assurance of the integrity of the file. The simple accounting proof method selects one or more key control fields, such as the accounts receivable balance, and then prepares a simple accounting proof for that field which begins with current balance, adds additions, subtracts deletions, and arrives at a new file balance.

Externally Maintained Control Totals. Control should be maintained outside of the automated applications if practical. These externally maintained control totals provide an independent control on the integrity of processing. For example, an externally maintained control total can be maintained on accounts receivable by using the data from the invoicing system and cash payments system. This external control total should be reconciled to the balance produced by the automated accounts receivable system. This independent total control has been successful in identifying problems in automated applications.

Access Control. The application resources should be restricted to those people who need to have access in the performance of their daily work. The needs of the systems user should be matched to the system's resources and accessibility enforced in accordance with those needs. Those individuals—or functions—who have no need for access to the application data should be denied access. For example, data base administrators, systems programmers, systems analysts, and application system programmers should be denied access to application data.

Processing Accountability. Individuals involved in application processing should be held accountable for their acts. Accountability must be maintained at the individual level, as opposed to the function. The kinds of accountability that should be required in application processing include people who:

Authorize transactions for processing

Override normal system processing rules

Delete, change, or add people to a list of authorized individuals to perform a privileged act

Grant special processing authorization

Application Audit Trail. Applications should maintain audit trail records sufficient to trace transactions to their control totals, and from control totals to all of the supporting transactions. In addition, the audit trail should be able to reconstruct and substantiate processing. However, audit trails that are uneconomical to use are little better than no audit trail. These cumbersome audit trails may satisfy legal requirements, but are not practical to use.

Audit trails pose special design problems in automated applications, including:

Transaction Time Span. If transaction processing is spread out over many days or months, the audit trail likewise is spread, making reconstruction difficult and costly.

Processing Logs. In advanced applications, such as data communication and data base, part of the audit trail is included on processing logs. This requires the coupling of two audit trails to identify and explain processing situations.

Scope of Audit Trail. Normally more audit trail data could be retained than is economical to store. Careful scrutiny must be made as to the minimum acceptable audit trail.

Obsolete Technology. Audit trails retained for an extended period may be recorded on media or use a technology that is no longer in use in the organization, making its use impossible.

User Documentation. Users need to understand how the system functions, and how to interpret and use system outputs. System strengths, weaknesses, or features are of little value until the user understands how to use those features, and how they fit into the day-to-day processing of the user organization. This system explanation can be accomplished with user documentation and training. The data processing project team share a joint responsibility with user management in developing this documentation.

Application Testing. Application systems contain a large number of instructions and processing paths. It has been estimated that thousands or even millions of possible processing paths exist in each application system. Assuring that each of these processing paths produces the desired results is a time-consuming and expensive process. Functional testing is a two-part process: first the user and the project team must agree on the processing reliability desired from testing; and then a testing program should be developed and implemented to achieve that level of reliability.

Accountants' Computer Guideline 17. Key controls are the key to controlling automated applications.

Origination/Authorization Control Solutions

The solution to adequate control is the examination of the risks in each application activity, and then determining that the controls are adequate to reduce those risks to an acceptable level. The development of the solution requires someone knowledgeable in both control practices and application processing. The control solution objective is to develop cost-effective controls so that it doesn't cost more to reduce the risk than the potential loss associated with the risk.

The types of controls that the accountant might look for or suggest in the origination/authorization activity are (note that these are in addition to the key controls):

Supervisory Review. A person in authority reviews the work performed by a subordinate. The review serves the purposes of verifying that the subordinate performed the work properly and applied reasonable judgment to the situation.

Prenumbered Forms. Using controlled forms so that if an input transaction were lost that fact would be known and an investigation could be undertaken.

Batch Totals. Develop a total over the input transactions so that the computer system can verify that all input transactions have been received.

Authorization Rules. Predetermined criteria have been established for how transactions are authorized and by whom.

Origination Forms. Using a preprinted form so that all of the needed data will be recorded during the origination process.

Field Definition Boxes. Providing the originator with a predetermined number of boxes for each field so that they cannot exceed field limits.

EXHIBIT 10-3 Origination/Authorization Activity Controls Checklist

Item	Yes	No
1. Have written procedures been established to govern the origination of transactions?		
2. Are the documents used to support transaction origination stored in an easily retrievable manner should they be needed to substantiate transactions?		
3. Have the transaction authorization rules been clearly established?		
4. Is a single individual responsible for each transaction?		
5. Is there reasonable supervisory review over the transaction origination and authorization process?		
6. Are prenumbered forms used for originating the transaction where appropriate?		
7. Are batch totals retained over transaction origination to ensure the complete and accurate entry of data into the system?		
8. Is the transaction origination process designed to ensure that all the needed data will be entered?		
9. Are appropriate measures used to ensure that the data entered will not exceed the number of characters allocated for a field or record?		
10. Are sufficient procedures established to permit the timely correction and resubmission of errors detected by the application system?		

Exhibit 10-3 is designed to help accountants assess the adequacy of origination/authorization activity controls.

Data Entry Control Solutions

Data entry commences the automated segment of the application system. Tight controls established during the origination/authorization activity will be reflected in control strengths throughout the entire application. One of the control objectives of data entry is to ensure that the controls established during origination remain intact during the remainder of processing.

Controls need to ensure that errors do not occur during the data entry process. The translation from people-readable information to machine-readable information is a high error activity. Even though the accuracy rate for data entry is usually greater than 99 percent, the number of bad characters entered per thousand keystrokes could still be harmful. The seriousness of those errors is dependent upon which field they occur in. Obviously, an error in a description field is not as serious as a dollar value field error.

The types of controls the accountant should place in the data entry activity include:

Key Verification.   Verification is performing the key entry process twice and then comparing the two results and correcting differences. The process assumes there is a very low probability that the same key entry error will be made twice by two different operators.

Check Digits.   A check digit is an extra character added to a numeric field which mathematically proves the accuracy of that mathematical field. Check digits are effective in catching both erroneous and transposed numbers.

Data Entry Instructions.   Data entry operators should be instructed not only on how to enter data, but provided guidance on normal input values, so they can be alert to unusual conditions.

Prompting.   A series of instructions provided terminal users to help them use the system properly in entering data.

Batch Totals.   Totals maintained over the number of transactions or value of entered transactions so that the processing segment can verify the accuracy and completeness of a grouping of input.

Turnaround Document.   Preparing a document which contains the input information that should be entered, assuming that the transaction is normally processed. For example, a company would bill a customer and at the same time provide a document to be returned with the payment on which the amount billed is recorded. Thus, ordinary transactions are already prepared and only exception input transactions need be prepared manually.

Job Training.   The data entry operators should be trained in their work before commencing the data entry function.

Transaction Identification Codes.   Adding a special code to the transaction which can be used to identify the type of transaction being processed.

Exhibit 10-4 is designed to help accountants assess the adequacy of data entry activity controls.

EXHIBIT 10-4 Data Entry Activity Controls Checklist

Item	Yes	No
1. Have formal procedures been prepared describing the data entry functions to be performed?		
2. Is the data key verified where applicable?		
3. Do key identification fields, such as customer number, product number, and so on, use check digits to ensure the accurate entry of those key identifiers?		
4. Are procedures established to ensure that data is entered only by authorized individuals?		
5. Are procedures established to verify that all data received by the data entry function is entered into the automated application?		
6. Are procedures established to ensure the timely reentry of errors?		
7. Do computer terminal procedures provide for prompting users to ensure accurate and complete entry of data?		
8. Are data entry operators and terminal users adequately instructed in how to use the data entry equipment?		
9. Can transactions entered into automated applications be easily identified?		
10. Are procedures established to ensure that data entered into an application system is received intact by the processing segment?		

Processing Activity Control Solutions

The processing activity is the most powerful activity in which to insert controls. Most of the controls in the previous activity are preventive in nature. In other words, the controls are designed to prevent erroneous information from entering the system. Within processing, detective controls can be used, which can use the power of the computer to draw upon the information available to the system to detect the problems that previous activities could not prevent.

Computer processing logic is complex, but controls need not be complex. The accountant can understand risk and recommend control solutions without fully understanding how those solutions are implemented within the computer processing activity.

An important part of the processing control solution is the notification to people of the control action taken. This interaction with people must be clearly developed. For example, the computer may go through some complex processing to detect problems. The information accumulated by this review should be made available to the people making the correction to avoid having them redo the steps already performed by the computer.

The kind of controls that the accountant should recommend in the processing activity include:

Error Messages. A complete description of the detected problem, together with supporting data and suggested action if possible.

Warning Messages. An indication that there may be a problem, but the processing activity does not have sufficient information to verify the integrity of the transaction. For example, if a very large quantity is ordered, a warning message may be produced indicating that the large quantity could have been entered erroneously. The transaction is processed with a warning message giving people the opportunity to stop the transaction before it is completed.

Anticipation Controls. The computer system using the information available in the computer files checks to determine that processing is within regular limits. For example, if a customer regularly orders between 100 and 500 of a particular product the controls would anticipate that an order from that customer would be within that quantity range. Should the customer order, say, 1,500 of that product, the processing activity would issue a warning message indicating a potential error.

Batch Total Verification. The computer reconciles the batch total to the total of the detailed records entered with the batch to determine that all the transactions have been entered.

Step-by-Step Totals. The development of a control total in the first processing program and then adding that control total to the transactions as they are passed from program to program. Each program that follows will verify that the detailed records are in agreement with the step-by-step total passed with those transactions.

Recalculation. The processing activity recomputes the totals that have been manually calculated, to verify their accuracy.

Audit Trail. The processing segment produces an audit trail showing how processing results were achieved. The audit trail can be produced in one portion of the processing activity, or it can be started in the early portion of processing and expanded as processing continues.

Positive Verification. Verifying entered data are correct. The processing activity can include a listing of all the authorized codes or condi-

EXHIBIT 10–5   Processing Activity Controls Checklist

Item	Yes	No
1. Have the processing instructions been documented and concurred with by the user?		
2. Have procedures been established to ensure that the operational system functions in accordance with the specifications?		
3. Are error messages adequately explained so that their intent will not be misinterpreted?		
4. Are messages produced which identify all conditions in which automated processing has changed the data entered by people?		
5. Are procedures adequate to ensure that the appropriate people receive all error and warning messages?		
6. Is the system designed to anticipate problems before they become serious?		
7. Is the accuracy and completeness of input verified against the control information provided by the data entry activity?		
8. Does the automated segment recalculate values manually calculated and entered?		
9. Are procedures established to ensure that errors are reentered on a timely basis?		
10. Are procedures established to ensure that processing can be reconstructed if necessary?		
11. Are identification fields positively verified?		
12. Are records produced which indicate each time the normal processing rules have been overridden by people?		
13. Can one individual be held accountable for the processing of each transaction?		

tions that can occur. For example, the processing segment can contain a list of all the customer numbers, all of the product numbers, and other information. When one of these identifiers is entered, the processing activity makes a positive identification to verify the authenticity of the identifier.

Exhibit 10-5 is designed to help accountants assess the adequacy of processing activity controls.

Storage Activity Control Solutions

Data are retained for the purpose of reuse in future processing, such as a recirculating payroll file, and as backup to substantiate or reconstruct processing. The amount of data stored by installations is usually voluminous. It is not uncommon for large installations to have over 50,000 tapes or disks in storage.

The application storage activity is concerned with the integrity of data. Part of the storage control solution is a physical solution, which is controlled by computer operations. The processing segment can provide control totals which can be used to ensure the accuracy and completeness of stored data.

The controls that the auditor should specify for the storage activity include:

Control Totals.   A total of one or more key fields of the stored information to verify the accuracy and completeness of the stored data upon reuse.

Hash Totals.   A total of meaningless data, such as the first four characters of an individual's name, to verify that substitutions have not been made for specific transactions, as well as to verify the accuracy and completeness of the file.

Off-Site Storage.   Retaining sufficient data away from the main site to enable reconstruction of processing should the main site be destroyed.

File Labels.   External and internal labels which identify the data and the storage criteria for the data.

Storage Check Digit Totals.   A special mathematical formula accumulating one or more characters of information within the storage file to verify that the sequence of records is unchanged and that substitutions have not been made in the storage file.

Longitudinal Check Digits.   A self-checking transaction character that verifies the information within a single transaction has not been transposed, altered, or deleted.

Transaction Dating.   Transactions within storage contain the date on which the transaction was entered into storage. This permits the length of time a transaction is stored to be monitored and notification given when transactions have been stored for an extensive time period.

Generation Code.   If processing rules change, a generation code can be added to a transaction to indicate in which version of the processing program the transaction was entered, or processed. For example, if

EXHIBIT 10-6   Storage Activity Controls Checklist

Item	Yes	No
1. Are physical files properly identified?		
2. Do physical storage files have an internal label which identifies the file?		
3. Does the storage label identify the period during which the file is to be retained?		
4. Are inventory records maintained on the physical files?		
5. Is a physical inventory of the data conducted periodically?		
6. Is sufficient data stored away from the main site so that if the main site should be destroyed processing could be reconstructed?		
7. Is access to the physical files restricted to authorized individuals needing that data?		
8. Are sufficient controls maintained over the data in the storage files to protect the integrity of data?		
9. Is sufficient information retained in storage to determine when transactions have been entered?		
10. Can a determination be made of the processing used to create a transaction?		
11. Are controls sufficient in the files to prevent data from being altered, such as changing the name of a payee on a check?		
12. Does the system have the capability to identify dormant transactions, accounts, and files?		

product prices change, the generation code could indicate which version of product prices was used in creating a billing amount. This would be helpful for back orders or credits for returned product.

Exhibit 10-6 is designed to help accountants assess the adequacy of storage activity controls.

Output Activity Control Solutions

The output activity produces information for people. The information should be designed to meet the specific needs of the individual. For example, it may not be necessary to provide all of the information; perhaps

EXHIBIT 10-7   Output Activity Controls Checklist

Item	Yes	No
1. Are procedures adequate to ensure that the report will be delivered to the intended individual?		
2. Is the report properly identified?		
3. Is the descriptive information on each page readily understandable?		
4. Are computer codes interpreted for the user wherever practical?		
5. Are only the required number of copies of the report prepared?		
6. Are carbons destroyed if they contain confidential information?		
7. Are procedures adequate to ensure that if parts of reports are lost they can be identified by the user of that report?		
8. Do users of reports have adequate instructions on the types of information contained in the report and how to use the report?		
9. Are procedures adequate to ensure that if reports are not prepared on time users will be aware of the fact and can take alternate action?		
10. Are procedures adequate to ensure that the information on the report is accurate and complete?		
11. Are procedures established to destroy reports when their useful life has ended?		
12. Are special procedures established to ensure the integrity of accountable documents, such as checks?		
13. Are procedures adequate to ensure that accountable documents damaged or destroyed during processing are properly accounted for?		

only the information on which action need be taken should be included in the report.

The controls over output should first ensure the accuracy, completeness, and authorization of output, and second ensure its usability. Usability controls involve timeliness of report preparation and delivery, the readability and explanations included on and with report information, as well as format of information.

The controls that the accountant should specify in the output activity include:

Report Dating.   The date on which the report was prepared.

Information Dating.   The period which the information in the report represents, such as the month of November, the week of February 22, and so forth.

Delivered to Name.   The name of the individual to whom the report is intended.

Use Qualification Statement.   If the information in the report could be misinterpreted, a statement should be included on the report explaining the scope or content of information. For example, the statement might indicate that the sales shown in the report include commitments by customers in addition to actual completed sales.

Page Numbering.   Each page on the report should be numbered to show sequence.

Report End Notification.   The last page on the report should indicate that it is the last page, or the pages should be numbered "page 1 of X." This is necessary, in case one or more pages are removed, so that the user will be aware that the report is not complete.

Descriptive Heading.   The name of the report and the columnar headings should be as complete as possible so that there is no misunderstanding as to the intent of the report.

Identifier Decoding.   Identifiers and codes used throughout automated processing, such as state codes, customer numbers, and so on, should be decoded wherever practical on the reports for people use.

Accountable Document Handling.   Special procedures to ensure the proper use and accountability of all accountable documents.

Exhibit 10-7 is designed to help accountants assess the adequacy of output activity controls.

Use Activity Control Solutions

Computer systems are designed to produce predetermined results. The results may be the completion of the intended processing, such as the preparation of an invoice, savings account statement, or a life insurance policy. In other instances, the results are input to people to take action, such as approve customer credit, ship product to a customer, or correct a condition that has not been predetermined by the computer system logic.

The type of controls the accountant should specify over the use of processing results include:

Anticipation Controls. Expecting information at predetermined times and taking action if the information is not received at that time.

Processing Procedures Manual. Detailed instructions defining each piece of information and the action to be taken based on the value of that information.

Processing Time Limits. User personnel should be given limits in which processing should occur. For example, all error messages should be resolved within forty-eight hours after receipt.

Information Storage. Rules regarding what information is retained, where it is retained, and how long it is to be retained.

Change Requests. A formal method for users to request changes to the application system.

Exhibit 10-8 is designed to help accountants assess the adequacy of use activity controls.

EXHIBIT 10-8   Use Activity Controls Checklist

Item	Yes	No
1. Are users of information produced by computer systems adequately instructed on how to use that information?		
2. Are procedures for use of information formally documented and in the hands of users?		
3. When information changes, are users notified of the type of change and the date of change?		
4. Are user personnel instructed in the time frame in which processing must occur?		
5. Have anticipation controls been established so that the user will be aware when needed information is not received on schedule?		
6. Are formal procedures established so that users can make requests to modify or enhance application systems?		
7. Have users been instructed on the appropriate retention period for computer-produced information?		
8. Are users notified when transactions that might have been included in output are not due to those transactions failing to meet systems specifications?		

PLAN OF ACTION

Good application controls don't just happen—they are planned. The accountant should be an active participant in applications that affect accounting. The following plan of action is recommended to improve the adequacy of control in automated applications through the involvement of accountants in designing, maintaining, and monitoring control:

1. *Identify Accounting Applications.* The accountant needs to identify the organization's system of accounting. This identifies the population of applications in which the accountant may wish to become involved.

2. *Identify Accounting Risks and Determine Magnitude of Risks.* The risks associated with those applications should be identified and measured. The accountant needs a basis for involvement and depth of involvement. Until the accountant can measure the severity of the risk in the application, it is difficult to justify the expenditure of the effort in designing, implementing, and monitoring controls.

3. *Select the Accounting Risks Requiring the Accountant's Attention.* If the severity of the risk warrants accounting involvement, the accountants should identify the specific application risks and then assist in the design, implementation, and monitoring of controls to reduce those risks to an acceptable level. This chapter has outlined an approach to accomplish this objective.

4. *Specify the Minimum Level of Accounting Controls.* Specify the minimum level of accounting controls for financial applications. Accountants may not have sufficient time or resources to work with all the project teams in designing and controlling controls. In those instances, if minimum levels of controls have been specified the accountants will be assured a minimum level control in all financial applications will exist. The key controls outlined in this chapter can form the basis for those minimum controls in financial applications.

Accountants' Computer Guideline 18. It is far better to ask embarrassing questions during the design process than try to answer embarrassing situations after poorly controlled applications are operational.

eleven

CONTROLLING COMPUTER OPERATIONS

The computer operations function is the kitchen of the data processing organization. If we were to compare the data processing function to the preparation of a meal, the systems requirements activity would specify the kind of meal wanted, the systems design function would order the food, the programming function would write the recipes, and computer operations would cook the meal. Computer operations, like the cook, gets the job done.

Computer operations is a job shop kind of operation. Rarely are there two operations that are identical. The time of running a system changes, the input mix changes, the mix of work running in a computer at a single point of time changes, and the results produce change. Computer operations has the responsibility to produce the desired results consistently and on time.

The computer operations function has changed dramatically during the past decade. Ten years ago, operators were continually on the go changing tape and disk drives, mounting different paper forms in the printer, and maintaining a continual dialog with the operating system. Today the central computer room may stand vacant while the computer interacts with remote operations. The busy activities at the central site have been replaced by operations activity at remote terminals, while the central site monitors the processing environment.

Computer operations in the past was operator directed. Today it is user directed. User personnel sitting at terminals initiate processing from remote locations. The central operation personnel have shifted from the mechanics of tending and feeding data to the equipment to one of monitoring to determine that operations are flowing flawlessly.

The role and responsibility of computer operations will continue to change as data processing becomes more intertwined into the day-to-day operation of the organization. The continual changing of the methods of operation provides a continual challenge to operations management to keep applications flowing smoothly. The types of operations support needed become increasingly complex. This chapter explains how computer operations supports the application activities.

COMPUTER OPERATIONS OBJECTIVES

The primary objective of computer operations is to operate computers. This responsibility includes all of the support functions necessary to supply data and keep the computers operational. These support functions include more than the day-to-day operation of the computer hardware.

The most common objectives for a computer operation group are:

Adequate Service Level.   Computer operations is charged with the responsibility of maintaining sufficient resources to accomplish the computing needs of the organization. The computer center is like a utility, in that when people want processing power they like to feel they can merely throw a switch and get it just as you can turn on a power switch and the lights go on. The service provided involves optimizing hardware and software, as well as smoothing user demands so that the resources maintain a steady workload throughout the operating period.

Continuity of Operation.   Computer operations is a continuous process. Computer operations must take those steps necessary to ensure minimal operational problems, and when problems occur take those steps necessary to restore the integrity of operations as quickly as possible. Continuity of operation not only involves hardware and software, but the ability to restore the integrity of application systems after that integrity has been lost because of operations problems.

Adequate Documentation Levels.   The operations function needs to be adequately documented to ensure that operations personnel perform all of the necessary tasks and in the proper sequence. Computer operations is a repetitious operation which requires the personnel to have adequate instructions on how to perform a variety of tasks correctly. It is not uncommon for a large computer center to execute many thousands of programs in the course of a week. These programs use a complex operating system which makes it impossible for a single operator to comprehend all of the intricacies of operation. Operations personnel depend upon consistent and adequate documentation to lead them through the steps necessary to perform the correct procedures.

Adequate Conversion. Computer operations involves a continual series of changes. Hardware changes, software changes, application systems change, and procedures change. The success of computer operations is often dependent upon how well the group can manage the changes.

Segregation of Functions. Computer operations resources offer the capabilities to manipulate, either intentionally or unintentionally, the application system and the data within the system. For example, using facilities available to the computer, records can be added, deleted, or modified in data files with virtually no audit trail records indicating such events had occurred. The capabilities are needed to recover from problems. However, the proper use of these capabilities requires the appropriate segregation of duties.

Maintenance of Computer Resources. Computer hardware and software require periodic maintenance. The hardware is machinery and as such wears out and malfunctions. Computer software also malfunctions, and is continually updated to include new features. Operations personnel have the responsibility to schedule and oversee the maintenance of the computer resources.

OVERVIEW OF THE OPERATING ENVIRONMENT

The computer operating environment involves the interaction between multiple software packages, the application system, and input/output devices. Over the years, the environment has become more complex as ever increasing segments of the application system have become generalized and placed into specialized software packages. A typical computer operating environment is illustrated in Figure 11-1. Let's look at how such an operation works.

This is an on-line data base environment. Many installations will not have all of the packages, but ordinarily the functions exist. When specialized software packages are not used, the functions are performed by the operating system.

The on-line process starts when the user has a request and initiates operation from the user terminal. The distance of the terminal from the computer is unimportant. The user initiates operations by depressing a *request* key. Since most terminals have some processing capability, the initial interaction between the user and the system is performed using terminal capabilities. The user indicates a request for action such as requesting the on-hand inventory for a particular product. This request re-

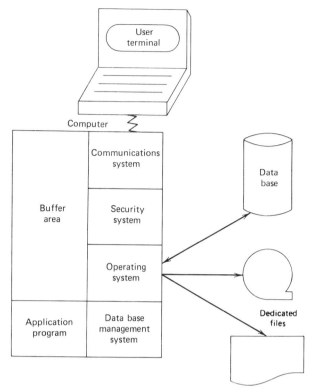

Figure 11-1.   Computer operating environment.

quires the processing capability of the central computer, so the terminal indicates to the communication system that a message is ready to be transmitted to the central location.

Before accepting and processing the message, the centralized security system is called into operation to verify that the user is authorized to process such a request. This might be performed by requesting the operator to enter a password and then verifying that against a profile of those users authorized to perform that action. Assuming the user is authorized, the message is accepted by the communication system for processing. The communication system stores the message in a queue and notifies the operating system that a message has been received.

The operating system needs to be told which application program is needed to process the message. That program is called from the program library into the main processing storage of the computer, sometimes called computer memory. The operating system then passes the message to the appropriate computer program for processing. The application program recognizes from the message type that the status of a product in inventory is requested. The needed data are located in a data base.

The application system then requests from the data base management system the on-hand quantity of the desired item of inventory. The data base management system searches through indices to find where that information is physically located in the data base. That information is passed to the operating system which initiates the read commands to get the information from the data base into the computer storage buffer area. The buffer area (a storage area in computer memory) is used because these records may be three to five thousand characters in length and several of the records will be in main storage at any one time. When the desired record has been placed into the buffer area, the operating system notifies the data base management system that the data are now available for usage. The data base management system selects the desired on-hand quantity from the physical record located in the buffer area and delivers it to the application program.

The application program prepares an outgoing message for the user terminal and notifies the operating system that a message is ready for delivery. The operating system takes the message from the application system and delivers it to the communication system. The communication system notifies the terminal that it has a message ready to be transmitted to the terminal. The terminal indicates an okay to transmit and the message is sent to the terminal. The terminal processing logic then displays the message onto the terminal screen. At the end of this process, the user has the on-hand quantity for the product. To the user, the response appeared within a fraction of a second or a few seconds at the most. The operations that occurred between the time the user entered the request and received the response were completely transparent to the user.

Several operations have occurred during this process which were not mentioned. These involve the use of dedicated files and the preparation of audit trail information. The communication system, the operating system, the security system, and the data base management system, as well as the application system may all produce audit trail logs. In addition, messages and other information may be sent to operator video terminals or printed for reference purpose or action. This simplified example has explained the processes that occur in today's computers to achieve the desired result. Actual practice may vary from the described practices, but the conceptual explanation should provide insight into the complexity of computer operations.

Technological Rule of Thumb 11. Computer operations, like the automobile engine, is complex. It is nice to know how a car works, but it is not necessary for driving a car, nor is it necessary to know how computer operations work in order to recommend controls.

CONTROLLABLE COMPUTER OPERATIONS ACTIVITIES

Computer operations involves the physical operation of the hardware and the support groups necessary to keep those operations functioning. The support functions in computer operations vary from organization to organization. Some operation departments have very distinct organizational structures dividing the support groups into organizational activities. Other operations groups combine many of the activities into two or three groups.

From a control perspective, the functions performed in the operations department can be divided into controllable activities. Although these activities may not coincide directly with the organizational structure of computer operations, the functions are usually identifiable, and thus controllable. The activities are necessary to reduce some of the specific computer operation risks.

The activities in computer operations which are controllable are:

Computer Operations. Computer operations has responsibility for running the computer hardware. This involves starting the computer operations during which the operating system is loaded into the computer so that it can take control of computer activities. Computer operators monitor the system to ascertain it is functioning properly, provide information needed by the operating system to continue the operations function, make any adjustments or corrections necessary to continue the proper functioning of operations, and shut down operations at predetermined times.

Data Library. The data library is the repository for the data used in the computer center. The data library is frequently a secure area isolated from the operations area. Even in smaller organizations, the information may be stored in a fireproof vault. The data library may be divided into on-site and off-site areas. The off-site location is used as a backup facility in the event the primary site is destroyed through a natural disaster. Among the functions performed by the data library are:

Maintain inventory of data
Provide physical protection for the data

Act as a librarian for computer operators to store and retrieve unneeded data

Restrict unauthorized individuals from accessing physical data

Develop and maintain a records retention policy

Destroy unneeded data

Monitor the performance and usefulness of computer media

Program Library. The programs used in the day-to-day operation of the
computer center are stored in the program library. The program library,
unlike the data library, is maintained on computer media, and itself may
be stored in the data library. The program library normally consists of a
source and object library. The source code library is the programming
statements written by the programmers, while the object library is the
executable machine instructions produced by the programmer's source
statements. The responsibilities of the program library include:

A repository for programs

A repository and identifier of multiple versions of the same program

A facility to modify programs

A protection against unauthorized modification to programs (optional)

Systems Software. The application system is only a portion of the processing logic needed to achieve user needs. Many of the functions needed
by the application program are performed by generalized system software. The main software package is called the operating system. It is this
system that determines which programs will be executed, communicates
with the operator regarding operating instructions, and reads and writes
the record from the input/output devices. Other software packages perform supporting tasks or specialized tasks such as managing data independently of the application programs (performed by the data base management system), providing security and limiting access to the computer and
associated resources, and special report-writing functions. In many instances, all of the user's needs can be satisfied through the systems software, making it unnecessary to write an application program.

Systems Software Support. Operating systems offer computer operations
with numerous capabilities. It is not necessary to incorporate all of these
capabilities into the operating environment because these capabilities utilize computing resources. Therefore, computer operations personnel
study the capabilities versus their operating needs, and make decisions as
to whether or not to incorporate those capabilities into the implemented

operating system. These decisions and the assembly of the software packages are performed by a systems support group. In addition, if problems are encountered in the systems software packages, the support group investigates and takes the necessary action to correct those problems. The individual staffing of the systems support group is usually the elite of the technical corps, and they are those individuals that work closest with the machine characteristics.

Data Control. The execution of many application systems requires the marshalling of resources both before and after the operation. For example, users prepare and submit data to computer operations, application systems require recirculating tapes to be withdrawn from the data library, and special instructions may need to be prepared. The data control group gathers these materials before running the application system. At the conclusion of operation, reports have been or need to be printed, and they may need to be bursted (have the carbon paper removed) and delivered to the users. In addition, inputs and recirculating tapes need to be returned to the appropriate storage location, and operating instructions need to be filed awaiting reuse. All of these functions can be performed by a data control group. In addition, the group may perform some control activities to verify such things as whether all of the needed data have been received, whether all of the reports that should have been produced were produced, and whether detected errors were corrected on a timely basis.

Recovery. Recovery is one of the most technically complex tasks performed by computer operations. As technology becomes more complex, so does the recovery operation. Let's look first at the ways in which an on-line data base system can fail:

Terminal operations can malfunction
Terminal hardware can fail
Communication lines can fail
Communication lines can malfunction
Communication software can malfunction
Data base software can malfunction
Operating system can malfunction
Centralized hardware can fail
Application system can malfunction
Computer operators can make mistakes
Data can be improper, causing system problems

Any or all of these events can occur simultaneously during operations. In addition, in large on-line systems many transactions are in various stages of completion. Terminal operations can be complete, but the transaction only partially completed by the central system. Thus, the terminal operator may think the operation has been completed when, in fact, it has not. All of these conditions must be incorporated into the recovery plan.

An essential part of the recovery process is the storage of sufficient backup data, programs, operating instructions, and the input data used in processing so that the integrity of the system can be restored quickly. Organizations that cannot afford to have the main system go down, such as many large banks, purchase duplicate facilities so that if one computer system fails, operations can be instantaneously switched to a backup computer.

Technological Rule of Thumb 12. The impact of computer operations failure on the organization must be determined (and quantified) so that adequate computer operating procedures and controls can be established to reduce that impact to an acceptable level.

COMPUTER OPERATION RISKS

The computer operation risks need to be identified by where they are most cost-effective to control. Many of the risks associated with computer operations are a result of inadequate controls in the application sys-

EXHIBIT 11-1   Operations Risks/Activities Matrix

Computer Operations Accounting Risks \ Computer Operations Activities	Computer Operations	Data Library	Program Library	Systems Software	Systems Software Support	Data Control	Recovery
Data Entry Error	✔						
Unidentified Data	✔	✔	✔			✔	
Inadequate Audit Trail	✔	✔	✔	✔	✔	✔	✔
Inadequate Service Level				✔	✔		✔

tem. For example, the data entry errors become the responsibility of computer operations to correct or have corrected, even though they originated in the application system. Controls in computer operations can deal with detected problems, and as such can address the problem at the point where action must be taken.

The computer operations risks and the activities where controls should be placed are illustrated in Exhibit 11-1. Note that some of these risks are shared with the application system. This sharing results from that application system detecting and computer operations correcting problems.

COMPUTER OPERATION KEY CONTROLS

Computer operation activities are not closely interrelated like application system activities. Rather, the computer operations activities are a loose network of related activities. The type of logical flow that occurs in systems development and application systems is not present in computer operations. For example, some of the activities such as recovery are only performed periodically, while other operations such as the execution of the systems software occur continuously.

The accountant should look for the implementation of key controls to ensure the integrity of computer operations. Unlike systems development and application systems, some of the key controls are planning procedures needed to address some of the more serious operation risks. While the key controls do not interact with each other, as frequently occurred in the application system, they are nevertheless equally as important in assuring a successful execution of application processing.

The key computer operation controls that the accountant should require in computer operations include (see Exhibit 11-2):

Operations Documentation. The multiplicity of programs and operations makes it impractical to operate a computer center without detailed documented instructions. Reliance upon the memory of computer operations personnel is a sure formula for failure. Most computer operations departments will not accept systems without detailed documentation being prepared. One large organization requires that the computer programmers and systems analysts be present in the operation room each time the system is run until the operations documentation is complete. The implementation of this policy solved getting operating documentation on a timely basis. The information needed by computer operations includes:

EXHIBIT 11-2   Computer Operations Key Controls

Key Control	Purpose of Control
1. Operations documentation	Explains how to execute the application
2. Operations logs	Lists all of the actions taken by computer operators
3. Error reporting and correction procedures	Ensures the timely and proper reentry of system errors
4. Contingency plans	Outlines the steps to be taken to ensure the integrity of operations after a problem
5. Software audit trail	Documents all the changes to operating software
6. Change management	Monitors the installation of changes
7. Capacity planning	Provides for sufficient operating capacity to provide the desired service level to users
8. Software package testing	Tests that operating software functions as specified
9. Media inventory control	An inventory of physical files such as tapes and disks
10. File labeling	External and internal labels identifying file contents

Input data files needed
Output data files produced
Programs used
Instructions to interface with the operating systems (sometimes called job control language)
Special operator instructions
Special forms used for the printer
Schedule for running the system
Report recipients

Operations Logs.   Millions of events may occur every hour during operations. These events involve the use of resources, messages to and from the operator, messages and transactions to and from programs, as well as changes in the data file. Most computer operating environments use logs to record all of these events. The logs are, in effect, a motion picture recording of the events that occur in the operating environment. These logs are an audit trail that can be used to reconstruct processing, or to recover the operation in the event of a problem. The operating software packages that produce operation logs include:

Operating system
Job accounting systems
Communication systems
Security systems
Data base management systems

Error Reporting and Correction Procedures. During the course of computer operations, problems will be encountered. Some of these problems can be corrected by the computer operator, while others may require a multidisciplined team to solve a complex operating problem. Computer operations needs a formalized method for identifying and dealing with problems. Operators should not be permitted to use their discretion in error correction. Several years ago, a tape file error occurred in the accounts receivable application of a large food-producing organization. The operator, recognizing that data could not be read from the file, went to the data library and got the backup file and mounted it. When the same problem occurred, the operator got another backup file and entered that. The process continued until there were no more backup files. A tape drive failure destroyed each backup file that was mounted, and the operator mounted every backup file. The organization lost thousands of dollars when other organizations failed to pay their accounts receivables and the company had lost their records so could not follow up on collections. Well-controlled computer operations formally document problems on an error form and then give that information to a supervisor to initiate action. Periodically, the forms are analyzed to look for trends and global solutions for those errors.

Contingency Plan. Computer operations must prepare for catastrophic events. The contingency plans describe in detail how computer operations will function in the event that a problem prevents normal operations from occurring. Contingency plans involve people, data, and processing capabilities. Some of the catastrophic occurrences that must be provided for in a contingency plan include:

Acts of God, such as flood, earthquake, and so forth
Fire and water damage
Major hardware malfunction
Loss of the on-site data library
Loss of the program libraries
Loss of key operating personnel

Software Audit Trail. Operating software systems are continually chang-ing. The change from one version of a software package to another is called moving to a new version or generation. An audit trail should be maintained documenting the changes made between two versions of soft-ware. This enables organizations to reconstruct the evolution of a soft-ware package, and to revert back to older generations should problems be encountered with the current generation. In addition, the audit trail should indicate who is accountable for the change, and when it occurred. The same type audit trail should be maintained for application system programs.

Change Management. Computer operations change daily. There is rare-ly a time that either operating instructions, programs, hardware, or proce-dures are not changing. The smooth implementation of those changes is essential to the proper functioning of computer operations. Each change has associated with it the potential for causing problems. Managing change is needed to ensure that problems are minimized and that the ap-propriate people are notified of the changes. Some computer operations have established an organizational group to oversee, monitor, and imple-ment changes in the operating environment. This commitment of re-sources to the management of change has substantially reduced the inci-dence of problems in those organizations.

Capacity Planning. The mix and volume of work handled by computer operations is consistently changing. Computer operations must provide resources for the hourly, daily, weekly, monthly, and yearly peaks as well as provide for trends of increased or decreased processing capacity needs. The lead time to obtain certain pieces of computer hardware may be 18 months or more. Thus, a request for a quick increase in capacity may not be possible. Many organizations have paid premiums of over 100 percent of the cost of equipment in order to obtain it quickly. The laws of supply and demand come into effect when hardware is limited, and those having the supply charge whatever the market will bear. Without adequate planning for increased capacity, organizations may be paying an enormous premium for not performing adequate capacity planning. On the other hand, too much capacity is equally as wasteful of computer resources. The objective of capacity planning is to provide sufficient computer resources at the times they are needed.

Software Package Testing. The majority of functions needed to satisfy user requests are performed by software packages obtained from vendors. Some are supplied without charge by the hardware manufacturer, while others need to be purchased. The vendors of these packages continually modify and issue new versions. The software packages are tested by the vendor, but still periodically introduce problems into the operating environment. The better the testing by the software vendor, the fewer problems introduced into the operating environment. However, the operations personnel should take measures to ensure that the vendor-supplied software packages function as specified. Some of the testing that operations personnel can perform to verify the functioning of vendor-produced software includes:

Verification that all of the software deliverables, such as documentation, tapes, diskettes, loading instructions, and so on, have been delivered

Running the software package in a nonproduction environment to ensure that it functions properly

Preparing test cases to verify most or all of the systems capabilities function properly

Conforming with other users of the software package regarding the correctness of operation

Some large computer operations groups have set aside a whole computer for test purposes. Not only do they let the programmers test application programs on that computer, but they test the new versions of vendor-operating software on them.

Media Inventory Control. Most computer operation departments have a large library of computer media. In large organizations, this may be over 50,000 tapes, disks, and diskettes, while in smaller organizations it may number only a few hundred. However, all organizations should initiate an inventory control procedure over computer media. Without such an inventory, they may be uncertain as to whether or not a particular file exists, they may retain information for too short or too long a time period, and may lose computer media and not be aware of the loss in time to conduct a meaningful investigation. The media inventory responsibility should be included within the data library responsibilities.

File Labeling. The data stored on computer media are electronically stored. The data are easily destroyed when the media are reused in the operating environment to create new output files. The means of protecting those files from premature destruction is file labeling. There are both external and internal file labels. External labels are descriptions of the file and the pertinent information about saving and storing that file for the use of people. The internal file label includes the same types of information but is for the use of the operating system. Both labels are designed to protect the files from premature destruction. The information contained in most file labeling procedures includes:

Name of file
Name of application system creating file
Date file was created or time of day if multiple files are created in a single day
File media identification number, which physically identifies the media
Security classification of file, if any
Program that created the file
Days the file is to be saved, or date on which the file can be destroyed

Accountants' Computer Guideline 19. Don't overlook the opportunity for general controls in computer operations to ensure the integrity of financial applications.

COMPUTER OPERATIONS CONTROL SOLUTIONS

The operation of the computer center is performed by the interaction of people and operating software. It is the combination of people interacting with that software that enables jobs to be completed. Therefore, controls involve people, operating procedures, and the interaction between the two.

The types of controls that accountants should specify for computer operations include:

Operator Accountability. An operator log should indicate what operators are responsible for what computer actions. This is particularly important when high-risk capabilities are available to the operator so that those procedures can be monitored. For example, there are routines which can insert instructions into programs immediately prior to operations. The use of these special programs should be monitored and operators held accountable for their use.

Two-Operator Rule.   A single operator should not be permitted to operate the computer unobserved. Two operators should always be in the computer room when the facility is in use.

Operator Log.   The operator and/or the computer should record the jobs executed by the operator. This audit trail of jobs executed can be used to substantiate that the job has been run, the amount of resources it consumed, and any special task performed during operation.

Error Notification Report.   Operators should be required to complete an error form when errors are detected. This form becomes the basis for initiating action to correct the errors.

EXHIBIT 11-3   Computer Operations Activity Controls Checklist

Item	Yes	No
1. Does each job run in computer operations have written operator instructions?		
2. Are operators trained in how to execute jobs on a computer?		
3. Is there adequate segregation of duties in the computer area?		
4. Are two operators always present when the computer is operational?		
5. Is a log used to record operator actions and jobs executed?		
6. Are procedures adequate to ensure that operators are accountable for their acts?		
7. Are operations adequately trained in the performance of their function?		
8. Are operators' duties restricted to operations, requiring them to obtain permission to perform nonroutine acts?		
9. Are formal procedures established to document operational errors?		
10. Do operators rotate the applications they execute on a regular basis?		

Operator Training. Operators should be required to go through a training session before operating the system. The training should familiarize the operator with both the equipment and the organization's procedures and standards for operating the equipment.

Exhibit 11-3 is designed to help accountants assess the adequacy of computer operations activity controls.

DATA LIBRARY CONTROL SOLUTIONS

Most data libraries are secure areas for storing data. In larger installations, they are staffed by full-time data librarians. Controls are designed to protect the integrity of data and provide a secure storage area for the data.

The kinds of data library controls the accountant should request include:

Off-Site Storage. Sufficient data and procedures should be stored off-site to permit reconstruction of processing in the event the primary site should be destroyed.

Media Location File. The data librarian should maintain a file indicating the location of each data medium. If the medium has been removed from the library, the name of the individual accountable for that medium should be recorded in the file.

Data Media Follow-Up. If data media are not returned to the library within a reasonable period of time, a follow-up procedure should be initiated to determine the whereabouts of the computer media.

Data Media Destruction Policy. The data librarian should have predetermined policies on how and when to destroy data media. Some media may be required to undergo electronic cleaning so that the data will not be on the media when they are reused, while other media can be returned for reuse without electronic cleaning at the end of the save period.

Media Inventory. Periodically, the data librarian should conduct an inventory of the computer media to determine that none has been lost. An investigation should be undertaken to locate the whereabouts of any missing computer media.

Media Translation Capability. The data librarian should ensure that there is a means of translating computer media to a people-readable format. For example, methods of recording data on tape ten years ago

EXHIBIT 11-4   Data Library Activity Controls Checklist

Item	Yes	No
1. Have adequate storage facilities been provided for computer media?		
2. Is the computer media in that storage facility recorded?		
3. Are periodic physical inventories made to determine that the storage media has not been lost?		
4. Are records maintained on who withdraws media from the storage area?		
5. If media is not returned within a reasonable period of time, are the follow-up procedures instigated?		
6. Is the media librarian organizationally independent of the operators, assuming the size of the organization permits this separation of functions?		
7. Are procedures established defining how each media is to be destroyed?		
8. Is sufficient data stored off-site to permit the reasonable reconstruction of processing should the data at the primary site be destroyed?		
9. Is sufficient hardware available to read all of the media retained in the storage area?		
10. Is that data library physically separated from computer operations?		

are no longer in use. Thus, it would be very difficult or impossible to have an old computer tape translated into readable data. The data librarian should ensure that the capability to translate that medium exists as long as it is necessary for that medium to be retained.

Exhibit 11-4 is designed to help accountants assess the adequacy of data library activity controls.

PROGRAM LIBRARY CONTROL SOLUTIONS

The program libraries store the application programs developed by the organization. These libraries control the programs that will be used during processing. The libraries must be protected against unauthorized modification, both accidentally and intentionally. Malfunctioning programs can subject an organization to extensive losses.

The types of controls the accountant should require for the program libraries include:

Restricted Access. Only programmers with an authorized need to access those programs should be permitted access. When the modification has been completed, the programmer should be denied access until the time there is need to again modify the program.

Supervisory Program Review. Supervisors should review programs on the library to provide general assurance that the programs only perform the specified functions.

Static Analysis. Programs should be subjected to a static analysis to look for code that cannot be entered during the normal processing of the program. This nonentrant code can represent both programming errors which could cause problems, or embedded Trojan horses, which can activate at some future time to defraud the organization.

EXHIBIT 11-5   Program Library Activity Controls Checklist

Item	Yes	No
1. Is one version of the program library maintained for source code, and another version for object code?		
2. Are programmers restricted in their access to the program libraries?		
3. Is each program uniquely identified?		
4. Is each version of a program uniquely identified?		
5. Is special approval required to move a version of a program from the source library to the object library?		
6. Are control copies of programs maintained for comparison against the production version to verify only authorized changes are made?		
7. Is an audit trail of changes to programs maintained?		
8. Must each change to a program be authorized?		
9. Are old versions of the production programs retained in case it is necessary to revert from a new version to an old version?		
10. Is a log maintained indicating each time a program is run in a production status?		

Program Identification.   Each program should be uniquely identified. This identifier is used by computer operations to select the program for operations.

Version Numbers.   Different versions of the same programs should be identifiable. A version identifier should be affixed to the program number to differentiate between two or more different versions of the same program.

Program Control Copy.   Periodically, control copies of programs can be made and stored in secure areas. To verify that programs have not been changed in an unauthorized manner, the control copy is compared to the production copy and differences investigated.

Exhibit 11-5 is designed to help accountants assess the adequacy of program library activity solutions.

SYSTEMS SOFTWARE CONTROL SOLUTIONS

Systems software is needed to run application systems. Many computer experts believe these software systems provide organizations with their greatest vulnerability to errors and abuse. The software systems are technically complex and thus the ability to understand and work with the systems is limited to a small corps of specialists. The organization may be dependent upon the honesty and skills of these people to provide a secure operating environment.

Unless carefully planned, the systems software will not leave the same audit trail of events as developed by most financial applications. However, because of the vulnerabilities associated with systems software, it may be more important to provide a systems software audit trail than an application system audit trail. Controls are essential to ensure the integrity of the implementation and operation of systems software.

The controls that the accountants should request for inclusion in systems software include:

Control Selection Procedures.   A formal method should be designed to determine which of the controls provided by the vendor are implemented in the operating software. Many of the controls provided by the vendor are optional, such as passwords, and without formal control selection procedures may be included or deleted at the discretion of the technical personnel.

Operations Log Reviews.   The events that occur in the operating environment are normally included on one of the operations logs. These

EXHIBIT 11-6 System Software Activity Controls Checklist

Item	Yes	No
1. Has a procedure been established for selecting system software?		
2. Is a formal procedure established for determining which vendor-provided controls and system software will be selected?		
3. Does the system software provide for an operations log?		
4. Does operations management regularly review the operations log in a search for unusual actions requiring investigation?		
5. Are powerful utilities restricted in their use?		
6. Are the use of powerful utilities logged and their usage monitored?		
7. Is a formal procedure established for reporting errors encountered in system software?		
8. Are vendors promptly notified of these system software problems?		
9. Is remuneration sought from the vendors where system software problems have resulted in losses to the organization?		
10. Is an inventory maintained of system software that is on rental?		
11. Is that inventory regularly reviewed by management to determine whether those system software packages are still needed?		

logs should be reviewed regularly by supervision. Much of these reviews can be performed automatically by eliminating noncontrol-oriented information from the few messages of control concern. It is the control concern messages that require investigation, such as when an operator shuts down the system and then the system runs for a while in an uncontrolled manner.

Utility Restrictions. Many of the utilities provided with the operating software are extremely powerful. For example, IBM has the utility called SUPER ZAP which provides for modifying operational code without following the normal procedures. Other utilities such as DEBE (Does Everything But Eat) are very powerful in adding, deleting, and modifying data to the files. Eliminating or restricting use of the more powerful utilities provides a degree of assurance that unauthorized modification will not occur.

Software Error Report. Errors occurring in vendor-produced software should be documented and given to the vendor for correction. If the software is purchased, the vendor might provide some kind of compensation for inconveniences caused due to the problem. In addition, good documentation of problems facilitates correction.

Exhibit 11-6 is designed to help accountants assess the adequacy of system software activity solutions.

SYSTEMS SOFTWARE SUPPORT CONTROL SOLUTIONS

The systems software support group has responsibility for the selection, assembly, and monitoring of systems software. In many instances, the recommendations of the systems software group are accepted without question, because unless the price is exorbitant few other people in the

EXHIBIT 11-7   System Software Support Activity Controls Checklist

Item	Yes	No
1. Has a group been established to select and maintain system software?		
2. Are procedures such as job rotation and mandatory action implemented in the system software support group to restrict people's ability to manipulate systems?		
3. Does the application team specify system software support needed?		
4. Does the system support group obtain software on a competitive bidding basis where applicable?		
5. Is a log of system support activities maintained to pinpoint accountability for actions?		
6. Is sufficient documentation maintained over software systems so that the organization is not dependent upon any single individual?		
7. Have the risks associated with system software use been identified?		

organization are knowledgeable enough to challenge the recommendations. Control should be implemented to ensure that the systems software support follows good business practices.

The types of systems software support controls that accountants should recommend include:

Job Rotation.   No one individual should work continuously on a single piece of software. Not only does job rotation increase control, but it also provides backup for other software systems in the event that a person leaves the company, is promoted, or transfers.

Mandatory Vacation.   The systems software support people should be required to take mandatory vacations for the same reasons that rotation of duties are recommended.

System Software Documentation.   The technical nature of systems software necessitates detailed standardized documentation if the organization is not to be dependent upon the capabilities of a single individual.

Application Software Specifications.   The application system's project team should decide the needed software system requirements, and then the system support group should be charged with the responsibility of obtaining software that satisfies those requirements.

Competitive Bidding.   Systems software should be obtained on competitive bidding wherever possible, to assure the organization that the maximum specifications are being obtained for the least cost.

Exhibit 11-7 is designed to help accountants assess the adequacy of systems software support activity controls.

DATA CONTROL SOLUTIONS

The data control activity is a control function. The function is charged with the responsibility of monitoring the accuracy, completeness, timeliness, authorization, data availability, and error correction processes. Accountants should support the data control function as an essential element of control in computer operations. The controls the accountant should require in the data control function include:

Data Run Control Sheets.   A control checklist should be prepared for each job run in the computer department. The control group should prepare the run sheets as a basis for ensuring that all the necessary steps are performed before, during, and after a job is run.

Data Reconciliations. Wherever possible, the control group should verify that all of the data have been processed. This may involve accumulating control totals by the data control group.

Change Anticipation Controls. The data control group should be informed when system changes have been made and the type of changes, so that they can look for and anticipate problems at those critical points where new processing capabilities and programs are introduced.

Error Message Follow-Up. Error messages should be processed through the control group to the individual with the responsibility for action. This permits the control group to monitor the timeliness and completeness of the correction process.

EXHIBIT 11–8 Data Control Activity Controls Checklist

Item	Yes	No
1. Has a data control function been established?		
2. Does the data control function have the responsibility to oversee the accuracy, completeness, timeliness, authorization, data availability, and error correction processes for application systems?		
3. Where possible, does the data control group maintain independent control totals?		
4. Does the data control group use formalized checklists to ensure that application processing is complete?		
5. Does the data control group develop anticipation controls to look for problems before they become serious?		
6. Is the data control group organizationally independent of computer operations and the application project team?		
7. Is the primary function of the data control group to monitor operations, rather than to participate in operations and the error correction process?		
8. Does the data control group follow up when any aspect of computer processing does not occur on a timely basis?		

Input/Output Anticipation Controls. The data control group should anticipate when input is to be received into the computer center, and output delivered from the computer center. If those schedules are not met, the data control group should investigate the delays and inform the people affected.

Exhibit 11-8 is designed to help accountants assess the adequacy of data control activity controls.

RECOVERY CONTROL SOLUTIONS

The recovery procedure is an essential part of the control of computer operations. The integrity of few applications would be retained for any length of time without adequate recovery procedures. The importance of planning and executing recovery cannot be overemphasized. The ac-

EXHIBIT 11-9   Recovery Activity Controls Checklist

Item	Yes	No
1. Has a determination been made as to whether or not the application needs to be recovered in the event of a problem?		
2. Has the period in which computer operations must be recovered been specified?		
3. Have the priorities been established regarding which applications are recovered in which order (note that these priorities may change depending upon the time of the failure)?		
4. Has a formal recovery plan been developed and documented?		
5. Has the recovery plan been tested?		
6. Have alternate processing procedures been designed for the time span in which the application system is not operational?		
7. Have recovery functions been assigned to specific individuals?		
8. Have procedures been established to determine both when a failure has occurred and when the integrity of the system has been restored?		
9. Are the problems documented so that long-range solutions can be developed to reduce problems?		

countant needs to determine that procedures are sufficient to recover financial applications within the necessary time requirements. The recovery controls that the accountant should require in computer operations include:

> *Recovery Specifications.* The time span in which recovery needs to be made must be determined as the basis for developing a recovery plan.
>
> *Recovery Priorities.* The order in which application systems are recovered should be specified. The order may change based on the day of the week or the week of the month. When problems occur, computer operations must know precisely in which order it needs to recover operations.
>
> *Recovery Plans.* A detailed plan needs to be established outlining in detail how recovery is to occur.
>
> *Recovery Testing.* The recovery process should be tested to verify that it works. This can be accomplished by periodically simulating a disaster and then restoring operations to verify the workability of the recovery plan.
>
> *Alternate Processing Procedures.* Users should know the methods to follow when the computer operations are not available. These procedures may involve not accepting transactions until the computer is operational again, or it may involve following alternate procedures until the computer is operational. When the system becomes operational, the transactions accepted during the downtime need to be entered into the computer.

Exhibit 11-9 is designed to help accountants assess the adequacy of recovery activity controls.

PLAN OF ACTION

A well-controlled computer operation is an essential link in the data processing system of control. The accountant should be concerned about the adequacy of controls in the computer operating environment. The shifting of application functions to the operating software involves shifting some of the controls from the application to the operating environment. This shift of controls necessitates increased emphasis by accountants on the adequacy of control in computer operations.

The following plan of action is recommended for accountants to become involved in establishing and monitoring computer operation controls:

1. *Understand Computer Operations Risks.* Identify and assess the severity of the computer operation risks.
2. *Isolate Financial System Risks.* Determine which of those risks affect the operation of financial applications, and concentrate control involvement on those risks.
3. *Specify the Minimum Level of Control.* Recommend that computer operations install the key controls described in this chapter as a minimum level of control.
4. *Monitor the Effectiveness of Controls.* Review the adequacy of control in the computer operations activities designed to reduce the identified financial accounting risks.

Accountants' Computer Guideline 20. The lack of involvement by accountants in computer operations may signal to operations personnel a lack of interest in the controls installed in the computer operations area.

twelve

CONTROLLING COMPUTER SECURITY

Computer security involves both the development and implementation of security procedures, and the enforcement of those procedures. Procedures without a security enforcement process are generally ineffective, and an enforcement process without good security procedures is likewise ineffective. Security begins with a management mandate and concludes with the enforcement process.

Trends are occurring that require organizations to devote more attention to data security. The need for security is increasing due to centralization of data, increased access to information through communication devices, more powerful processing utilities, and increased government privacy regulations. In addition, many corporations believe that good security provides them a competitive advantage in the marketplace.

Data base technology combines into a single repository large amounts of data. Communication lines make the data accessible to anyone having access to a public telephone. The increased concentration of data, coupled with the accessibility of the data through communication lines, increases the need for security.

The development of powerful computer utilities enables those gaining unauthorized access to computer resources to perform complex processing procedures. For example, using query languages to manipulate data managed by a data base management system provides processing capabilities that can, within a matter of minutes, perform actions that might have taken months to design, code, implement, test, and operate in a non-data base environment.

The increased accessibility of data, coupled with processing capabilities, has raised regulatory agency concern over the violation of privacy rights of individuals. This has led to legislation which restricts retaining and/or making available certain kinds of data about people. In addition, some legislation requires organizations to make available the information that they possess about people to those individuals. This trend is expected to accelerate as more data become centralized and readily available for analysis.

COMPUTER SECURITY OBJECTIVES

The perceived need for computer security varies extensively between organizations. Some organizations are vitally concerned over computer security and devote substantial resources to providing security. Other organizations do not perceive major security threats and give only minimal attention to computer security.

The overwhelming reason for the lack of concern over security is the "it hasn't happened here yet" syndrome. Psychologists tell us that people have great difficulty identifying and being concerned about events which have not occurred in their lifetime. This is one of the reasons why such a low percentage of people wear seatbelts in automobiles. They have not been personally involved in a serious automobile accident, and thus believe that because they have not been involved in an accident they will not be involved in the future. To these people, a catastrophe is always a surprise.

Controls and control mechanisms are traditionally designed to prevent the recurrence of unfavorable events which have already occurred in the organization. Many of the risks associated with the computer are caused by the new capabilities, and thus the problems associated with those capabilities have not yet occurred. The accountant needs to understand and be supportive of security controls designed to reduce some of the new computer risks.

The objectives of security remain the same whether the environment is manual or automated. However, the security threats and the method of prevention and detection change. The basic objectives of computer security include prevention of:

Data Destruction.   The unauthorized or unintentional destruction of data resources. Causes of destruction can be from disgruntled employees, dishonest employees, or outsiders. The data resources are a major asset to the organization and should be protected. The cash assets stored physically in a bank ordinarily represent less than 1 percent of the total assets of the bank. Yet, those banks place the cash in vaults with five-foot-thick concrete walls and one-foot-thick steel doors. At the same time, they leave computer terminals unattended which have access to over 99 percent of the bank's resources.

Data Compromise. Computerized data can be taken but still be there. When someone steals cash from a cash register, the merchant recognizes instantly that the funds are gone. On the other hand, the compromise of computer data is not easily detected. The value of some types of data is in the possession of the data and not in the destruction or modification of the data. For example, the names, addresses, salaries, and employment history of an organization's engineers would be a valuable commodity in the headhunting industry. Having this information, a good search firm should be able to pry away a reasonable number of an organization's engineers. In a marketing organization, the customer base, the products they purchase, and prices they pay are other valuable commodities. Compromise is gaining access to information for improper purposes.

Data Modification. Organizations can be damaged through the modification of data. Even slight changes to data can result in large personal gains to individuals. For example, the "salami technique" is slicing a small percentage of funds from an account. The "roll of salami" looks no different when a small slice has been cut off. For example, in a salami technique fraud it is only necessary to take a few pennies from the calculated interest of each savings account to accumulate many thousands of dollars for personal use over the course of the year. The modification of data can involve:

Changing financial amounts

Changing payees

Deleting records

Adding records

Changing effective dates of records

Removing small amounts of funds from many records and placing the "salamied" funds into a single account

Changing reports produced about financial information (for example, changing the amounts on W-2 statements sent to the government but not changing internal payroll department records)

Improper Use of Facilities. The use of computer resources is a valuable asset to an organization. Many employees have been able to run service centers and do contract programming for outside groups using their employer's time and resources. The computer facilities that can be misused include:

Hardware

Systems software such as compilers

People time

Organization experience and know-how

Technological Rule of Thumb 13. The security provided by people in a manual environment must be shifted to automated security in an automated environment.

COMPUTER SECURITY ACTIVITIES

The security activities should be performed by a security officer function. The security officer function has responsibility for the physical and logical security of the data processing resources. Physical security includes the hardware, the computer room, and communication lines and remote terminals. Logical security includes the data, the application programs, and the operating systems software.

The activities within security are different from the activities in most of the other data processing areas. For example, in computer operations there may be several different groups, each headed by a supervisor handling an activity. However, within the security all of the tasks are usually performed by a single individual or a single group of individuals.

The security officer function should be considered a responsibility as opposed to an organizational group. Many financial institutions, such as banks and insurance companies, have recognized the need for assigning people full time to the security officer function. Other organizations only have the responsibility as a part-time responsibility of an individual or group.

Many industrial firms have established a security committee. The committee is comprised of multiple disciplines, including in some organizations computer operations, management, systems analysts, plant security, internal audit and, frequently, someone from a user area.

The full-time security officer, the part-time security officer, and the security committee all have the same basic responsibilities. The difference between the organizational approach is one of management interest and allocation of resources. Experience has shown that the more resources allocated to the security officer function, the more successful the organization's security program.

The key to good security in the data processing area is the designation of a security officer function. Unless someone is assigned responsibility for security, it is difficult to establish, operate, and monitor an effective security program. People implementing security programs without the strong support of management have difficulty building effective security problems.

The activities performed by the security officer function include:

Security Policies and Procedures.   The security officer has the responsibility to develop the policies and procedures governing security over the data processing resources. An organizational policy should be established regarding security in the data processing area. The policy should outline the following:

Management support for security
The employee's responsibility for security
The employee's responsibility for reporting security violations
The organizational philosophy for implementing and operating security programs
The security violation policy

Security Hardware.   The security officer should be reviewing security hardware technology, and recommending security hardware where appropriate. Numerous hardware devices, such as cryptography, are available to protect both the physical installation and the data and programs within that installation. Based on the security needs, the security officer should work with computer operations or systems personnel to select hardware if the security needs warrant that degree of protection.

Security Software.   In an on-line data base environment, some of the stronger security measures are implemented through software. Security measures can be included within systems software packages, within application systems, or through the use of stand-alone security needs, and then the security tools best designed to meet those needs can be selected. Security software is usually cheaper and often more effective than security hardware.

Security Test Program.   Security, unlike other aspects of data processing, is difficult to evaluate. If no security violations are detected, one could assume that either no one attempted to break security or that the security procedures were effective. Those who feel security measures are an unnecessary expense will come to the conclusion that the organization is subject to attempts by perpetrators. While testing cannot provide an exact simulation of a perpetrator in action, it does provide some degree of assurance that the security program is working.

Security Education.   Security education programs are not widely utilized. Many organizations assume that computer security is the prob-

EXHIBIT 12-1   Security Risks/Activities Matrix

Security Accounting Risks \ Security Activities	Security Policies and Procedures	Security Hardware	Security Software	Security Test Program	Security Education
Unauthorized Transaction	✔	✔	✔	✔	✔
Control Level Violation	✔	✔	✔	✔	✔
Fraud	✔	✔	✔	✔	✔

lem of the security personnel or a few key people in the operations area. Other organizations believe that security is everybody's problem and, therefore, training is necessary to create the awareness of the need for security and the measures that people should take to help ensure an effective security program. Education usually pays good security dividends.

Accountants' Computer Guideline 21.   The appointment of a security officer is the most important security control.

COMPUTER SECURITY RISKS

Security permeates all aspects of data processing. It is difficult to isolate the control points for security because the perpetrator looks for the weak points. The Security Risks/Activities Matrix (Exhibit 12-1) illustrates that installing controls in all security activities is important. Security exists only if all activities contribute to the program.

Accountants' Computer Guideline 22.   Perpetrators search out and break the weakest security link.

COMPUTER SECURITY KEY CONTROLS

The key controls in security are designed to protect the assets of the organization. The installation of the key security controls should substantially reduce the risks from destruction, modification, and compromise of data.

EXHIBIT 12-2   Security Key Controls

Key Control	Purpose of Control
1. User profile	Matches users with the resources needed in the performance of their job
2. Resource accountability	Makes people accountable for the resources they use
3. Security reviews	Tests the adequacy of security procedures
4. Cryptography	Codes information
5. Chargeout procedures	Bills users for the resources they consume
6. Bait records	Records included on a file for the purpose of detecting improper use of those files
7. Observed destruction	Monitors the destruction of data
8. Security prosecution	Prosecutes security violators
9. Data classification	Classifies data in accordance with its importance
10. Security awareness program	Educates people about the importance of security
11. Physical forms security	Physically protects important forms

Controlling the security of data involves controlling the resources that have access to that data.

The key controls that the accountant should request to safeguard the data processing resources include (see Exhibit 12-2 for a brief description of the key security controls) the following.

User Profile.   A user profile matches the resources of the organization with the needs of the user. The user profile should be prepared by the security officer who begins the process by identifying the resources requiring security, such as data, programs, hardware, and so forth. The security officer will assure that a single individual is accountable for each resource. That individual is then requested to identify which users can have access to those resources. This produces the user profile. A typical user profile for data is illustrated in Exhibit 12-3. This shows not only the data resources, but the kind of access permitted to those resources (to read data, write data, add data, or delete data). The users who can have

EXHIBIT 12-3   User Profile Examples

Data Item	Data Uses			
	Read Data	Update Data	Delete Data	Add New Data
Data Item 1	3	4	5	6
Data Item 2	1	2	2	18
Data Item 3	8	9	9	9
Data Item 4	21	26 27 28		31
Data Item 5	2 7 13 14	51		52

access to the data are identified within the matrix by their employee number.

Resource Accountability.   One individual should be accountable for each data processing resource requiring security. The types of resources that require accountability include:

Physical assets	Documentation
Data files	Program libraries
Data elements	Systems documentation
Communication lines	Negotiable instruments

Security Reviews.   Periodically, the adequacy of the security program should be tested by conducting security reviews. The review should be conducted by individuals knowledgeable in both data processing and security violations and procedures. In some organizations, the security officer may conduct the review, in others it could be the auditor or independent security consultants.

Cryptography.   Cryptography is a method of encoding and decoding data. Cryptography uses an encryption key which encodes data so they are unintelligible by people. The data stay in coded form until they are decoded using the same key. Cryptography can be performed using software, or it can use hardware cryptographic devices for the coding and decoding. A standardized cryptography key has been recommended by the National Bureau of Standards. Data can be encrypted for the following purposes:

During Transmission. The data are encoded immediately before transmission and decoded immediately after receipt by the receiving location.

Storage in Computer Files. Requires encoding before placing the data in the computer file and then decoding the data when they are read back for use.

Chargeout Procedures. Users of data processing resources should be charged for those uses. Chargeout is a method of making users accountable for the resources that they use. It also makes it difficult for unauthorized individuals to use those resources, because they may not have the appropriate charge numbers to use the facilities. This technique can be effective in reducing the improper use of computer hardware and software. Even those having a charge number and using the computer improperly could be detected if there are flagrant violations of use.

Bait Records. Bait records are records placed on computer files for the purpose of detecting when those files are improperly used. Bait records are most effective on files involving people or organizations. A security person uses his home address or address of a friend's business as the bait record. For example, if an organization was concerned over its customer file, a fictitious business or bait business would be added to the customer file, using some unique identifier such as misspelling the name of the organization or adding a fictitious middle initial to a person's name. Should that individual be contacted or receive information from other than regular sources, it would be immediately known that the file has been compromised, and appropriate investigation and action can be taken.

Observed Destruction. Organizations need to destroy unwanted data. The data can be on computer tape, paper, disks, or other media. Based on the security classification of the data, the decision must be made as to the means of destruction. If the data require destruction other than normal disposal through the trash process, then that destruction should be logged and observed. Destruction should not be performed by a single individual, because that does not provide the necessary control that the destruction actually occurred. An observed destruction requires developing an inventory of the data resources to be destroyed, and then having two or more individuals witness that they did, in fact, observe the destruction of that information.

Security Prosecution. Security programs are as effective as management's backing of those programs. If management truly wants the program to be effective, they will identify violators, and then punish those violators. As soon as management takes strong action against violators, the security of the organization will increase immediately. Some organizations have policies that state that if people give other people their passwords they will be fired on the spot. Violators should not only be punished, but the punishment should be made known to the other employees of the organization.

Data Classification. Data should be classified according to their importance to the organization. Many organizations have developed classifications for data, such as business confidential, manufacturing confidential, people confidential, and accounting confidential. Obviously, not all accounting documents are classified accounting confidential. Those documents that need to be classified should have stated policies on how to protect and destroy that information.

Security Awareness Program. Employees need to be continually reminded of the need for security. Associated with this awareness program are the responsibilities expected from employees in protecting the security of the organization's data processing resources. The methods used in organizations to create an awareness for security include:

Security posters
Security responsibilities stated in job descriptions
Security briefings
Security training sessions, usually not longer than one hour
Security video presentations

Physical Forms Security. Some computer forms are negotiable instruments or documents which enable people to perform privileged acts. These forms should be uniquely identified, e.g., with prenumbering, and then inventoried and accounted for during processing. Many organizations store these forms in a locked area. Some organizations have two different locks with two different individuals each having one key. This then requires the two individuals to be present to unlock the secure cabinet and remove the documents. These individuals should then be present

when the accountable forms are being used. In addition, they should periodically inventory the forms to be assured that none is missing.

COMPUTER SECURITY CONTROL SOLUTIONS

Security is like a chain that holds a vessel to the dock. It is comprised of a
series of links and each link is important in keeping the boat secure. If one
link in the chain breaks, the boat will drift away from the dock. If one link
is weaker than the other links, it will break first. Thus, in designing the
security control solution the security officer must look at the total chain
and not independent links.

Perpetrators look for the weakest link in the security chain and penetrate at that point. If an organization spends a lot of money building one or
two very strong links, those funds may be wasted. To have several strong
links and several weak links does not provide good security. The perpetrator will search out the weak links and penetrate at that point, avoiding
the strong security links.

Let's look at an example of a security program which includes cryptography, surveillance devices, and key locks. All three are strong security
links. At the same time, the program does not include operator training
programs, security violation penalties, and strong terminal access controls. In such an installation, it would be difficult to get into the computer
areas without an escort either during or after hours, and information taken
during transmission may be meaningless. However, due to lack of training, operators may permit someone to talk their way into the computer
room because they may feel security is unimportant because of the lack of
punishments for violations. In addition, people may be able to gain access
to the system through unattended terminals. Some are strong controls and
some weak controls, with the perpetrators concentrating on the weak
controls.

The bottom line of a security solution is a security chain of equally
strong links. If all the links in a chain appear weak, the security program
can comprise two or more chains of security. Having to break a series of
chains, even though they are weak, may be more difficult than breaking a
single link in a single chain of security. For example, a combination of a
medium-strength physical security program at the terminal plus a medium-
strength access method may be better than a very strong access method
and no physical security.

The security program requires planning. Security measures should not
be installed independent of one another but, rather, installed in conjunction with one another so that the total program can be assessed as a pack-

age. The planned integrated approach justifies the assignment of the security responsibility to a single security officer function, rather than spreading that function among several people, none of whom has oversight responsibility for the organization's total data processing security program.

The security controls that the accountant should expect in an effective computer security program are:

Physical Hardware Protection.   Computer hardware and the physical computer media should have controls to protect them from accidental destruction. For example, reels of computer tape have a ring that can be inserted to prevent tapes from being written on, and computer rooms have Halon gas installed to prevent damage from fire.

Supervised Terminals.   Placing terminals so that a supervisor can observe who is using that terminal provides protection from unauthorized use.

Automatic Shutdown.   One of the methods of breaking access to a computer system is to piggyback usage on a terminal once it has been opened. Piggybacking means that an authorized user opens the terminal, and then leaves the terminal without closing it. This permits an unauthorized individual to use that terminal for unauthorized purposes. Automatic shutdown can stop piggybacking. Automatic shutdown can be used in two ways: first, if an unauthorized person makes X invalid attempts to open the terminal it is shut down from all further use until reopened by a supervisor; and second, the terminal can be shut down after X minutes or seconds of inactivity requiring a supervisor to reopen the terminal.

Automatic Callback.   In systems where the receiving terminal is unsure of the location of the incoming call, the call can be accepted, the identity of the caller requested, and then the connection broken. The receiving terminal then calls back to the authorized location of the caller. This prevents someone from gaining access from an unauthorized location even with the appropriate passwords.

Surveillance Devices.   Hardware can be used to provide surveillance of an area when people are not in attendance. Surveillance devices can be laser beam devices or sonic devices. Either one will sound an alarm when an object moves in a surveillance area.

Privileged Persons Reviews.   Those individuals that have privileged positions, such as systems programmers, auditors, systems analysts/ programmers, should be subject to extra scrutiny. If permitted by law, their personal accounts in the organization should be reviewed, as well as their activities within the automated environment.

Job Accounting Log. Job accounting logs automatically record the use of computer resources by individuals using those resources. These logs can be periodically reviewed to determine whether or not unauthorized access has occurred.

Security Log. Security systems produce a log of accesses to computer resources as well as invalid attempts for which access has been denied. This log should be periodically reviewed to determine areas of security concern such as numerous invalid attempts to gain access from a particular terminal.

Voiding Negotiable Documents. Negotiable documents that are used for printer alignment or damaged in the printing process should be voided. Procedures should require the voiding of unusable negotiable forms immediately following the printing process.

Negotiable Instruments Reconciliation Form. The use of all negotiable instruments should be reconciled. The reconciliation should include the number of forms taken out of storage for use, the number of forms used, the number destroyed, and the number returned to storage.

Exhibit 12-4 is designed to help accountants assess the adequacy of security controls.

COMPUTER SECURITY PLAN OF ACTION

The centralization and accessibility of computer resources require an in-depth assessment of security. The accountant should be a participant in this program. The accountant understands the value of financial information and is experienced in control design assessment.

A plan of action for building an effective computer security program is:

Establish a Security Officer Function. A single individual should be assigned the responsibility for computer security. This need not be a full-time function, but the responsibility should be centralized in a single individual or group, and that individual or group made accountable for the adequacy of security.

Design and Implement a Security Program. Security cannot be implemented on a piecemeal basis. Even if minimal resources are allo-

EXHIBIT 12-4   Security Activity Controls Checklist

Item	Yes	No
1. Has one individual been appointed responsible for data processing security?		
2. Has a security plan been developed which incorporates all aspects of data processing security into a single plan?		
3. Have security procedures been developed and disseminated to the involved personnel?		
4. Has management developed a policy on data processing security?		
5. Are security violators punished?		
6. Are procedures established to record security violations?		
7. Has the security level of data processing resources been identified, and appropriately classified?		
8. Are security procedures consistent with the value of the resources to the organization?		
9. Have the procedures to destroy important information been defined?		
10. Has a user profile been established indicating which users have access to which resources?		
11. Are individual people accountable for the resources they use?		
12. Are individuals charged for the resources they consume as a method of accountability?		
13. Are bait records included on key files to detect file compromise?		
14. Are programs established to create employee awareness of management's desire for security over data processing resources?		
15. Are procedures established to study and implement hardware and software security devices?		
16. Is the destruction of secure information observed by two or more people?		
17. Are procedures established to ensure that only authorized people can use computer resources?		

EXHIBIT 12-4 (Continued)

Item	Yes	No
18. Are the accounts of activities of individuals in privileged positions monitored?		
19. Are logs maintained of security actions and violations?		
20. Are the security logs periodically reviewed by management to detect unauthorized acts?		
21. Does supervision take an active role in the implementation of security programs?		
22. Are negotiable instruments adequately controlled?		

cated to security, a plan should be developed and implemented to make effective use of the total dollars allocated to security.

Create Security Awareness. Employees need to be advised of management's desire for an effective security program and their part in that program. Employees cannot be expected to give a high priority to security until they are aware of their management's desire for that security priority.

Monitor Security. It is difficult to verify the adequacy of security procedures without testing. Unless a perpetrator attempts to break security and is detected, one cannot be sure whether the security procedures are effective or ineffective. The security officer should periodically attempt to break security to determine the adequacy of security procedures.

Accountants' Computer Guideline 23. Security, like a metal chain, must be built of links of equal strength.

part four

THE AUTOMATION OF ACCOUNTING CONTINUES

thirteen

MANAGING CHANGE

Many accountants ask, "Whatever happened to the good old days?" These accountants dream of the simpler, less complex methods of accounting; however, tomorrow's good old days are today. Whatever system you are using today for accounting won't be there tomorrow. Change is a way of life and accountants must learn to manage that change.

There are three types of accountants. Those who make things happen, those who watch things happen, and those who don't know what's happening. You can't manage change if you don't know what's happening.

It is very possible that the major responsibility of tomorrow's accountant will be managing change. The computer has taken the drudgery out of accounting, and left in its place a much higher skilled job of problem identification, analysis, and correction. Not only are the roles and responsibilities of the accountants changing, but with that change has come need for new skills.

I LOVE YOU TOMORROW

Recall the closing line of the song "Tomorrow" from the musical *Annie:* "Tomorrow, tomorrow, I love you tomorrow, you're always a day away." No need to worry about tomorrow because it is always a day away. Unfortunately, without planning, the accountants' tomorrow may not include a position in the organization chart unless they survive the redefined accounting role.

Let's look at tomorrow and see what's coming:

Voice-Activated Equipment. Accountants will be able to converse orally with machines. The voice-activated typewriter is already operational and should be available during the mid-1980s. The current barriers to the accountants' interfacing with the computer, namely the keyboard, will give way to a much easier and direct interface between accountant and machine.

Intercompany Processing Networks. Computers in one company will talk to computers in another company. The banking industry transfers funds electronically; marketing personnel and customers can order products over touch-tone telephone; and treasurers of corporations have terminals in their office directly connected to their bank's computers. The trend will accelerate and more business between companies will be conducted directly by computers.

Authorization via Personal Identifiers. Machines can recognize people's fingerprints, voiceprints, lip prints, and signatures. The cumbersome methods of authorization using magnetically encoded cards and passwords will be gradually replaced with these newer personal identifiers. These will increase the ability of systems to restrict access to resources to authorized individuals.

Information Management. The information of an organization will be managed as a true resource of the organization. Senior-level management functions will be established to administer the organization's data. The process will increase the consistency, integrity, and reliability of data while making them more readily available for use by any authorized individual.

Data Banks. All of the organization's data for periods of years will be readily accessible within seconds. Low-cost, limitless computer storage will make it cost-effective to store and retrieve on command all of the data generated by the organization.

Tomorrow is going to be different from today. These changes in capabilities will significantly change the methods of doing business. Change cannot be delayed because the competitive advantage tomorrow will go to the company whose information systems enable them to be more responsive to the needs of their customers.

THE ACCOUNTANT AS A CHANGE MANAGER

Accounting monitors and evaluates operations. Changes in the methods of operation are quickly reflected in the changes in the methods of accounting. However, rather than a follower, the accountant should be a leader in managing change in accounting systems.

An accountant's plan of action for managing change is outlined below.

Following these few simple steps will let you manage change rather than have change managing you:

RECOGNIZE: An Increased Reliance on Control.   The lack of hard-copy evidence and lesser involvement by people in automated systems means that increased reliance must be placed on the automated controls for accurate, complete, and authorized processing.

RECOGNIZE: That Hard-Copy Evidence Will Be Limited.   Computer systems will rely more heavily on direct input and direct output to and from users of the systems. In addition, with the ready abundance of terminals and easy access to information, people will want fewer documents to store when the same information can be obtained quickly using a computer terminal.

RECOGNIZE: Rapid Change in Technological Capabilities.   The technological capabilities of automated equipment will continue to outpace people's ability to use that technology. This trend means that technological capabilities may also outpace the accountant's ability to control that technology.

RECOGNIZE: Increased Systems Capabilities.   Systems are becoming more integrated and complex as they take advantage of the new technological capabilities and by using improved systems development techniques.

RECOGNIZE: The Need for Data Processing Skills.   The interaction between computers and people will increase as automated systems assume a greater share of information processing. People will find it more difficult to remain competitive with their peers without data processing skills.

OBTAIN: Data Processing Skills.   Accountants should obtain an understanding of computer concepts and systems design. In addition, it is advisable for accountants to learn a computer language. An easy method to obtain these basic computer skills is to acquire and practice the skills on a small home computer.

IDENTIFY: The Accounting Structure.   The automated accounting structure is the lifeblood of the accountant. It is essential that the accountant understand how accounting data are accumulated, fed into automated systems, processed, stored, and incorporated into accounting reports.

IDENTIFY: The Risks of Automation. Risk is the basis for control, and until accountants understand the new and increased risks in an automated environment they cannot assist in the development of, or evaluation of, the adequacy of automated controls.

SPECIFY: Accounting Systems. Accountants should be in charge of their own destiny, which means becoming directly involved in the specification, development, and operation of automated accounting systems.

SPECIFY: Automated Accounting Controls. Only the accountant can understand and design controls to reduce accounting risks in the organization. The adequacy of accounting control is dependent upon the accountant's direct involvement in the design of accounting controls.

PARTICIPATE: In Long-Range Automation Planning. The long-range success of automated applications is dependent upon effective long-range planning. The accountant as guardian for the organization's assets and having primary responsibility for control has an essential role in the planning process. The complex nature of tomorrow's systems requires that tomorrow's control needs be specified today as part of long-range planning.

PREPARING FOR TOMORROW

Accountants need "accountant-friendly" systems. Data processing personnel talk of "user-friendly" systems, meaning systems that are easy to use and integrated into the day-to-day work of the user. The computer should be the tool of the accountant, and one of the accountant's systems design objectives should be to make the computer as friendly as possible.

Tomorrow's systems will be "less forgiving" than today's systems without the accountant's involvement in the development of those systems. When larger and more complex systems malfunction, the effect will be far more dramatic than the problems occurring in today's less complex systems.

Tomorrow, tomorrow, I love you tomorrow; you're always a day away. However, you can only love tomorrow if you prepare today. The course charted for automated systems is clear; an ever increasing segment of the accountant's work will be absorbed into the organization's automated systems. Accountants thus have a unique opportunity to help move their organization through the choppy waters of new automation risks into the safe harbors of adequate controls. Don't miss the boat.

INDEX